1

Salmon Mousse on Cucumber
Strathboro Paste
Zucchini Pizzas
Recipes on pages 8 and 9

Celebrity All-Occasion Cooking

Recipes for Every Occasion

Edited by Sally Sullivan

Originally published by Epilepsy Ontario
Suite 207
5385 Yonge Street
Willowdale, Ontario
M2N 5R7

Published in 1985 by Stoddart Publishing
A Division of General Publishing Co. Limited
30 Lesmill Road
Don Mills, Ontario
M3B 2T6

Canadian Cataloguing In Publication Data
Main entry title:

Celebrity All-Occasion Cooking
Originally Published by:
Epilepsy Ontario

Includes index

ISBN: 0-7737-5033-9

1. Cookery.   I. Epilepsy Ontario.
TX715.C44 1985   641.5   C85-098133-6

Printed and bound in Canada

ALL-OCCASION COOKING
A Retrospective

Volume I of All-Occasion Cooking became an instant best seller and the subsequent ongoing demand for the book over a 3 year period was gratifying beyond all expectations. Not only did the revenue generated from sales allow us to expand our services, particularly to areas where programs were minimal or non-existent, but the extensive television, radio and news coverage brought Epilepsy before the public as never before.

Epilepsy, as previously outlined, is still a "closet" disorder due to widely held misconceptions and the discrimination experience by those who have the problem. If All-Occasion Cooking has directly and/or indirectly helped to alleviate these problems in some small way, then we have accomplished a very great deal.

CELEBRITY ALL-OCCASION COOKING
An Introduction

In volume II of Celebrity All-Occasion Cooking we have retained much of the physical appearance of volume I due to the many comments and letters we received applauding the clarity of layout and a print size that everyone could read.

The addition of metric was an endless debate by the Committee members, but for our Canadian cooks, whose grocery products are now measured solely in metric, it was decided to include the measure.

Recipes were sought and obtained over a two year period from International cooks who generously shared with us their family favourites. Because of the high calibre of recipes we received, the final selection of those to be published was extremely difficult. Preference was ultimately shown to those recipes that provided a mix of day-to-day fare to more elaborate cooking which would reflect our all occasion cooking theme.

You may have noticed on the front cover the statement, "A Fund-raising Project for non-profit organizations". The concept of offering the book to other charitable organizations as a fund-raising vehicle evolved through the interest shown in the first book by such groups. It was evident in our discussions that there was a need for a risk free quality product that could be sold across North America. Hence we have chosen to make this book "generic" in nature which will allow sister organizations to add their own name to the book to sell to their friends.

THE COOKBOOK COMMITTEE

Mrs. Gary Bond	Mrs. Gordon Isserstedt	Mrs. Brian McGrath
Mrs. A.M. Burka	Mrs. Margaret Marcar	Mrs. R. Thomas Merry
Mrs. Bev Collombin	Mrs. Roger W. Matthews	Mrs. Peter S. Morine
Mrs. Roberto del Rosal	Mrs. Douglas McCutcheon	Mrs. William J. Plaxton
Mrs. C. Ross Healy	Mrs. James W. McCutcheon	Mrs. Stephen Secord

From the kitchens of:

To all the busy men and women who took time to share their recipes with us go our sincere thanks and gratitude.

H.R.H. The Princess of Wales
Mrs. Ralph A. Aceto
Mrs. Alberta L. Agnew
Julie Andrews
Miss L. Angermann
Ed Asner
Richard Attenborough
Elizabeth Baird
Mrs. Michael Barber
Mrs. Stanley Blair
Mrs. G.W. Bond
Pat Boone
Mrs. A.E. Boothe
Miss Sarah Bowman
Mrs. S.J. Bowman
Mrs. Ian Boyd
Liona Boyd
Mrs. Jane Bunting
Mrs. A.M. Burka
Carol Burnett
Mrs. Ronald Burrows
Leo Buscaglia
Mrs. Donald Cannon
Mrs. Christopher Cape
Mrs. D.H. Carlisle
Mrs. James Caylor
Mrs. Peter Chubb
Mrs. G.H. Collins
Mrs. Beverly Collombin
Mrs. J. Connor
Mrs. Terry Corcoran
Mrs. Joan Costa
Mrs. Douglas Cottier
Mrs. Susan Cotton
Mrs. Joan Crossen
Dr. Rosalind M. Curtis
Mrs. George Darling
Mrs. Marion Davis
Marsha Davis
Mrs. Roberto del Rosal
Dom DeLuise
Bronwyn Drainie
Mrs. Kenneth Duck
Mrs. David Eaton
Mrs. Robert Elder
Mrs. W. Eplett
Anne Farrell
Susan Ferguson
Dianna Findlay
Mrs. Douglas Florence
Mrs. Gerald R. Ford
Mrs. Dolliver H. Frederick
Mrs. Elaine Gay
Mrs. Douglas Gibson
Diana Goad
Mrs. Douglas Goodkey
Mr. and Mrs. Robert Goulet
Lorne Greene
Wayne D. Gretzky

Mrs. George Gretzner
Mrs. George Guy
Mrs. David Hackett
Mr. Michael Halloran
Hagood Hardy
Mrs. Peter Hatcher
Mrs. C. Ross Healy
Mrs. Elsie Healy
Miss Pearl Heldmann
Mrs. Joyce Hisey
Bob Hope
Mrs. Russell Horsfall
Mrs. William Hubler
Bobby Hull
Mrs. M.B. Hutcheson
Mrs. Gordon Isserstedt
Glenda Jackson
Mrs. Carl Jellett
Mrs. Murray Kingsburgh
Ted Knight
Mrs. Grace Kornacher
Mrs. Pearl Kump
Mrs. Edwin Langdon
Mrs. Edith Lawford
Vicki Lawrence
Yvonne Le Blanc
Mrs. David Lewis
Art Linkletter
Mrs. Charles Loewen
Mrs. Virginia Lucas
Mrs. T.G. Lutton
Mrs. H.C. Lyons
Mrs. Betty Macdonald
Mrs. Philip MacDonnell
Mrs. Margaret Marcar
Neville Marriner
Patrick Martin
Mrs. D.C. Matheson
Johnny Mathis
Miss Cathy Matthews
Mrs. Lynn Matthews
Mrs. P.D. Matthews
Mrs. Robert G. Matthews
Mrs. Roger Matthews
Mrs. J.L. McAlpine
Mrs. Richard McCoy
Mrs. Douglas McCutcheon
Mrs. James McCutcheon
Caroline McEwan
Mrs. Brian McGrath
Mrs. D.C. McKay
Ed McMahon
Mrs. J. McMurray
Mrs. Barry Mercer
Miss Marianne Merry
Mrs. R. Thomas Merry
Mrs. Victoria Meurer
Susan Milligan
Mrs. Maryian Milson
Mrs. P.J. Misener

Roger Moore
Mrs. Peter Morine
Mrs. Harvey Morris
Anne Murray
Jim Nabors
Carroll O'Connor
Mrs. Desmond O'Rorke
Judy Paisley
Mrs. Alice Parker
Mrs. Ann Paul
Mrs. Margaret Peacock
Mrs. Barry Percival
Mrs. Alan Plaxton
Mrs. William Plaxton
Mrs. Jane Pletsch
Steve Podborski
Mrs. William Porritt
Mrs. John C. Preston
Charley Pride
Mrs. Ronald Reagan
President Ronald Reagan
Mrs. N.H. Regan
Lee Remick
Mrs. Hugh Rennie
Burt Reynolds
Mrs. Edward Ritcey
Joan Rivers
Mrs. A.W. Robinson
Beth Roode
Mrs. Helen Ross
Mrs. Murray Ross
Mrs. Frank Rush
Mrs. Arthur Scace
Mrs. P.F. Schaffer
Barbara Ann Scott
Mrs. Stephen Secord
Mrs. Kenneth Selby
William Shatner
Mrs. Thomas Shea
Frank Shuster
Beverly Sills
Mrs. D.G. Sirola
Mrs. H.M. Sisley
Mrs. Joseph Smith
Mrs. Randall G. Smith
Sir Georg Solti
Jean Stapleton
Mrs. C.E. Stewart
Sally Sullivan
Elizabeth Taylor
Mrs. John H. Taylor
Mrs. E.W. Thompson
Brenda Vaccaro
Mrs. Peter VanBuskirk
Mrs. A.E. Van Clieaf
Johnny Wayne
Clara Wilkins
Henry Winkler
Mrs. A.R. Winnett
Shelley Winters

Patrons

Our special thanks to our Patrons who so generously supported us.

Mr. and Mrs. Ralph A. Aceto
Mr. Colin Acton
Mr. and Mrs. T.C. Agnew
Lillias Cringan Allward
Mr. and Mrs. David Ashworth
Mr. and Mrs. J. Alberto Bacardi
Dr. Joan Bain
Mr. and Mrs. J.M. Bankes
Mr. and Mrs. G.W. Bascombe
Mr. and Mrs. Richard C. Berndt
Mr. and Mrs. Klaus Bindhardt
Mrs. Marion J. Birch
Patricia A. Black
Dr. and Mrs. Gordon Blair
Mr. Blair C. Bongard
Mr. William E. Boothe
Mr. and Mrs. James Bunton
Mr. and Mrs. A.M. Burka
Mr. and Mrs. Michael Burns
Mr. and Mrs. Ronald G. Burrows
Mr. and Mrs. John G. Byrne
Mr. and Mrs. Maynard E. Capes
His Honour Judge and Mrs. R. Ian
Cartwright
Mr. and Mrs. Ralph S. Caswell
Dr. and Mrs. Lionel Chisholm
Dr. Sheila G. Cohen
Mr. and Mrs. J. Ian Crookston
Mr. and Mrs. R. Gordon Cummings
Dr. Rosalind M. Curtis
Mr. and Mrs. Juan del Rosal
Mr. and Mrs. Roberto del Rosal
Mr. and Mrs. Elvio Del Zotto
Mr. and Mrs. R. James Elder
Mr. and Mrs. John H. Eliot
Mr. and Mrs. Douglas C. Ellis
Mr. and Mrs. Eric Exton
Mr. and Mrs. Douglas Florence
Mr. and Mrs. E. Ewart Fry
Dr. and Mrs. John D.M. Gillies
Mr. and Mrs. Lionel J. Goffart
Mr. and Mrs. Peter S. Gooderham
Dr. Noelle Grace
Mr. and Mrs. B.T. Grant
Mr. and Mrs. Thomas G. Halford
Miss J. Moyra Haney
Mr. D. Harbottle
Mr. and Mrs. Robert W. Harris
Mary and Dennis Hawley
Mr. and Mrs. C. Ross Healy
Mr. W.A. Heaslip
Mr. and Mrs. V. Heinrichs
Mr. and Mrs. Lyman Henderson
Mr. and Mrs. Lawrence R. Heron
Stefanie Hill
Catherine Hill
Mr. and Mrs. S.K. Hisey
Mrs. Ann M. Hogarth
Mrs. Russell Horsfall

Madge Humphries
Mr. and Mrs. Donald H. Hunter
Mr. and Mrs. Michael B. Hutchison
Mrs. Gordon Isserstedt
Mr. and Mrs. John Judson
Mrs. Marianne D. Kelley
Mr. and Mrs. Kenneth W. Kernaghan
Mr. and Mrs. E. George Kneider
Mr. and Mrs. Peter J. Labbett
Dr. Nadira Lakdawalla
Mr. and Mrs. Edwin Langdon
Mr. and Mrs. Lee W. Larkin
Mr. and Mrs. David A. Lemmon
Mr. and Mrs. T.G. Lutton
Dorothea Manson
Dr. and Mrs. Joseph T. Marotta
Mr. and Mrs. C.L. Marshall
Mr. and Mrs. John L. McAlpine
Mrs. A. McD. McBain
Dr. and Mrs. W. Greg McCain
Mr. and Mrs. Douglas McCutcheon
Mr. and Mrs. James W. McCutcheon
Mr. and Mrs. H. John McDonald
Mr. James H. McGuinness ·
Mr. and Mrs. Sidney S. McMurray
Dr. and Mrs. Keith Meloff
Miss Marianne Merry
Mrs. R. Thomas Merry
Mr. and Mrs. W.H. Milne
Dr. Sandra Moody
Mr. and Mrs. Peter S. Morine
Miss Camilla M. Murphy
Dr. and Mrs. M.J. O'Brien
Mr. and Mrs. Rocco Pantalone
Mr. and Mrs. Donald D. Paterson
Mr. and Mrs. R. Douglas Paterson
Mr. and Mrs. William J. Plaxton
Dr. John S. Prichard
Mr. and Mrs. Donald B. Redfern
Dr. and Mrs. S.R. Ross
Mrs. Eloise Schmidt
Doris S. Scott
Mr. and Mrs. Stephen Secord
Mr. and Mrs. Robert A. Shea
Mr. and Mrs. Thomas Shea
Mr. Zoltan D. Simo
Mr. and Mrs. Joseph Smith
Mr. and Mrs. Alan N. Steiner
Mr. and Mrs. Robert T. Stephens
Mr. and Mrs. Paul Sullivan
Mr. and Mrs. F.R.S. Tomenson
Mr. and Mrs. John A. Watt
Mr. and Mrs. Frank W. Welch
Mr. and Mrs. David B. Weldon
Mr. and Mrs. Bill Wilburn
Mr. and Mrs. R.C. Wilkins
Mr. and Mrs. W.J. Young
Mr. and Mrs. David Yule

Contents

Appetizers

MEATBALLS IN BARBECUE SAUCE

Serves 8 to 10

1 pound ground round steak	500 g
⅓ cup finely chopped onion	75 mL
⅓ cup bread crumbs	75 mL
1 egg	1
⅓ cup cream	75 mL
salt and pepper to taste	
¼ teaspoon garlic powder	1 mL
butter or oil	

Mix all ingredients and form into small balls. Brown in butter or oil.

Sauce

1 cup brown sugar	250 mL
½ cup cider vinegar	125 mL
2-10 ounce cans condensed tomato soup	2-284 mL
1 tablespoon chili powder	15 mL
1 tablespoon celery salt	15 mL

Mix all ingredients. Simmer for one hour. Pour over meatballs. Refrigerate. Heat to serve.

Serve in Italian bread boat. (Remove top from loaf and scoop out inside.)

ZUCCHINI PIZZAS

Serves 4 to 6
low calorie

1 large zucchini, sliced, ¾ inch (2 cm) thick	1
1-5 ounce can tomato paste	142 mL
Mozzarella cheese, cut into cubes	
Parmesan cheese	
garlic powder	
oregano	

Parboil zucchini slices in water 1½ minutes, or until tender and crisp; drain on paper towels. Place slices in single layer on cookie sheet. Top each with ½ teaspoon (2 mL) tomato paste, cubed Mozzarella, Parmesan, garlic and oregano. Broil 3 to 5 minutes or until cheese is melted and bubbly.

STRATHBORO PASTE

Makes 2¼ cups or 550 mL

A delicious alternative to pâté!

2 cups, cooked beef, cubed (well-done)	500 mL
10 anchovy fillets	10
1 small onion cut in quarters	1
2 teaspoons garlic, sliced	10 mL
1 teaspoon crushed thyme	5 mL
1 bay leaf, crumbled	1
salt and pepper, to taste	
½ cup soft butter	125 mL

In food processor, mix beef, anchovy, onion, garlic, thyme, bay leaf, salt and pepper, until evenly chopped. Add butter and process until mixture is smooth. Transfer to a serving dish and serve with cocktail breads or crusty French loaf.

SALMON MOUSSE ON CUCUMBER

Serves 6 to 8

¼ cup water	50 mL
1 envelope unflavoured gelatine	1
1 tablespoon lemon juice	15 mL
½ medium onion	½
¼ cup mayonnaise	50 mL
1 tablespoon prepared horseradish	15 mL
½ teaspoon dill weed	2 mL
¼ teaspoon salt	1 mL
⅛ teaspoon paprika	pinch
1-7 ounce can salmon, well drained, picked over to remove bones	220 g
½ cup whipping cream	125 mL
1 English cucumber	1

Dissolve gelatine in ¼ cup water and blend in blender with lemon juice and onion. Add mayonnaise, horseradish, dill, salt, paprika and salmon. Pour whipping cream over all and blend until smooth. Lightly oil 2 cup (500 mL) mould. Pour mousse in and refrigerate until set. Serve as spread on cucumber slices. 30 calories per tablespoon.

CHEESE WAFERS, WITH A TWIST!

Makes 6 to 8 dozen

¼ pound butter	125 mL
½ pound Cheddar cheese, grated	250 g
½ package dehydrated onion soup mix	½ package
½ teaspoon salt	2 mL
1 cup white all-purpose flour	250 mL

Let butter and cheese come to room temperature, then mix thoroughly. Add remaining ingredients and blend. Shape into two or three rolls, one inch (2 cm) in diameter. Wrap in waxed paper and chill. Slice roll into slices ¼ inch (.5 cm) thick. Bake on an ungreased cookie sheet for 10 to 12 minutes in 375°F (190°C) oven.

Wafers should be slightly brown on edges. These are good hot or cold. Freezes beautifully.

SPINACH DIP

Serves 8 to 10

1 package frozen chopped spinach, thawed	1
3 green onions, chopped	3
1 package dry vegetable soup mix	1
1 cup mayonnaise	250 mL
1 cup sour cream	250 mL
1-10 ounce can water chestnuts or sliced almonds	1-284 mL

Thaw spinach and drain well. Chop green onions in food processor and add mayonnaise, sour cream and spinach. Put in bowl and stir in vegetable soup mix and water chestnuts or almonds. Chill overnight.

ABC DIP

Serves 6 to 8

⅓ cup chopped almonds	75 mL
3 strips bacon (well done and crumbled)	3
1½ cups grated sharp Cheddar cheese	375 mL
¾ cup mayonnaise	175 mL
1 teaspoon minced onion	5 mL
¼ teaspoon salt	1 mL

Combine all ingredients in blender or food processor. Serve with crackers, vegetables or melba toast. Always popular and easy as the name implies!

DELICIOUS TACO DIP

Serves 15 to 20 people

2-8 ounce packages cream cheese	2-250 g
⅓ cup hot taco sauce	75 mL
¼ cup dry minced onion	50 mL
red or green chili, small amount to taste	

Mix above ingredients together and serve as a dip with tortilla chips or add the following for tacos.

shredded lettuce
2 tomatoes, finely chopped
½ can black olives, chopped
shredded sharp Cheddar cheese

Stuff taco shells with a layer of lettuce, add chopped tomatoes, olives, and cream cheese mixture. Top with shredded sharp Cheddar cheese. Serve on a platter.

MUSHROOM CAVIAR

Serves 6 to 8

Can be made the day before.

½ medium onion, finely chopped	½
1 tablespoon butter	15 mL
¼ pound finely chopped fresh mushrooms	125 g
½ teaspoon Worcestershire sauce	2 mL
salt and fresh ground pepper to taste	
1 tablespoon lemon juice	15 mL
mayonnaise (enough to hold mixture together)	

Sauté onion in butter, until golden. Add mushrooms and sauté 5 minutes, stirring lightly to mix well. Add lemon juice and Worcestershire sauce. Mix well. Remove from stove. Add enough mayonnaise to bind and mound in a serving dish. Chill well. Serve with melba rounds or crackers. Easy, inexpensive and a winner!

MUSHROOM TURNOVERS
Makes 12

3 tablespoons butter	45 mL
1 medium onion, finely chopped	1
½ pound mushrooms, finely chopped	250 g
2 tablespoons flour	25 mL
¼ teaspoon thyme	1 mL
½ teaspoon ground black pepper	2 mL
¼ cup sour cream	50 mL
rich pastry	

In skillet heat butter and sauté onions until lightly browned. Add mushrooms and cook for about 3 minutes, stirring frequently. Stir in flour, thyme, salt and pepper.

Gradually stir in cream and cook, stirring, until mixture is thick. Cool.

Place 1 teaspoon (5 mL) of mixture in centre of 3 inch (7 cm) round of pastry. Fold dough over and press edges together with tines of a fork. Freeze unbaked, separating layers with freezer paper.

When ready to be used, defrost and bake at 400°F (200°C) for 15 to 20 minutes, or until browned. Serve hot.

MUSHROOM MOUSSE
Serves 8

½ pound mushrooms, sautéed in butter	250 g
1½ teaspoons gelatine, dissolved in ¼ cup (50 mL) chicken broth	7 mL
1 tablespoon sherry	15 mL
1 egg, separated	1
¼ cup mayonnaise	50 mL
2 drops tobasco sauce	2
1½ tablespoons chopped onion	20 mL
optional — a few capers	
garlic salt to taste	
pepper to taste	
½ cup whipping cream	125 mL

Blend everything but the egg white in processor. Beat egg white until stiff and fold into mixture. Chill in a mould. Serve on crackers.

CAROL BURNETT'S "PARTY MENU"

Serves 6

Broiled Devilled Clams (see recipe)
Tossed green salad
Turkey Fillets with Pistachios (see recipe)
Buttered egg noodles
Fresh steamed asparagus with lemon butter
Fresh Peach Soufflé (see recipe)

"BROILED DEVILLED CLAMS"

24 small hard-shelled clams	24
¾ cup softened butter	175 mL
¼ cup minced shallots	50 mL
3 tablespoons Dijon mustard	45 mL
2 tablespoons lemon juice	25 mL
salt and pepper to taste	
stale bread crumbs	
rock salt	

Clean and shuck clams, discarding the top shell, and release them from the bottom shells. In a bowl, combine the butter, mustard, shallots, lemon juice, salt and pepper. Divide the mixture among the clams, spreading it evenly over each clam, so clam is completely covered. Cover clams with plastic wrap and chill 30 minutes. Sprinkle 2 teaspoons (10 mL) of bread crumbs over each clam and arrange the clams on a bed of rock salt in a shallow baking pan. Broil clams 2 inches (5 cm) from flame for 3 to 4 minutes until the crumbs are golden.

PRAWN PATÉ

3 pounds cooked prawns	750 g
⅓ cup butter	90 g
4 ounces cream cheese	125 g
1 tablespoon plus 2 teaspoons mayonnaise	45 mL
crushed garlic, lemon juice, black pepper to taste	

Shell and devein the prawns. This yields about 1½ pounds (375 g) of prawn meat. Chop this finely (preferably with a knife, a cuisinart will also do). Cream butter and cheese together. Mix in the prawn's and mayonnaise and other seasonings. Check carefully for taste while adding these. Chill in bowl it is to be served in. This tastes even better the day after it is made and keeps for several days.

Serve with lemon wedges on crackers or melba toast.

CHEESE STRAWS
Makes 2 to 3 dozen

1 cup Cheddar cheese, grated	250 mL
1 cup flour	250 mL
¼ cup butter	50 mL
7 tablespoons sour cream	75 mL
1 egg white	1
salt, to taste	
paprika, to taste	

In a large bowl, cut butter into flour. Mix in grated cheese. Blend in sour cream. Chill dough for 30 minutes.

On a floured board roll out dough to ¼ inch (.5 cm) thickness. Brush with egg white. Cut in strips 4 inches (10 cm) long and ½ inch (1 cm) wide. Twist into spirals. Bake on an ungreased cookie sheet at 350°F (180°C) for 15 minutes or until golden.

Excellent warm or cold.

ESCARGOTS EN PHYLLO

Makes 16

32 mushroom caps	32
¼ cup snail butter	50 mL
32 escargots	32
8 sheets Phyllo pastry	8
¼ cup melted butter (approximately)	50 mL
pinch caraway seeds	pinch

Quarter mushrooms. In a skillet, heat snail butter; add mushrooms and sauté over high heat for a minute. Add escargots and heat through. Remove from heat; let cool.

Cut pastry into rounds 4 inches (10 cm) in diameter, a total of 48 pieces. Brush each piece lightly with melted butter.

Stack 3 rounds of pastry, one on top of the other; place 2 escargots and some mushroom mixture on half of pastry; fold other half over. Seal edges by pressing hard. Brush melted butter on top and sprinkle with caraway seeds. Repeat with remaining pastry rounds. Bake in a 350°F (180°C) oven for 8 to 10 minutes or until golden brown.

Escargot Butter

¼ cup butter	50 mL
2 tablespoons finely chopped parsley	25 mL
1 tablespoon lemon juice	15 mL
1 teaspoon finely chopped garlic	5 mL
1 teaspoon grated onion	5 mL
dash of Worcestershire, Tobasco, salt and pepper	dash

In a small bowl, mix ingredients together.

COCKTAIL QUICHE

Makes 90

Crust

3-3 ounce packages cream cheese	3-125 g
¾ pound butter	375 mL
3 cups flour	750 mL

Filling

8 ounces Mozzarella cheese, grated	250 g
4 ounces Cheddar cheese, grated	125 g
⅓ cup Parmesan cheese, grated	75 mL
2-4½ ounce cans devilled ham	2-128 g
3 eggs, well beaten	3
1½ cups milk	375 mL
1 generous dash Worcestershire sauce	1
½ cup onion, chopped	125 mL
1 tablespoon Dijon mustard	15 mL
salt and pepper to taste	

Mix cream cheese, butter and flour. Chill at least 3 hours. Divide into balls between 1 inch to 1½ inches (1 cm); flatten into miniature muffin pans. Mix filling ingredients, spoon into shells. Bake at 350°F (180°C) for 30 to 35 minutes. Let cool before removing from pan. If freezing remove 1 hour ahead of serving time and bake at 350°F (180°C) for 8 to 10 minutes.

POTATO SKINS

Serves 4

2 baking potatoes	2
1½ tablespoons melted unsalted butter	20 mL
½ cup freshly grated Cheddar or Parmesan cheese	125 mL
4 strips crumbled cooked bacon	4

Preheat oven to 400°F (200°C). Scrub and dry potatoes. Pierce each one with a fork. Bake 1 hour and 10 minutes or until very tender. Remove potatoes from oven and reduce heat to 375°F (190°C). Cut potatoes inhalf lengthwise. Scoop out the potatoes leaving ¼ inch (.5 cm) shell, (reserve the scooped out potatoes for another use).

Brush the inside of the skins generously with the melted butter. Sprinkle on the cheese and top with the crumbled bacon. Return the potatoes to the oven and bake for 30 minutes or until the tops are golden and the skins are very crisp.

Serve as a side dish or cut into strips and serve as an appetizer. May be doubled or tripled.

AN OLD FAVOURITE

Serves 4

1-10 ounce can consommé, condensed	1-284 mL
8 ounces cream cheese, softened	250 g
½ teaspoon curry powder	2 mL
sour cream, optional	
red lumpfish caviar, optional	

Heat ½ can (142 mL) of consommé, and mix with cheese and curry. Place in attractive individual glass dishes. Cool in refrigerator overnight. Carefully spoon remaining consommé (room temperature) over consommé mix. Set in refrigerator. Garnish with a dollop of sour cream and red lumpfish caviar. A delight to behold.

MEATBALL HORS D'OEUVRE

Serves 8

1 pound hamburger, or ground steak	500 g
1½ cups ginger ale	375 mL
½ cup tomato ketchup	125 mL

Form tiny meatballs and place in a casserole dish. Mix ginger ale and ketchup in a bowl, (adding more ketchup if you like sauce spicier) and pour over meat. Cover and cook on top of stove over medium heat 20 to 30 minutes, mixing very gently after 10 minutes. Serve with a toothpick in each. Don't be put off by the ginger ale — it really makes "the difference".

SMOKED SALMON
OR TROUT PATÉ

Makes 3 cups

You can use any smoked fish to make this pâté.

12 ounces smoked salmon	350 g
1½ cups whipping cream	375 mL
1 bunch watercress	1

In food processor purée salmon to fine texture. Whip cream to soft peaks. Fold salmon into cream. Spoon into serving dish; cover and refrigerate for at least 1 hour.

May be prepared a day in advance. Serve with watercress and French bread or toast strips.

RIBBON PATÉ
Serves 25

2 envelopes unflavoured gelatine	2
2 cubes beef bouillon	2
1 tablespoon lemon juice	15 mL
2-8 ounce packages cream cheese	500 g
½ cup dairy sour cream	125 g
1 tablespoon grated onion	15 mL
2-4½ ounce cans liver pâté	2-128 g
¼ cup mayonnaise	50 mL
2 tablespoons chopped parsley	25 mL
2-4½ ounce cans devilled ham	2-128 g
¼ cup prepared sweet mustard relish	50 mL
3 pitted ripe olives, sliced	3

Make aspic by combining gelatine and beef broth with 1 cup (250 mL) in small saucepan. Heat, stirring constantly just until gelatine dissolves. Measure ¼ cupful (50 mL) into a 6 cup (1.5 L) mould and stir in lemon juice. Set mould in pan of ice and water to speed setting. Reserve remaining ¾ cup of broth.

Make cheese mixture by combining cream cheese, sour cream, onion and ¼ cup (50 mL) aspic.

Make liver mixture by combining pâté, mayonnaise, parsley and ¼ cup (50 mL) aspic.

Make ham mixture by combining ham, mustard relish and ¼ cup (50 mL) aspic.

Assembly

When gelatine in mould is slightly firm arrange a ring of olive slices on top. Let set until sticky firm. Spoon half of cheese mixture on top. Let set until sticky firm. Repeat with all of the ham mixture, remaining cheese mixture, then all of liver mixture, waiting each time until layer on top is sticky firm. Remove mould from ice and water. Cover with foil and chill several hours until firm. When ready to serve set mould in lukewarm water for a few minutes. Turn onto serving plate. Surround with your choice of crisp crackers.

This recipe takes time, but what a showoff!

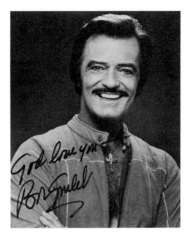

ROBERT AND VERA GOULET'S "CAVIAR SPREAD"

Yields 2 cups (500 mL) of spread

1 cup creamed cottage cheese	250 mL
1 cup sour cream	250 mL
1-4 ounce jar red caviar (lumpfish)	113 g
3 tablespoons sherry	45 mL
2 tablespoons chopped chives	25 mL
1 teaspoon lemon juice	5 mL
¼ teaspoon dry mustard	1 mL
watercress	
English biscuits, melba toast or crackers	

In a large bowl combine cottage cheese, sour cream, caviar, sherry, chives, lemon juice and dry mustard. Place in serving bowl. Cover and chill at least one hour.

When ready to serve, garnish with watercress and accompany with unseasoned crackers or melba toast.

PORT AND CHEDDAR SPREAD

Serves 6

¼ cup port or sherry	50 mL
2 tablespoons sour cream (or regular cream)	25 mL
¼ teaspoon paprika	1 mL
½ pound sharp Cheddar cheese, diced	250 g

Blend above ingredients until smooth. This is nice moulded in a small bowl. Serve with crackers. Stores well in the refrigerator.

CHEESE BALL

Serves 6

1-8 ounce package cream cheese	250 g
8 slices smoked beef	8
1½ bunches green onions	1½
1 teaspoon garlic salt	5 mL
1 tablespoon monosodium glutamate	15 mL

Whirl in food processor; form into a ball. Chill overnight. Garnish with chopped beef; serve with melba rounds.

OPEN FACE SANDWICHES

Serves 6

12 slices rye bread	12
½ cup sour cream	125 mL
¼ bottle creamy Italian salad dressing	250 mL
½ cup pecans	125 mL
½ teaspoon mustard	2 mL
1½ cups Cheddar cheese, shredded	375 mL
12 slices cooked ham	12
2 tablespoons gelatine	25 mL
3 tablespoons water	45 mL
2 cups mayonnaise	500 mL
⅓ cup whipping cream, whipped	75 mL
olives	

Trim crusts. Combine sour cream, nuts, dressing, mustard and cheese. Spread on bread. Cover with sliced ham. Chill.

In a saucepan, mix gelatine and water. Heat until dissolved. In a bowl, mix mayonnaise, whipped cream and fold in cooled gelatine mixture.

Place sandwiches on a serving plate, ice with mayonnaise mixture (over edges of bread) and garnish with olives. Chill until set.

HONEY DIP FOR CRUDITÉS

Serves 12

1 cup Hellman's mayonnaise	250 mL
1 clove garlic, crushed	1
½ teaspoon ginger	2 mL
1 teaspoon curry powder	5 mL
2 tablespoons liquid honey	25 mL
1 to 1½ tablespoons lemon juice (or to taste)	15 to 20 mL

Mix all ingredients. Flavour improves with standing and so should be prepared a day in advance. Keep covered in refrigerator. Serve with raw vegetables.

DEVILLED HAM DIP

Serves 4 to 6

1-4½ ounce can devilled ham	128 g
1-4 ounce package pimento cream cheese, softened	125 g
1 teaspoon dry mustard	5 mL
½ cup sour cream	125 mL
1 tablespoon green pickle relish	15 mL
1 tablespoon dried minced onion	15 mL

Combine all in food processor or blender. Chill and serve as dip for crudités or on crackers.

ARTICHOKE DIP

Serves 6

1 cup mayonnaise	250 mL
1 cup Parmesan cheese	250 mL
1-14 ounce can artichoke hearts (not marinated), drained	398 mL
pinch of garlic to taste	

Chop artichoke hearts and combine with mayonnaise and cheese. Place in heat proof dish and heat in 350°F (180°C) oven for approximately 20 minutes or until lightly browned. Stir before serving. Serve with crunchy crackers. This recipe can be doubled.

SUPER MAKE AHEAD APPETIZER

Serves 6 to 8

7 English muffins (split)	7
1-14 ounce can pitted black olives, drained and chopped	1-398 mL
½ cup mayonnaise	125 mL
½ cup green onions, finely chopped	125 mL
8 ounces old Cheddar cheese (orange), grated	250 g
½ teaspoon curry powder	2 mL
½ teaspoon salt	2 mL

Mix all of the above together (except English muffins). Spread mixture on muffin halves. Freeze briefly to make it easier to cut into quarters. Freeze or use immediately. Cook in preheated oven 350°F (180°C) for 20 minutes if frozen, 10 minutes if fresh (or thawed).

CAVIAR MOULD

Serves 6 to 8

1-10 ounce can beef bouillon	1-284 mL
1 envelope unflavoured gelatine	1
1-4 ounce jar black caviar or lumpfish	113 g
1-8 ounce package cream cheese	250 g
1 tablespoon green onions, chopped	15 mL
mayonnaise	

Dissolve gelatine in bouillon over low heat, stove. Pour ⅓ (75 mL) of mixture into a one quart (1 L) mould. Chill. When set spread the caviar over the bouillon. Mix cream cheese with green onions and enough mayonnaise to soften. Pour on top of caviar. Pour on rest of bouillon. Chill well. Serve with melba rounds. This gives you miles out of 1 jar of caviar and is wonderful with drinks.

FLORENTINE BALLS
Makes 48

2-10 ounce packages frozen chopped spinach, thawed but not cooked. Drain very, very well.	2-284 g
2 cups packaged stuffing mix	500 mL
1 cup grated Parmesan cheese	250 mL
salt and pepper, to taste	
6 eggs, beaten	6
¾ cup softened butter	175 mL

Combine all ingredients, mixing well. Roll into balls, the size of walnuts. Freeze.

To serve, place frozen balls on a cookie sheet and bake at 350°F (180°C) for 15 minutes.

SMOKED OYSTERS

Open a tin of smoked oysters	104 g
Open a can of Pillsbury buttermilk biscuits	227 g

Cut each biscuit in half. Wrap each half around a smoked oyster and seal. Place on a cookie sheet and bake according to directions on roll package. Serve hot with mustard.

VIRGINIA DIP
Serves 6

1 cup pecans, chopped	250 mL
2 teaspoons butter	10 mL
1-8 ounce package cream cheese, softened	1-250 g
4 tablespoons milk	50 mL
1 package dried beef, minced	1
1 teaspoon garlic salt	5 mL
1 cup sour cream	250 mL
4 teaspoons chopped onion	20 mL

Sauté pecans in butter, reserve. Mix remaining ingredients thoroughly. Add pecans. Chill until serving time. Bake at 350°F (180°C) for 20 minutes. Serve with crackers.

SHRIMP APPETIZER

Serves 8

1-10 ounce can condensed tomato soup	1-284 mL
1-8 ounce package cream cheese	250 g
1 envelope unflavoured gelatine	1
¼ cup cold water	50 mL
¾ cup chopped celery and green onion, combined	175 mL
12 ounce bag of frozen, precooked, salad shrimp, thawed	340 g
½ cup mayonnaise	125 mL

Soften gelatine in water. Bring soup to boil and dissolve gelatine in it. Put cream cheese in blender, add soup, and blend. Add mayonnaise and blend. Pour into bowl and add vegetables and shrimp. Combine. Turn into a mould. Refrigerate until firm. Serve with crackers.

DELICIOUS CHEESE SPREAD

8 ounces creamed cottage cheese, well drained	250 g
⅔ cup soft butter	150 mL
1½ teaspoons anchovy paste	7 mL
10 to 12 chopped, drained, green pimento stuffed olives	10 to 12
2 teaspoons caraway seeds	10 mL
2 tablespoons minced green onions	25 mL
1 tablespoon paprika	15 mL
garlic powder and salt to taste	

Mix all ingredients together in food processor. Chill at least 5 hours. Excellent on dark bread.

CHEESE PUFFS

Serves 8 to 10

1 unsliced loaf of white bread	1
2 cups sharp Cheddar cheese	500 mL
Hellman's mayonnaise to moisten	
paprika	

Cut crusts off unsliced loaf (day old is best) and cut the loaf into cubes. Grate the cheese and add Hellman's to moisten. Ice the cubes of bread. Sprinkle with paprika. Bake at 350°F (180°C) until cheese melts (about 12 minutes).

SALMON SUPREME
(gravlax)

Serves 12 as an appetizer

3 to 3½ pounds fresh salmon fillets, centre cut, cleaned and scaled	1.5 Kg
1 large bunch of fresh dill	1
¼ cup salt	50 mL
¼ cup sugar	50 mL
2 tablespoons coarse black pepper	25 mL

Slice salmon in half lengthwise and place fish, skin side down in a large glass dish. Combine dill, salt, sugar and pepper and sprinkle over the top of the fish. Cover with the second piece of fish, skin side up. Weight salmon and refrigerate 48 hours. Turn every 3 hours and baste all over, keeping weight in place for entire time. Scrape away seasonings and serve, sliced very thin with brown bread.

CHEESE CHUTNEY

Serves 6

6 ounces cream cheese	170 g
4 ounces grated Cheddar cheese	125 g
3 tablespoons sherry	45 mL
2/4 teaspoons curry	4 mL
salt to taste	
mango chutney to taste	
chopped chives to taste	

Process first five ingredients. Place in crock or glass dish and refrigerate until ready to serve. Can be made the day before. Before serving garnish with a little mango chutney and chives to taste. Serve with melba rounds or crackers.

TEXAS CRABGRASS

Serves 6 to 8

⅓ cup butter	75 mL
½ cup finely chopped onion	125 mL
1-7½ ounce can crabmeat, drained	213 g
¾ cup Parmesan cheese	175 mL
1 package frozen chopped spinach, drained	1

Melt butter and add onion, sauté until soft. Add remaining ingredients. Heat through, serve hot with melba toast.

ANCHOVY ROLLS

Serves 6 to 8

1-8 ounce package cream cheese, softened	250 g
1-3 ounce tin anchovy fillets, drained and finely chopped	84 g
3 tablespoons pimentos, chopped finely	45 mL
2 tablespoons sour cream	25 mL
dash of pepper	
16 slices sandwich bread	16
melted butter	

Combine first five ingredients. Cut crusts from slices of the sandwich bread. Spread each slice with anchovy mixture. Roll up as for jelly-rolled sandwiches. Cut in half. Brush with melted butter. Pack rolls in shallow pan. Broil until lightly browned on all sides.

This freezes. If frozen, take out ½ hour before broiling.

MARVELLOUS MUSHROOMS

Serves 8 to 10

40 medium-sized mushrooms	40
1-8 ounce package green onion cream cheese	250 g
16 slices bacon	16
¼ cup softened butter	50 mL

Wash mushrooms and remove stems. Broil bacon until crisp. Chop bacon and mix with cheese and butter. Fill mushroom caps with mixture. Bake at 350°F (180°C) for 20 minutes. Note: cream cheese and bacon mixture may be done ahead of time.

NUTS AND BOLTS

Makes 7 quarts (6.5 L)

1 pound butter	500 g
1 tablespoon garlic salt	15 mL
1 tablespoon celery salt	15 mL
2 pounds skinless salted peanuts	1 Kg
1 large box Shreddies	1
1 large box Cheerios	1
1 large box pretzels	1

Melt butter, garlic and celery salt together. Pour in other ingredients and mix. Put in 200°F (100°C) oven for 2 hours, stirring occasionally.

Soups and Salads

CURRIED CARROT AND LEEK SOUP
Serves 10 to 12

4 medium leeks	4
2 pounds carrots (about 14 medium)	1 Kg
½ cup butter	125 mL
4 teaspoons curry powder, or to taste	20 mL
1 teaspoon cumin	5 mL
½ teaspoon nutmeg	2 mL
5 cups chicken stock	1.25 L
¼ cup frozen orange juice concentrate	50 mL
2 cups whipping cream	500 mL
2 teaspoons salt, or to taste	10 mL
freshly ground pepper, to taste	

Slice leeks (white part and about 1 inch (2.5 cm) of green). Peel carrots, then slice into rounds. In large saucepan, melt butter; add leeks and carrots and cook over medium heat, stirring, for about 15 minutes.

Stir in curry powder, cumin, nutmeg, chicken stock and orange juice. Bring to boil, reduce heat and simmer, covered, for 20 minutes or until vegetables are tender.

Purée soup in food processor or blender or pass through food mill. Just before serving, return soup to saucepan; add cream, salt and pepper to taste. Bring to boil. Add more chicken stock if desired.

GREEN TOMATO SOUP
Serves 8

¼ cup butter	50 mL
2 onions, sliced	2
8 green tomatoes, cut in chunks	8
1 cup chicken stock	250 mL
1 tablespoon flour	15 mL
1 cup milk	250 mL
1 teaspoon sugar	5 mL
salt and pepper, to taste	
chopped chives	

In a skillet, melt butter. Add onions and tomatoes, sauté until soft, (about ½ hour). Blend in food processor. Add the chicken stock.

In a small bowl, blend flour and milk, add to soup mixture. Pour into saucepan, boil until thick. Season with salt, pepper, and sugar.

Garnish with chopped chives. A September treat!

BILL SHATNER'S "CARROT VICHYSSOISE"

Serves 4

2 cups peeled, diced potatoes	500 mL
2 cups sliced carrots	500 mL
1 leek, sliced	1
3 cups vegetable stock	750 mL
1 cup milk or ½ cup milk and ½ cup cream	250 mL

Combine first four ingredients in a saucepan. Bring to a boil. Reduce to a simmer for 25 to 30 minutes. Purée half of the vegetables and liquid in a blender. Empty into a bowl, add milk and a pinch of salt and pepper. Stir. Serve cold in chilled bowls. Garnish with cold sliced scallions very sparingly.

HARVEST ASPARAGUS–TOMATO SOUP

Serves 6 to 10

1½ cups asparagus, cooked	375 mL
5 cups chicken stock	1.25 L
1 medium onion, chopped	1
1 carrot, coarsely chopped	1
1 tablespoon chopped parsley	15 mL
1 bay leaf	1
2 cups canned or fresh tomatoes	500 mL
⅛ teaspoon pepper, freshly ground	pinch
½ teaspoon thyme	2 mL
1 teaspoon salt	1 mL
pinch of ground cloves	pinch
½ teaspoon sugar	2 mL
2 tablespoons flour	25 mL
2 tablespoons melted butter	25 mL

Garnish
½ teaspoon butter	2 mL
½ teaspoon fresh parsley or	2 mL
1 tablespoon sour cream	15 mL
½ teaspoon chives, minced	2 mL

Combine all soup ingredients except butter and flour. Cover, simmer for 45 minutes.

Purée in food processor or blender until fairly smooth. This may need to be done in 2 or 3 batches. Return to pot over low heat. Blend butter and flour together, stir into soup. Simmer 20 to 30 minutes. Garnish.

CRÈME SENEGALESE

Serves 6

2 tablespoons butter	25 mL
½ cup chopped onion	125 mL
1 tablespoon mild curry powder	15 mL
1 cup chopped leeks (white parts only)	250 mL
1 clove finely minced garlic or ½ teaspoon garlic flakes	1 or 2 mL
½ cup diced bananas	125 mL
¼ cup chopped, peeled apples	50 mL
1½ cups peeled, chopped tomatoes	375 mL
1 cup peeled, cubed potatoes	250 mL
salt and freshly ground pepper	
4 drops Tobasco sauce	4
3½ cups chicken broth	875 mL
1 cup whipping cream	250 mL
½ cup finely diced cooked breast of chicken	125 mL
1 tablespoon unsweetened coconut	15 mL

In heavy pot heat butter, add onion. Cook, stirring until glossy. Add curry powder and stir to coat onion. Add leeks, garlic, bananas, apples, tomatoes, potatoes, salt and pepper, to taste. Add Tobasco. Stir well. Add chicken broth and simmer for 20 minutes. Pour little at a time into a blender. When blended pour into a bowl and chill overnight. When ready to serve add cream and chicken, mix well. Serve thoroughly chilled. Sprinkle with coconut on top before serving.

AVOCADO AND GRAPEFRUIT SOUP, CHILLED

Serves 6

2 ripe avocados	2
2 tablespoons coriander, freshly chopped	25 mL
¾ teaspoon salt	7 mL
2 cups grapefruit juice	500 mL
1½ cups plain yogurt	375 mL
6 teaspoons red caviar or lumpfish	25 mL

Peel the avocados. In a bowl, mash the avocados with the coriander and salt, beat in the grapefruit juice and yogurt, one half of a cup at a time, blending the mixture thoroughly.

Chill and pour into 6 soup bowls. Garnish each serving with 1 teaspoon (5 mL) red caviar. Fresh and festive!

TOMATO-DILL SOUP

Serves 8 to 10

8 tablespoons unsalted butter	125 mL
3 cups onions, peeled and sliced	750 mL
2 garlic cloves, minced	2
1 bunch fresh dill, finely chopped	1
salt and pepper to taste	
2 quarts chicken stock	2 L
3 pounds Italian plum tomatoes, drained, seeded	1.5 Kg
1 teaspoon allspice	5 mL
pinch sugar	pinch

Garnish
sprigs of dill	
1 cup sour cream	250 mL

In a large pot melt butter. Add onions, cook slowly over low heat covered until tender. Add garlic, cook another 5 minutes. Add half the dill, season to taste and cook uncovered 15 minutes. Add chicken stock, tomatoes, allspice, sugar. Bring to a boil, reduce heat, simmer covered 45 minutes. Purée the soup. Return soup to pot, add remaining dill, simmer 5 minutes. Serve immediately or refrigerate overnight. Delicious hot or cold. Garnish with a dollop of sour cream and a sprig of dill.

CARROT AND ONION SOUP

Serves 4

In heavy pot or pressure cooker, sauté for 5 minutes:
3 tablespoons butter	45 mL
4 to 5 medium carrots, grated	4 to 5
1 medium onion, minced	1

Add and stir until coated:
½ cup dry rice (brown or white)	125 mL

Add:
4 cups seasoned water or vegetable stock	1 L

Have ready:
1 cup hot milk	250 mL

Cook until rice is very well done, about 45 minutes (or 25 in pressure cooker). You may wish to sieve the soup or blend it into a purée.

Return it to the pot and add the hot milk. Do not boil.

2

Savory Lamb and Spinach Roll
Recipe on page 77

NANCY REAGAN'S
"ONION WINE SOUP"
Serves 6 to 8

¼ cup butter	50 mL
5 large onions, chopped	5
5 cups beef broth	1.25 L
½ cup celery leaves	125 mL
1 large potato, sliced	1
1 cup dry white wine	250 mL
1 tablespoon vinegar	15 mL
2 teaspoons sugar	10 mL
1 cup light cream	250 mL
1 tablespoon minced parsley	15 mL
salt and pepper, to taste	

Melt butter in large saucepan. Add chopped onion and mix well. Add beef broth, celery leaves and potato. Bring to boiling. Cover and simmer for 30 minutes. Purée mixture in a blender. Return to saucepan and blend in wine, vinegar and sugar. Bring to boil and simmer 5 minutes. Stir in cream, parsley and salt and pepper to taste. Heat thoroughly but do not boil. With best wishes!

FISH CHOWDER
Serves 6

1 pound white fish	500 g
juice of 2 limes	2
3 tablespoons butter	45 mL
½ pound salt pork, minced	250 g
1 pound onions, sliced	500 g
1-10 ounce can of tomatoes	1-284 mL
1 tablespoon butter	15 mL
2 pounds potatoes, sliced	1 Kg
½ pound unsalted crackers, crushed	250 g
1 cup sherry	250 mL
¼ cup Worcestershire sauce	50 mL
flour, salt and pepper	

Marinate the fish in lime juice for 1 hour. Drain and pat dry. Dip fish in flour. Sauté fish in butter on both sides, season with salt and pepper.

Brown onions in pan with salt pork. Add tomatoes, butter and a little water. Cook slowly for 15 minutes.

Cook potatoes until almost tender. Add fish to half the tomato mixture. Add crackers, potatoes, sherry and Worcestershire sauce. Add remaining tomato mixture.

If necessary add sufficient boiling water to cover. Simmer slowly for 15 minutes.

WATERCRESS SOUP
Serves 4 to 6

3 large potatoes	3
2 large chopped onions	2
1½ pints chicken stock	750 mL
1 bunch watercress	1
1 large knob (about 1 dessert spoonful) butter	15 mL

Boil potatoes and chopped onions in the chicken stock. When vegetables soft add watercress (less a few leaves for garnish).

Cook for 10 more minutes. Season with salt to taste. Put the above in blender little at a time. Reheat the above with large knob of butter.

Serve with chopped watercress sprinkled over.

(The socially secure may add a clove or two of garlic to the soup when cooking. Remove before serving!) Serve hot.

LEEK AND BROCCOLI SOUP

Serves 6 to 8

¼ cup butter	50 mL
2 cups chopped leeks (white and pale green)	500 mL
½ cup chopped onion	125 mL
1 garlic clove, minced	1
½ cup chopped celery	125 mL
1 bunch broccoli (1½ pounds, 750 g), chopped	1
2 tablespoons flour	25 mL
½ teaspoon salt	2 mL
¼ teaspoon pepper	1 mL
5 cups lightly salted chicken stock	1.25 L
2 cups whipping cream	500 mL

Melt butter in saucepan, add leeks, onion, garlic and celery, sauté 15 minutes. Prepare broccoli (peel stems before chopping), reserving ¼ cup (50 mL) for garnish. Add broccoli to vegetables. Add flour, salt and pepper, cook 3 minutes. Pour in stock, bring to a boil and simmer uncovered for 15 minutes, or until tender. Purée.

To serve, pour in cream and heat. Steam reserved broccoli, float on soup. A wonderful winter soup!

FISH SOUP

Serves 4 to 6

2 pounds white fish (cod, sole, halibut or flounder)	1 Kg
5 medium-sized potatoes, peeled and sliced	5
1 large onion, peeled and sliced	1
2 medium-sized tomatoes, peeled and chopped	2
2 cloves garlic, peeled and crushed	2
bouquet garni of parsley, bay leaf, celery and strip of orange peel	
½ cup olive oil	125 mL
1 teaspoon salt	5 mL
freshly ground black pepper	
fresh parsley, finely chopped	

Place all ingredients in an iron casserole or a heavy pot. Pour boiling water over contents to cover (6 to 8 cups — 1.5 to 2 L) and cook, uncovered, over medium heat for 20 minutes.

FRENCH CANADIAN PEA SOUP

Serves 6 to 8

2 cups split peas, washed	500 mL
1 very meaty ham bone	1
2 quarts water	2 L
1 large onion, sliced thinly	1
2 sticks of celery, sliced	2
2 cloves garlic, chopped	2
4 cloves	4
2 bay leaves	2
salt, to taste	
¼ teaspoon white pepper	1 mL

In a large saucepan place the water, washed peas, ham bone and all other ingredients except the salt. Bring to boil and skim, if necessary. Reduce the heat, and cook for 2½ hours, stirring now and again. If the ham has not made the soup as salty as you like, add more salt to taste. Remove the ham bone, cut off any bits of meat still remaining and dice finely. Put the soup through a blender or food mill, removing the bay leaves and cloves. Return the soup to the pot with the diced ham pieces, and if the mixture is too thick, dilute with broth, cream or sherry. If you wish you may add crispy bacon bits, sliced spicy sausage, croutons or toasted almond slivers.

Always a favourite.

MUSHROOM-ALMOND SOUP

Serves 4 to 6

1-10 ounce can condensed onion soup	1-284 mL
4 chicken bouillon cubes	4
2 tablespoons butter	25 mL
¼ pound fresh mushrooms	125 g
2 cups boiling water	500 mL
a dash each of garlic powder, celery salt, and freshly ground black pepper	
juice of one lemon	1
⅓ to ½ cups sherry	75 to 125 mL
toasted almonds	

Dissolve bouillon cubes in boiling water. Combine in top of double boiler with onion soup, seasonings, lemon juice and mushrooms which have been sautéed in 2 tablespoons butter. Reserve remaining butter to toast almonds. Heat mixture. Add sherry. Pour into heated soup bowls and garnish with almonds.

STILTON AND CELERY SOUP

Serves 10

1 medium onion, finely chopped	1
3 sticks of celery or 1 celery heart, chopped	1
2 ounces butter	50 g
2 ounces flour	30 g
¼ pint dry cider	150 mL
2 pints chicken stock	1.1 L
1½ pints homogenized milk	850 mL
5 ounces Stilton cheese	150 g
salt and pepper to taste	
¼ pint cream	150 mL

Prepare the onion and celery and chop them finely. Heat the butter until foaming. Add the flour and stir for 1 minute. Take off the heat and mix in the cider and stock. Put back over gentle heat and bring to a boil, stirring continuously, and simmer for 45 minutes. Mash the cheese thoroughly and mix into the milk, then add to the soup and heat until it is just below boiling point, stirring all the time. Taste for seasonings then liquidize or sieve. Add the cream and bring to just under boiling point and serve hot.

This is a most lovely soup, creamy and with a most elusive flavour.

BEER-CHEESE SOUP

Serves 4

4 tablespoons unsalted butter	50 mL
2 tablespoons minced shallots	25 mL
¼ cup flour	50 mL
½ teaspoon dry mustard	2 mL
pinch of cayenne pepper	pinch
2 cups chicken stock, or broth	500 mL
2 cups milk	500 mL
¼ cup beer	50 mL
3 cups sharp Cheddar cheese, grated	750 mL
¼ teaspoon salt	50 mL

In a large saucepan, melt butter and sauté shallots until soft, about 5 minutes. Whisk in flour, mustard, and cayenne. Gradually stir in chicken stock, milk, beer, cheese, and salt. Cook gently, stirring constantly, until cheese has melted and serve piping hot.

ROBUST VEGETABLE SOUP

Serves 6

1 tablespoon butter	15 mL
1 cup sliced mushrooms	250 mL
½ cup chopped onions	125 mL
2 large carrots, sliced	2
1 small cauliflower, separated into florets and sliced	1
2 large stalks celery, chopped	2
1 teaspoon basil	5 mL
½ teaspoon nutmeg, freshly ground	2 mL
1 bay leaf	1
1 teaspoon salt	5 mL
8 cups chicken stock	2 L
½ cup butter	125 mL
½ cup barley	125 mL
1 cup diced cooked chicken or turkey	250 mL
½ cup sour cream	125 mL
chopped parsley	

Melt butter in saucepan. Add onions and mushrooms and cook over low heat, covered for 10 minutes, until soft.

Set aside. Bring carrots, cauliflower, celery, seasonings and stock to a boil in a large saucepan. Reduce heat to low and simmer for about 10 minutes, or until vegetables are just beginning to get tender. Strain, reserving stock.

Melt butter in saucepan. Add barley and stir until coated. Add reserved stock, cover, and simmer about 1½ hours or until barley is tender. Add mushrooms, juices and vegetables to pan with chicken and heat thoroughly.

Remove from heat, stir in sour cream. Sprinkle generously with parsley and serve.

ROBERT AND VERA GOULET'S "FRESH CAULIFLOWER SOUP"

Serves 4

1 small cauliflower (about 1¼ pounds)	1
1 small onion, thinly sliced	1
¼ teaspoon dried thyme leaves	1 mL
2 cups of chicken broth (home-made or canned)	500 mL
2 tablespoons butter or margarine	25 mL
1 tablespoon flour	15 mL
1 teaspoon salt	5 mL
dash of ground mace, or nutmeg	dash
dash of white pepper	dash
2 cups of light cream	500 mL
½ cup of shredded Fontina cheese	125 mL
chopped parsley for garnish	

Cut out cauliflower core, remove outside leaves and separate into small florets. Combine cauliflower in medium saucepan with onion, thyme, and chicken broth. Bring to a boil. Reduce heat. Simmer, partially covered, until cauliflower is tender, about 10 minutes.

Remove and reserve about a third of the cauliflower.

Transfer remaining cauliflower mixture to food processor or blender.

Whirl until smoothly puréed.

In a 3 or 4 quart (2 L) saucepan, melt butter over medium heat; stir in flour, salt, mace or nutmeg and pepper. Cook until bubbly. Remove from heat. Gradually mix in cream. Cook stirring constantly until mixture boils. Blend in cauliflower purée and cheese. Heat, stirring occasionally, until soup is steaming and cheese melts.

Add reserved cauliflower. Cook just until heated through, about 3 minutes. Serve sprinkled with parsley.

VICHYSSOISE
Serves 4

6 cups chicken stock (Swiss Knorr cubes are lightest coloured)	1.5 L
4 medium Jerusalem artichokes (or 4 medium potatoes if Jerusalem artichokes not in season)	4
1 medium onion sliced very thin	1
3 leeks (use white parts only) sliced very thin	3
1 cup light cream	250 mL
salt and white pepper (over-salt slightly as salt loses flavour with potatoes and when chilled)	
1 tablespoon chopped chives	15 mL

Heat stock to boiling, then add vegetables. Cover and cook gently until vegetables are very tender (approximately 10 minutes). Whirl in blender (a little at a time) until very smooth. Stir in cream. Add salt and pepper to taste.

Chill overnight.

Serve with a sprinkling of chopped chives.

COLD KIWI FRUIT SOUP
Serves 4 to 6

5 or 6 large kiwi, peeled and diced	5 or 6
2 cups Sauterne	500 mL
1 cup water	250 mL
¼ cup sugar	50 mL
1 tablespoon cornstarch	15 mL
1 cup melon balls	250 mL
pinch of salt	pinch

In a medium saucepan, place kiwi, 1 cup (250 mL) of Sauterne, water, sugar and salt. Boil for 5 minutes. Dissolve cornstarch in ¼ cup (50 mL) of remaining Sauterne. Stir into soup and boil one minute, stirring constantly. Remove from heat and add remaining Sauterne. Put ½ of mixture in the soup. Add melon balls and chill. Serve with whipped cream.

ICED LEMON SOUP A LA GREQUE
Serves 12 Generously

4 cups chicken stock	1 L
2 cups light cream	500 mL
2 tablespoons cornstarch	25 mL
6 eggs, lightly beaten	6
1 cup lemon juice (about 8 lemons)	250 mL
1 teaspoon monosodium glutamate	5 mL
dash cayenne pepper	dash
thin slices of lemon	
chopped parsley	

In a saucepan, combine chicken stock and cream. Heat the mixture gently, stirring constantly, and stir in cornstarch. Cook the soup over low heat until it begins to thicken. Gradually pour a little of the hot soup into the egg yolks, stirring briskly. Pour the egg yolk mixture into the soup and add the lemon juice and monosodium glutamate and a dash of cayenne. Let the soup cool and chill it for at least 8 hours. Serve very cold, garnished with thin slices of lemon and chopped parsley.

ICED STRAWBERRY SOUP
Serves 4 to 6

1 quart fresh strawberries	1 L
½ cup dry white wine	125 mL
½ cup water	125 mL
½ cup sugar	125 mL
⅛ teaspoon allspice	pinch
⅛ teaspoon nutmeg	pinch
1 cup buttermilk	250 mL

Wash, pat dry, and hull strawberries. Set aside 8 strawberries for a garnish. Purée remaining strawberries in blender or food processor with wine and water. Pour purée into a large bowl and stir in sugar, allspice, nutmeg, and buttermilk. Chill 4 to 6 hours. At serving time, slice 8 strawberries and stir into soup.

BIBB LETTUCE SALAD WITH CANDIED ALMONDS

Serves 6 to 8

4 to 5 heads of bibb lettuce	4 to 5
2 bunches watercress	

Wash and pat dry bibb lettuce, tear into bite-sized pieces. Wash and dry the watercress, cut off the coarse stems. Just before serving place in a large chilled bowl, add dressing, toss. Sprinkle with candied almonds.

Dressing

2 shallots or green onions, chopped	2
½ cup olive oil	125 mL
2 tablespoons white wine vinegar	25 mL
1 tablespoon Dijon mustard	15 mL
¼ teaspoon freshly ground black pepper	1 mL
½ teaspoon salt	2 mL
3 to 4 tablespoons mayonnaise	45 to 50 mL

Mix together and chill — keeps well in refrigerator.

Candied Almonds

½ cup cold water	125 mL
1½ cups white sugar	375 mL
1 pound blanched almonds, whole or slivered	454 g

Combine water and sugar in saucepan. Simmer over low heat until practically all liquid has evaporated. Stir almonds in sugar mixture, until generously coated. Spread evenly on cookie sheet to harden. Store in tightly covered container.

These are excellent for nibbling or use as a topping for ice cream.

COLESLAW-NUT SALAD
Serves 8

6 cups shredded cabbage	1.5 L
1 cup bean sprouts	250 mL
1-5 ounce can water chestnuts (sliced and drained)	1-142 mL
¾ cup dry roasted peanuts	175 mL
Toasted sesame seeds	

Dressing

½ cup mayonnaise	125 mL
¼ cup sour cream, or yogurt	50 mL
2 tablespoons sugar	25 mL
2 tablespoons lemon juice	25 mL

To prepare salad: Toss cabbage, sprouts and water chestnuts. Add dressing. Refrigerate for 1 to 2 hours. Mix in peanuts, sprinkle with sesame seeds. Serve.

To prepare dressing: Blend together ingredients and let stand.

CURRIED VEGETABLE SALAD
Serves 4

1 cup turnip strips	250 mL
1 cup celery slices	250 mL
1 cup carrot strips	250 mL
2 cups cauliflower florets	500 mL
1 small green pepper in strips	

Cover vegetables with water and 1 teaspoon (5 mL) salt. Bring to boil, cover and simmer no longer than five minutes. Drain and cool.

In a jar combine:

½ cup white vinegar	125 mL
⅓ cup sugar	75 mL
¼ cup salad oil	50 mL
1 teaspoon salt	5 mL
¼ teaspoon freshly ground black pepper	1 mL
2 teaspoons curry powder	10 mL

Shake well and pour over vegetables. Marinate in refrigerator for at least 10 hours.

Will keep for four or five days.

FLAMING SPINACH SALAD

Serves 4

4 cups spinach torn into bite-size pieces	1 L
¼ cup sliced celery	50 mL
4 tablespoons sliced green onions	50 mL
4 slices bacon, cut into ½ inch (1 cm) pieces	4
2 tablespoons vinegar	25 mL
2 tablespoons packed brown sugar	25 mL
¼ teaspoon salt	1 mL
⅛ teaspoon tarragon leaves	pinch
pinch of pepper	pinch
2 tablespoons brandy	25 mL

Place spinach, celery and onions in serving dish. Fry bacon until crisp, drain on paper towel and reserve. Remove all but 1 tablespoon (15 mL) bacon fat from skillet. Stir brown sugar, vinegar, salt, tarragon and pepper into fat in skillet, Heat just to boiling, stir in bacon. Heat until bacon is hot, pour on spinach, celery and onions.

Heat brandy just until warm, ignite and pour on salad. Toss and serve immediately.

SALAD NICOISE

Serves 6 to 8

1 large head of romaine lettuce, cut into bite size pieces	1
4 medium sized tomatoes, quartered	4
2 large green peppers, sliced	2
1-7 ounce can tuna, packed in olive oil, drained	1-220 g
3 hard boiled eggs, quartered	3
12 black olives, pitted	12
1 cup garlic croutons	250 mL
1 can anchovies, drained	1
¼ cup green onions, sliced	50 mL
parsley	

Dressing
Stir into 3 tablespoons (45 mL) wine vinegar, salt, pepper, mustard, and slowly beat in 2 cups (500 mL) of olive oil and ¼ teaspoon (1 mL) lemon juice. Add Parmesan cheese.

AVOCADO RING SALAD
Serves 4

1 tablespoon gelatine	15 mL
½ cup boiling water	125 mL
1 medium avocado, peeled and sliced	1
1 tablespoon lemon juice	15 mL
1 teaspoon sugar	5 mL
¼ teaspoon salt	1 mL
pinch of ground pepper	pinch
½ cup mayonnaise	125 mL
dash of Tobasco	dash
few drops of green food colouring (optional)	

Blend gelatine and boiling water in a blender for 15 seconds. Add remaining ingredients and blend until smooth. Pour into oiled 3 cup (750 mL) ring mould and chill until firm.

Excellent with a fish luncheon.

PINEAPPLE COTTAGE CHEESE MOULD
Serves 6

1 package lime jelly powder	1
¾ cup boiling water	175 mL
1 cup drained crushed pineapple	250 mL
1 teaspoon lemon juice	5 mL
1 teaspoon sugar	5 mL
1 cup cottage cheese	250 mL
½ cup chopped pecans	125 mL
½ cup chopped celery	125 mL
½ cup mayonnaise	125 mL
1 cup evaporated milk	250 mL

Dissolve jelly powder in water, when cooled, add milk and stir in rest of ingredients. Pour in an 8 inch (20 cm) mould and chill.

MOROCCAN CARROT SALAD

Serves 6

1 pound carrots, trimmed and scraped	500 g
¼ cup olive oil	50 mL
3 tablespoons lemon juice	45 mL
1 clove garlic, finely minced	1
½ teaspoon cumin	2 mL
¼ teaspoon dried mint leaves	1 mL
salt and freshly ground pepper to taste	
½ teaspoon confectioners' sugar (or more to taste)	2 mL
¼ teaspoon cayenne pepper	1 mL

Use the julienne cutter of a food processor to cut the carrots into fine shreds (or cut the carrots on a flat surface into ⅛ inch thick slices), stack the slices and cut them into very fine strips. There should be about 6 cups (1.5 L).

Blend the remaining ingredients and pour the sauce over the carrots. Toss to blend.

KOREAN SALAD

Serves 4

1 bag spinach, washed, dried and stemmed	
1-10 ounce can water chestnuts, drained and sliced	1-284 mL
1-10 ounce can bean sprouts (or fresh)	1-284 mL
2 hard boiled eggs, sliced	2
5 strips bacon, crisp and crumbled	5

Marinade
½ cup sugar	125 mL
1 cup oil	250 mL
2 tablespoons Worcestershire sauce	25 mL
⅓ cup ketchup	75 mL
¼ cup vinegar	50 mL
1 onion, grated	1

Mix marinade, pour over salad. Let stand for 15 minutes. Drain, chill and serve.

A summer delight.

SHELLEY WINTERS'
"CAESAR SALAD"

Serves 4

1 head of Romaine Lettuce	1
2 cloves of garlic	2
1 teaspoon salt	5 mL
1 teaspoon black pepper	2 mL
raw egg	1
1 lemon	1
½ cup of salad oil	125 mL
1 tablespoon Worcestershire sauce	15 mL
1½ cups of croutons	375 mL
⅓ cup Italian cheese, grated	75 mL
Anchovies as desired	

Wash and chill lettuce in refrigerator until ready. Rub salad bowl with garlic. Add salt and pepper, and break in raw egg. Squeeze in juice of 1 lemon. Combine salad oil with Worcestershire sauce, add to above. Place chilled lettuce in bowl. Add croutons, cheese and anchovies. Stir lightly.

BROCCOLI SALAD

Serves 6

1 large head broccoli, parboiled and chilled	1
½ pound bacon, cooked and crumbled	250 g
2 garlic cloves, crushed	2
½ pound fresh mushrooms, sliced	250 g
½ cup sour cream	125 mL
¼ cup Italian dressing	50 mL

Break parboiled broccoli into bite-size pieces. Place in a large salad bowl. Add sliced mushrooms and crumbled bacon. Mix together crushed garlic, sour cream and Italian dressing and pour into salad bowl. Serve chilled.

BLENDER GREEN GODDESS DRESSING

Yields 2 cups

2 small or 1 large avocado	2 or 1
1 small package slivered almonds	1
1 cup mayonnaise	250 mL
2 tablespoons anchovy paste	25 mL
1 tablespoon lemon juice	15 mL
¼ cup chopped fresh parsley	50 mL
1 clove garlic	1
3 tablespoons chopped chives	45 mL
3 tablespoons vinegar (preferably tarragon wine)	45 mL
½ cup whipping cream	125 mL

Blend ingredients well. Add ½ cup whipping cream at the end and blend until foamy. Chill several hours before serving. Creamy dressing with a crunch and zesty flavour.

GAZPACHO SALAD
Serves 8

2 medium cucumbers	2
10 medium-sized mushrooms	10
4 scallions	4
½ cup parsley, minced	125 mL
3 large tomatoes, peeled and cut into wedges	3
1 medium green pepper, seeded, thinly sliced	1
½ pound Swiss cheese, cut into thin strips	250 g
4 hard boiled eggs, sliced	4

Peel and thinly slice cucumbers and put in a bowl. Sprinkle with 1 teaspoon salt, let stand for 30 minutes.

Add mushrooms, scallions and drained cucumbers to a bowl. Top mixture with parsley and mix. Add tomato wedges and green pepper. Add dressing (listed below). Chill for 4 hours, covered. Just before serving add Swiss cheese and garnish with hard boiled eggs.

Dressing
Combine:

⅔ cup olive oil	150 mL
⅓ cup wine vinegar	75 mL
1 garlic clove, minced	1
1 tablespoon fresh basil	15 mL
or	
1 teaspoon dried basil	5 mL
1 teaspoon salt	5 mL
½ teaspoon pepper	2 mL

RICE AND BEET SALAD
Serves 6

2 cups boiled rice (1 cup raw)	500 mL
2 cups diced whole canned beets	500 mL
4 tablespoons minced green onions	50 mL
¾ cups vinigrette — french dressing	175 mL
1½ cups mayonnaise	375 mL
salt and pepper to taste	

Toss rice, beets, onion and vinigrette together — cover and refrigerate 24 hours. Just before serving add mayonnaise. Toss and put in bowl and garnish with black or green olives and hard boiled eggs.

FANTASTIC SALMON MOUSSE
Serves 6

½ cup green pepper, chopped	125 mL
¼ cup celery, chopped	50 mL
½ cup green onions, chopped	125 mL
¼ cup vinegar	50 mL
½ cup ketchup	125 mL
1-15 ounce can salmon	1-425 g
1 cup mayonnaise	250 mL
2 tablespoons unflavoured gelatine	25 mL
½ cup cold water	125 mL

Drain fish and reserve liquid. Mash and mix with vegetables. Chill. Soften gelatine in cold water for 5 minutes. Combine salmon liquid, ketchup and vinegar in a saucepan and bring to boil. Add gelatine and stir into salmon mixture. Whisk until smooth. Add mayonnaise and mix well. Spoon into mould. Cover with wax paper and refrigerate overnight.

Perfect for a summer buffet.

TABULA
Serves 6

½ cup brown rice, washed	125 mL
3 large tomatoes, chopped	3
1 cup mild onions, chopped	250 mL
1 cup parsley, chopped	250 mL
⅓ cup lemon juice	75 mL
⅓ cup olive oil	75 mL
2 teaspoons salt	10 mL
1 clove garlic, crushed	1
2 tablespoons mint, chopped	25 mL
or	or
1 tablespoon dried mint	15 mL

Cook rice and set it aside to cool. Chop tomatoes, onions, parsley and mint. Once rice has cooled combine all of these ingredients and add garlic (crushed, not minced). Add lemon juice, olive oil and chopped mint. Refrigerate.

"EVERYTHING" SALAD DRESSING

Yields 4 cups

2 to 2½ cups vegetable oil	500 to 625 mL
1 cup vinegar	250 mL
1 medium-sized onion	1
2 large cloves of garlic	2
1 tablespoon dry mustard	15 mL
1 teaspoon celery salt	5 mL
1 egg	1
½ teaspoon lemon pepper	2 mL
1 teaspoon salt	5 mL
1 teaspoon paprika	5 mL
2 tablespoons prepared mustard	25 mL
2 tablespoons ketchup	25 mL
2 teaspoons anchovy sauce	10 mL
½ teaspoon Worcestershire sauce	2 mL
1 teaspoon soya sauce	5 mL
4 drops Tobasco	4
1 tablespoon lemon juice	15 mL
2 tablespoons Parmesan cheese	25 mL
1 tablespoon sugar	15 mL

Mix all ingredients in a blender. Add a dollop of mayonnaise to thicken if you wish. Will keep for weeks in the refrigerator.

ORANGE AND PINEAPPLE JELLIED SALAD

1 small package lemon gelatine	1
1-10 ounce can Mandarin oranges	1-284 mL
1-14 ounce can crushed pineapple	1-398 mL
1 cup evaporated milk (thoroughly chilled)	250 mL
1 or 2 tablespoons lemon juice	15 to 25 mL

Drain juice from oranges and pineapple. Measure 1 cup (250 mL) of fruit juice and heat. Add lemon gelatine, stir until dissolved. Cool until slightly thickened. Whip evaporated milk. Add lemon juice. Add thickened gelatine. Beat together. Add drained fruit. Pour into large mould. Chill.

JAPONAISE SALAD
Serves 4 to 6

3 oranges, sectioned, seeded and diced	3
½ pineapple, diced (or 1 small can)	½
2 apples, diced	2
1 banana, diced	1
1 mango or papaya, diced	1
strawberries (if desired)	
1 kiwi fruit for decoration	1
½ pint whipped cream	250 mL
½ pint thick mayonnaise with lemon juice	250 mL
1 Boston lettuce	
1 ounce Cointreau	

Fruit should be diced, well-drained and mixed together. Whip cream. Mix liqueur into mayonnaise and then mix fruit and mayonnaise into whipped cream. Add cream mixture to the fruit (only enough to bind the fruit).

Serve on a lettuce leaf. Top with kiwi fruit.

FRUIT SALAD DRESSING
Yields 1¼ cups

1 cup olive oil	250 mL
juice of one lemon	1
juice of one orange	1
¾ teaspoon salt	4 mL
¾ teaspoon paprika	4 mL
¾ teaspoon dry mustard	4 mL
1 teaspoon Worcestershire sauce	5 mL
2 tablespoons vinegar	25 mL
⅓ cup sugar	75 mL
½ clove garlic (optional)	

Mix and shake well, refrigerate.

BARBARA ANN SCOTT'S "STRAWBERRY MOULD"

2-3 ounce orange jelly powders	2-85 g
2-3 ounce strawberry jelly powders	2-85 g
add 6 cups hot water and mix	1.5 L
1-19 ounce can crushed pineapple	540 mL
2-11 ounce packages frozen strawberries	312 g each
3 mashed bananas	3

Mix together and put in large round mould. Unmould on round platter and put a bowl of sour cream in center of fruit mould.

BUTTERMILK DRESSING

Yields 1 cup

In a salad bowl put:

1 teaspoon salt	5 mL
1 teaspoon sugar	5 mL
½ teaspoon dry, mustard powder	2 mL
fresh ground pepper	
1 clove garlic, ground	1

Slowly add and mix with a whisk:

2 tablespoons wine or cider vinegar	25 mL
½ cup corn oil or any good vegetable oil	125 mL
⅓ cup buttermilk	75 mL

Mix until fairly thick.

RUSSIAN DRESSING

Yields 1¼ cups

Similar to, but a pleasing change from, the more usual Thousand Island dressing.

½ cup mayonnaise	125 mL
½ cup chili sauce	125 mL
2 tablespoons chopped celery	25 mL
2 tablespoons chopped green pepper	25 mL
2 tablespoons chopped pimento	25 mL
2 tablespoons chopped olives	25 mL

Combine ingredients and chill thoroughly. Serve over lettuce wedges.

THOUSAND ISLAND DRESSING

A rich, creamy dressing. Adds zest to plain lettuce wedges.

1 cup mayonnaise	250 mL
2 tablespoons chili sauce	25 mL
2 tablespoons pimento, chopped	25 mL
2 tablespoons ketchup	25 mL
2 tablespoons olives or gerkins, chopped	25 mL
2 hard cooked eggs, finely chopped	2

Combine and chill very well before serving.

CREAMY DIJON DRESSING

Makes 1 cup (250 mL)

1 small egg yolk, room temperature	1
2 teaspoons Dijon mustard	10 mL
2 teaspoons white wine vinegar	10 mL
½ teaspoon minced garlic	2 mL
½ teaspoon salt	2 mL
¼ teaspoon freshly ground pepper	1 mL
1 teaspoon dried tarragon	5 mL
3 drops hot pepper sauce	3
1 cup olive oil	250 mL
1 teaspoon fresh lemon juice	5 mL
1 tablespoon warm water	15 mL

Combine egg yolk, mustard, vinegar, garlic, salt, pepper, and hot pepper sauce in small bowl and blend well. Slowly whisk in oil in thin stream. Blend in lemon juice and water.

Dressing can be prepared 1 day ahead and refrigerated. Re-blend before using.

CUCUMBERS IN SOUR CREAM

Yields 2 cups

1 or 2 English cucumbers	1 or 2
salt	
1 onion, finely chopped	1
1 cup sour cream	250 mL
1 tablespoon vinegar	15 mL
3 tablespoons sugar	45 mL
freshly ground black pepper	
chives	

Peel cucumbers and slice thinly. Place in a colander and sprinkle with salt. Put a saucer on top and press with a weight. After several hours drain off excess juice. Mix cucumbers with remaining ingredients (except chives). Place in a small dish and sprinkle with chives. Chill and serve.

Can be used as an accompaniment for cold meat, fish, hamburgers, etc.

SUNSHINE FRENCH DRESSING
Yields 3 cups

2 cups salad oil	500 mL
1 large lemon (juice only)	1
3 regular oranges (juice only)	3
½ cup white vinegar	125 mL
1 tablespoon Worcestershire sauce	15 mL
1 tablespoon dry mustard	15 mL
¾ tablespoon paprika	10 mL
¾ tablespoon salt	10 mL
¾ cup sugar	175 mL
½ clove garlic	½
1 small onion	1

Mix in blender until smooth.

ZIPPY TOMATO DRESSING
Yields 3 cups (750 mL)

1½ teaspoon salt	7 mL
1 teaspoon dry mustard	5 mL
3 tablespoons sugar	45 mL
1¾ cups cooking oil	425 mL
¾ cup malt vinegar	175 mL

Mix ingredients together, and alternately beat in oil, and malt vinegar. Beat until fairly thick.

Add:

1-10 ounce can condensed tomato soup	1-284 mL
1 small grated onion	1
1 teaspoon Worcestershire sauce	5 mL
1 garlic clove	1

Refrigerate overnight, then remove garlic clove. Refrigerate again until ready to use.

Entrées

MARINATED FLANK STEAK

Serves 4 to 6

1 flank steak, scored	1

Marinade — Combine:

2 tablespoons brown sugar	25 mL
3 tablespoons sesame seeds (optional)	45 mL
3 tablespoons salad oil	45 mL
¼ cup soya sauce	50 mL
¼ cup sliced green onions	50 mL
1 chopped garlic clove	1
¼ teaspoon pepper	1 mL
¼ teaspoon ginger	1 mL
¼ cup sherry	50 mL

Place steak in marinade and refrigerate overnight. (Can be frozen in marinade.) Barbecue or broil 2 to 3 minutes on each side. Slice diagonally. Serve hot or cold. Perfect for a picnic and a family favourite.

STEAK SAUCE, SCRUMPTIOUS

Makes 3 to 4 pints or 1.5 to 2 L

12 large tomatoes, chopped and skinned	12
4 medium cucumbers, skin and slice paper thin, or 2 English cucumbers	4
6 onions, chopped	6
½ cup pickling salt	125 mL
2 cups white vinegar	500 mL
4½ cups white sugar	1.1 L
½ teaspoon curry	2 mL
½ teaspoon turmeric	2 mL
½ teaspoon celery seed	2 mL
¼ teaspoon cayenne pepper	1 mL
3 tablespoons flour	45 mL

In a large crock, put pickling salt over tomatoes, cucumbers, and onions, and leave overnight. Drain off salty fluid.

Bring to a boil vinegar, sugar, curry, turmeric, celery seed, and cayenne. Add vegetables and simmer until cucumbers are clear.

Make a paste of some of the liquid and the flour. Stir in, and cook a few minutes longer. Bottle in sterilized jars, seal. Ummmmm good ...

BURT REYNOLDS' "BEEF STEW"
Serves 4

3 slices of bacon, cut in small pieces	3
4 tablespoons flour	50 mL
1 teaspoon salt	5 mL
¼ teaspoon pepper	1 mL
2 pounds lean beef (chuck is juicy) cut in 1 inch (2.5 cm) pieces	1 Kg
1 large onion, chopped (1 cup)	1 (250 mL)
1 clove of minced garlic	1
1 can tomato sauce	1-213 mL
½ can condensed beef broth	½
1 cup good dry Burgundy wine	250 mL
1 bay leaf (optional)	1
1 pinch of thyme	pinch
2 carrots, cut up coarsely (1 cup)	2 (250 mL)
2 stalks of celery, cut up coarsely (¾ cup)	2 (175 mL)
2 potatoes, pared and cut in 4 pieces	2
6 to 8 mushrooms, sliced	6 to 8

Cook bacon until crisp in a large, heavy pot. Combine flour, salt and pepper; dip beef in flour mixture to coat completely. Brown in bacon fat, turning often. (Add a little vegetable oil if needed.) Add onion, garlic and brown a little. Add tomato sauce, broth, wine, bay leaf and thyme. Cover and cook slowly for about 1½ hours. Add carrots, celery, then potatoes and mushrooms. Uncover and cook until meat and vegetables are tender.

THREE MEAT GOULASH

Serves 6 to 8

4 tablespoons butter	50 mL
3 cups onions, thinly sliced	750 mL
1 pound boneless beef cut in 1 inch (2 cm) cubes	500 g
1 pound veal (cut as the beef)	500 g
1 pound pork (cut as the beef)	500 g
2 teaspoons salt	10 mL
½ teaspoon black pepper, freshly ground	2 mL
2 teaspoons paprika	10 mL
2 tablespoons tomato paste	25 mL
1 cup dry white wine	250 mL
1 cup sour cream	250 mL

Melt butter in casserole. Sauté the onion 10 minutes. Add the meat and brown well. Stir in salt, pepper, paprika, tomato paste and ¼ cup (50 mL) wine. Cover and cook over low heat for 30 minutes. Add remaining wine and cook 1½ hours. Stir the sour cream into the pan juices. Heat but do not boil.

Serve with a red Bordeaux or Valpolicello.

SEASONED FLOUR

2 cups all-purpose flour	500 mL
2 tablespoons salt	25 mL
1 tablespoon celery salt	15 mL
1 tablespoon pepper	15 mL
2 tablespoons dry mustard	25 mL
4 tablespoons paprika	50 mL
2 tablespoons garlic powder	25 mL
3 tablespoons monosodium glutamate	45 mL
1 teaspoon ginger	5 mL
½ teaspoon thyme	2 mL
½ teaspoon oregano	2 mL
½ teaspoon sweet basil	2 mL

Sift all ingredients together and blend evenly. Store in a covered jar in the refrigerator. For a crumb coating, combine 1½ tablespoons (20 mL) of seasoned flour with 1 cup (250 mL) fine bread crumbs. Perfectly wonderful for coating fish fillets, pork chops, veal cutlets, etc.

BOBBY HULL'S "SWISS STEAK"

Serves 4

2 to 2½ pounds round, flank or chuck steak, sliced 1 to 1½ inch (2 to 3 cm) by 2½ inch (4 cm) thick cubes	1 Kg
½ cup flour (seasoned with salt and pepper)	125 mL
3 tablespoons cooking oil	45 mL
½ chopped medium onion	½
½ cup chopped celery	125 mL
1 minced garlic clove	1
2 tablespoons chopped parsley	25 mL
1-19 ounce can tomatoes or tomato juice	540 mL
1 bay leaf	1

Trim any fat or membrane from meat. Spread seasoned flour on work surface and over meat. Pound the flour into the meat with the dull edge of a large knife (on both sides). Brown meat on both sides in oil, add chopped vegetables. Add tomatoes or tomato juice plus enough water to surround steak. Heat until liquid bubbles. Lower heat to a gentle simmer, cover and simmer for 1½ to 2 hours. Turn meat over once or twice. Slice the meat on the diagonal and pour gravy over meat.

BUSY-DAY BEEF
Serves 4 to 6

4 to 5 pound short-rib, blade roast or brisket, well trimmed	2-2.5 Kg
1 clove of chopped garlic	1
1-12 ounce can of beer	1-341 mL
¼ cup water	50 mL
3 sliced onions	3
2 to 3 lemons, sliced	2 to 3

Preheat oven to 425°F (220°C).

In roasting pan, place all ingredients. Sear uncovered for 10 to 15 minutes. Cover and cook at reduced heat 300°F (150°C) for 3 to 4 hours or 250°F (120°C) all day. (If beef is frozen, cook 1 hour longer.)

If you wish, ½ hour before serving, add vegetables, carrots, potatoes, onions.

Serve sliced beef and vegetables over a bed of rice.

LIVER AND VEGETABLES
Serves 4

1 pound baby beef liver, cut in strips	500 g
½ cup back bacon, cut in strips	125 mL
½ cup Hungarian sausage, substitute with other spicy sausage	125 mL
1 medium onion, coarsely chopped	1
¼ medium green pepper, coarsely chopped	50 mL
2 medium tomatoes, coarsely chopped	2
1 cup fresh mushrooms, sliced	250 mL
1 tablespoon fresh parsley, finely chopped	15 mL
salt and pepper	

In pan on medium heat sauté sausage and bacon until quite well done, remove from pan and set aside. In bacon drippings sauté liver until quite brown and cooked through, remove from pan and set aside with other meats. In same bacon drippings, fry onions, mushrooms, green pepper until brown, add tomatoes and spices. Add meats back to pan and simmer until done, about 5 minutes.

Add a little water if tomatoes do not give enough liquid. Serve with parsley boiled potatoes or steamed rice and a tossed mixed salad.

BARBECUED BEEF AND BEAN CASSEROLE

Serves 8 to 10

2 pounds ground beef	1 Kg
½ cup sliced onions	125 mL
½ teaspoon salt	2 mL
¼ teaspoon pepper	1 mL
1-12 ounce can pork and beans	340 mL
1 teaspoon celery salt	5 mL
½ cup ketchup	125 mL
1 tablespoon Worcestershire sauce	15 mL
2 tablespoons vinegar	25 mL
¼ teaspoon Tobasco	1 mL
¼ teaspoon paprika	1 mL

In a large skillet, brown beef and onions. Pour off excess fat. Stir in all remaining ingredients and mix well. Bake 25 minutes at 350°F (180°C) in an uncovered 3 quart (3 L) casserole.

HAM AND BROCCOLI CASSEROLE

Serves 8

6 eggs, unbeaten	6
2 pounds creamed cottage cheese	1 L
6 tablespoons flour	75 mL
½ pound Cheddar cheese, diced	250 g
½ cup butter, softened	125 mL
5 whole green onions, chopped	5
¼ teaspoon dry mustard	1 mL
1 large head broccoli, uncooked and chopped	1
2 cups ham, chopped	500 mL

Mix all the ingredients, except the broccoli and ham in a large bowl.

Fold in broccoli and chopped ham. Pour into a greased 9 × 12 inch (23 × 30 cm) baking dish. Bake at 350°F (180°C) for one hour, or until knife comes out almost clean. Let set for ten minutes before serving.

The casserole should be brown and bubbling on top.

For luncheon or informal supper.

BEEF STEW PROVENÇAL

Serves 8

3 pounds boneless beef chuck, cut into 1½ inch cubes	1.5 Kg (3.5 cm) cubes

Marinade

1 naval orange	1
1½ cups dry red wine	375 mL
1½ tablespoons dried thyme leaves	20 mL
½ cup flour	125 mL
salt to taste	
½ teaspoon pepper	2 mL
1 leek, washed, sliced, ⅛ inch thick	1
¼ cup butter	50 mL
2 tablespoons olive oil	25 mL
10 small white onions, peeled	10
1 clove garlic, crushed	1
2 bay leaves	2
1-28 ounce can tomatoes, undrained	1-786 mL
10 small new potatoes, scrubbed	10
4 zucchinis, washed and sliced	4
12 ripe olives	12
chopped parsley	

Marinade

Cut a strip of orange peel 1 inch (2.5 cm) wide, 3 inches (7.5 cm) long. In a large bowl, combine orange peel, red wine, thyme. Mix well. Add beef, coat well. Refrigerate tightly covered 2 to 3 hours. Drain well. Reserve marinade and peel. Coat beef with flour, salt, pepper.

In a 6 quart (6 L) Dutch oven, heat butter and oil over high heat. Add beef (do not overcrowd). Brown all sides over medium heat, remove when browned. Add leeks, onions, garlic to drippings, stirring until golden. Remove. Return beef to Dutch oven, add bay leaves, tomatoes, marinade.

Stir well. Bring to boil, reduce heat, simmer covered 1 hour. Add onions, leek potatoes, cook 40 minutes. Add zucchini, olives, cook 20 minutes, or until beef and vegetables are tender. Stir the flour into ¼ cup (50 mL) water until smooth. Stir flour mixture into beef. Simmer uncovered 10 minutes. Garnish with parsley and peel.

3

Crown Roast of Pork with
Cranberry-Apple Stuffing
Recipe on page 78

JULIE ANDREWS' "RICE WITH BEEF AND EGGS (ITOKO DOMBURI)"

Serves 4

Preparation time: 5 minutes
Cooking time: 10 minutes

3/8 pints stock	175 mL
4 tablespoons sake (Japanese Rice Wine)	50 mL
4 tablespoons soya sauce	50 mL
2 tablespoons sugar	25 mL
1 small onion, sliced thinly	1
½ pound thinly sliced beef	250 g
4 eggs	4
8 ounces cooked rice	250 g
4 Asatsuki or spring onions	4
1 sheet Nori (dried seaweed, optional)	1

Put the stock, sake, soya sauce, sugar and onion into a frying pan and bring slowly to a boiling point. Put in the meat and cook until the meat changes colour and is tender. Add the beaten eggs and tilt the pan so that the whole surface is covered with the eggs. Cover and cook for 2 to 3 minutes until the eggs are just set. Place the rice in four serving bowls and put one-fourth of the egg and meat mixture in each. Sprinkle with Asatsuki. If Nori is used, hold it over heat for a few minutes to crisp. Put in a cloth and rub so that it crumbles and then sprinkle over the beef and egg mixture.

Note: Chicken and egg on rice is called Oyako-Domburi (Parent and Child Bowl) and Beef and Egg on Rice is called Itoko-Domburi (Cousin Bowl). When pork is used, it is called Tanin-Domburi (Stranger Bowl). Thinly sliced boiled bamboo shoots can also be used. Each serving may be made separately in a frying pan or the four servings may be cooked together and then divided.

BEEF OR PORK SATE
WITH PEANUT SAUCE

Serves 4

1 pound lean pork butt or beef steak	500 g
½ teaspoon ground coriander	2 mL
½ teaspoon ground cumin	2 mL
½ teaspoon garlic powder	2 mL
2 ounces (¼ cup) sweet soya sauce (Indonesian, if available)	50 mL

Cut meat into ¾ inch (2 cm) cubes, mix with remaining ingredients and allow to marinate for 1 hour. Drain, reserving marinade. Soak skewers (bamboo if available), 5 minutes in cold water to prevent burning while cooking. Spear meat cubes on skewers, leaving small spaces between for even cooking. Barbecue or broil, to desired degree, brushing with marinade. Serve with peanut sauce.

Peanut sauce

1 pound fried peanuts, coarsely ground, or 2 cups crunchy peanut butter	500 g or 500 mL
2 cloves mashed garlic	2
3 small sweet or hot red peppers, minced fine	3
1 teaspoon hot sauce	5 mL
2 ounces (¼ cup) vegetable oil	50 mL
1 cup water	250 mL
2 ounces (¼ cup) soya sauce	50 mL
2 bay leaves (Indonesian, if available)	2
2 slices ginger root or Laos if available	2

Crush peanuts or stir peanut butter until softened. Sauté garlic, peppers and hot sauce in oil. Add water, peanuts and remaining ingredients. Cook slowly over low heat, stirring and adding a little water if necessary, to make a smooth sauce for dipping. Serve meat skewers on bed of rice with a little sauce drizzled over and the balance of sauce in gravy boat. Serve with salad.

Buy less familiar ingredients at specialty shops or large chain stores.

SIR GEORG SOLTI'S "GOULASH"

Serves 6

½ pound onions	250 g
2 ounces lard	50 mL
2½ pounds braising steak (cut in ½ inch (1 cm) cubes)	1 Kg
½ pound beef heart (optional) (cut in ½ inch (1 cm) cubes)	250 g
2 garlic cloves	2
pinch caraway seeds	pinch
salt	
4 pints beef stock	2 L
2 tablespoons paprika (finest quality)	25 mL
½ pound tomatoes	250 g
2 green peppers	2
1 pound potatoes (cut into ½ inch (1 cm) cubes)	500 g

Peel and dice onions. Melt lard in heavy-bottom saucepan; sauté onions but do not colour. Add beef (and heart if used) and sauté for about 10 minutes.

Chop and crush garlic, caraway seeds and salt. Remove beef from heat and stir in paprika and garlic mixture. Add beef stock and return to heat with lid on and simmer for at least 1 to 1½ hours.

Peel and dice tomatoes, core and cut peppers into rings and add to meat; simmer for a further 30 minutes adding more stock if required to keep to a soup-like consistency. Add potatoes and cook till all is tender.

Serve with little dumplings.

CHEESEBURGER PIE

Serves 4 to 6

1 pound lean ground beef	500 g
½ cup evaporated milk	125 mL
½ cup ketchup	125 mL
⅓ cup fine dry bread crumbs	75 mL
¼ cup chopped onion	50 mL
¾ teaspoon salt	3 mL
½ teaspoon oregano	2 mL
⅛ teaspoon pepper	pinch
1-8 inch pie shell, unbaked	1-20 cm
4 ounces grated Cheddar cheese	125 g
1 teaspoon Worcestershire sauce	5 mL

Combine meat, milk, ketchup, bread crumbs, onion, salt, oregano and pepper. Spread in unbaked pie shell. Bake at 350°F (180°C) for 35 to 40 minutes. Mix together cheese and Worcestershire and spread on top. Bake 10 minutes longer. Let stand 10 minutes before serving.

DAY AHEAD MEAT LOAF

Serves 4 to 6

Have your butcher grind twice:

1 pound round steak	500 g
1 boneless pork chop	1
2 ounces veal	60 g
2 ounces salt pork	60 g

Ingredients

1-19 ounce can tomatoes, drained, reserving liquid	540 mL
1 teaspoon salt	5 mL
½ teaspoon sage	2 mL
½ teaspoon thyme	2 mL
½ teaspoon onion salt	2 mL
¼ teaspoon dry mustard	1 mL
¼ teaspoon pepper	1 mL
1 tablespoon Worcestershire sauce	15 mL
¾ cup bread crumbs	175 mL

Mix ingredients thoroughly, press into a loaf pan and refrigerate overnight. Before cooking, pour reserved tomato liquid over top. Cook in a 350°F (180°C) oven for 1 hour and 15 minutes.

ANNE MURRAY'S FAVOURITE
RECIPE "HEARTY HODGEPODGE"

(Great for a crowd)
Serves 12 to 14

1½ pounds ground chuck	750 g
¾ cup chopped onion	175 mL
1 clove garlic (I use garlic powder)	1
3 cans condensed minestrone soup	3-284 mL
1-28 ounce can beans and pork in tomato sauce	1-796 mL
1½ cups chopped celery	375 mL
1 tablespoon Worcestershire sauce	15 mL
½ teaspoon oregano	2 mL

Sauté beef, onion and garlic in skillet until beef is browned and onion is tender. Stir in soup, beans, celery, Worcestershire sauce and oregano in big pot. Simmer, covered for 15 to 20 minutes.

FLEMISH BEEF

Serves 6

Butter	
3 large onions	3
3½ pounds of round steak, 1½ inch (4 cm) thick	1.75 Kg
¼ cup flour	50 mL
1 bay leaf	1
½ teaspoon dried rosemary	2 mL
2 whole cloves	2
1 teaspoon salt	5 mL
1 teaspoon pepper	5 mL
2 cups beer	250 mL
parsley or chives for garnish	

Butter a 9 × 13 inch (23 × 33 cm) covered casserole dish. Cut 3 large onions into thick slices and place in the bottom of casserole. Pound flour into the steak with a meat mallet. Place meat on top of onions. Bake uncovered in 450°F (230°C) oven for 40 minutes. Reduce heat to 325°F (160°C). Add bay leaf, rosemary, cloves, salt, pepper and beer. Cover tightly and bake for 1½ to 2 hours, or until meat is very tender. Sprinkle with chives or parsley before serving. Serve with buttered noodles, green salad and beer.

BARBECUED SAUCE SUPERIOR

Yields 1½ cups (375 mL)

2 tablespoons brown sugar	25 mL
1 tablespoon paprika	15 mL
1 teaspoon salt	5 mL
1 teaspoon prepared mustard	5 mL
¼ teaspoon chili powder	1 mL
⅛ teaspoon cayenne pepper	pinch
2 tablespoons Worcestershire sauce	25 mL
¼ cup vinegar	50 mL
1 cup tomato juice	250 mL
½ cup water	125 mL

Combine all ingredients in a saucepan. Bring to a boil. Simmer until slightly thick.

Brush on meat of your choice and grill. Baste as meat cooks.

Refrigerate leftover.

ED ASNER'S "MEDITERRANEAN STEW"

Serves 6 to 8

1 pound chuck steak, cut into 1½ inch (3 cm) cubes	500 g
1 pound sweet Italian sausage	500 g
1½ cups Burgundy wine	375 mL
2 cups water	500 mL
1-6 ounce can tomato paste	1-170 mL
¾ teaspoon pepper	4 mL
3 minced garlic cloves	3
2 teaspoons paprika	10 mL
1 pound cooked ham, cubed	500 g
3 coarsely chopped medium onions	3
1 coarsely chopped sweet red pepper	1
¼ cup chopped fresh parsley	50 mL
2-1 pound cans drained garbanzo beans (chick peas)	2-540 mL
1 teaspoon grated lemon rind	5 mL
1 head of cabbage, cut into wedges	1

In a large skillet, sauté beef cubes and sausage until brown. Drain meats and slice sausage; transfer to Dutch oven. Add wine, water, tomato paste, salt, pepper, garlic and paprika. Bring to boil, cover and simmer 1½ to 2 hours or until meat is tender.

Add remaining ingredients except cabbage. Cover and cook about 20 minutes; add cabbage and cook until crisp-tender, about 15 to 20 minutes. Refrigerate overnight to develop flavours. Skim off fat. Bring stew to room temperature. Reheat in microwave oven 4 or 5 minutes; top of range 15 to 20 minutes or until hot.

SAUSAGE-BEEF CASSEROLE

Serves 4 to 6

6 sweet Italian sausages (about 1 pound)	6 (500 g)
1 pound beef chuck, cut in 1 inch (2.5 cm) cubes	50 g
1 large onion, sliced	1
2 medium cloves of garlic, minced	2
2 medium green peppers, seeded and cut in eighths	2
4 medium potatoes, peeled and cut in quarters	4
2 cans (1 pound each) red kidney beans, drained	2-540 mL
1 teaspoon basil	5 mL
½ teaspoon salt	2 mL
¼ teaspoon pepper	1 mL
2 beef bouillon cubes dissolved in 1 cup boiling water	2-250 mL

In a heavy skillet, over medium heat, brown sausages well. Cut each link in thirds and place in 2½ to 3 quart (2.5-3 L) casserole. Drain fat from skillet, reserving 2 tablespoons (25 mL). Brown beef in 1 tablespoon (15 mL) fat, then turn out into casserole. Cook onion and garlic in remaining 1 tablespoon (15 mL) fat until tender; add green peppers and cook 1 minute longer, stirring; turn out into casserole. Add potatoes and beans. Sprinkle with seasonings and mix lightly. Add bouillon; cover and bake in 350°F (180°C) oven for 1 hour 15 minutes or until beef and potatoes are tender. Good with warm crusty bread, tossed salad, beer or red wine.

SPICED BEEF

Serves 15 to 20

1-15 pound round steak roast or rump roast of beef	7.5 Kg
6 tablespoons saltpetre (available at drug store)	75 mL
¾ cup brown sugar	175 mL
4 tablespoons ground cloves	50 mL
1 bottle of allspice	1
2 nutmegs, grated	2
3 handfuls of salt	3

Place beef in a crock, in a cool place. Rub with above ingredients. Turn and rub every day for 3 weeks.

Roast at 350°F (180°C) until meat thermometer registers between rare and medium. Serve cold, sliced very thin.

WAYNE GRETZKY'S "CHILI À LA WAYNE"

Serves 6 to 8

Are you ready for a bachelor's delight — a chili dish that can't fail. It's called (by me anyway) "Chili à la Wayne". Here it is.

2 pounds ground beef	1 Kg
3 large onions, chopped	3
3 stalks of celery, sliced	3
1 large green pepper, diced	1
1-5½ ounce can tomato paste	156 mL
1-28 ounce can tomatoes	796 mL
1-19 ounce can kidney beans	540 mL
2-14 ounce cans baked beans	398 mL
1 cup dry red wine (optional)	250 mL
3 dashes Tobasco sauce	3
2 teaspoons Worcestershire sauce	10 mL
salt and pepper, to taste	
1½ to 2 tablespoons chili powder	20 to 25 mL
1-19 ounce can pineapple chunks	540 mL

Sauté ground beef, onions, celery and green pepper until vegetables are soft and beef has begun to brown. Add canned ingredients, wine and seasonings. Simmer over low heat 30 to 45 minutes, stirring frequently.

Add pineapple chunks just before serving. Use liquid depending upon desired thickness of chili.

Variation — add sliced carrots, broccoli and cauliflower before simmering stage.

A sure score, Gretzky scores again!

SAVOURY LAMB

Serves 6

1 lamb leg – about 5 pounds, cut in 1 inch (2.5 cm) cubes	2.5 Kg
2 cups Spanish onions, chopped	500 mL
1 cup red Burgundy wine	250 mL
¼ cup Cognac	50 mL
1 tablespoon powdered sugar	15 mL
1 teaspoon salt	5 mL
½ teaspoon nutmeg	2 mL
½ teaspoon thyme	2 mL
¼ teaspoon ground cloves	1 mL
½ teaspoon pepper	2 mL
3 tablespoons gin	45 mL
2 cloves of mashed garlic	2
2 bay leaves	2
½ cup chicken stock	125 mL
2 tablespoons olive oil	25 mL
2 tablespoons butter	25 mL

Combine lamb, oil, red Burgundy, Cognac, sugar, salt, nutmeg, thyme, cloves, pepper, gin, garlic and bay leaves in a large bowl. Refrigerate covered 2 or 3 days and continue to turn the meat twice a day.

Add chicken stock and let stand at room temperature 1 hour. Preheat oven 250°F (120°C). Drain lamb; sauté in butter and oil in large skillet until brown. Deglaze skillet and set meat aside.

Heat marinade in Dutch oven until liquid is reduced to 1¾ cups (425 mL). Add lamb; heat to boiling and bake until tender, 1½ to 2 hours.

Serve with new potatoes. Wonderful combination of flavours.

LEG OF LAMB
WITH GARLIC SAUCE

Serves 6 to 8

1-5 pound leg of lamb	2.5 Kg
3 tablespoons olive oil	45 mL
2 teaspoons rosemary	10 mL
1 teaspoon thyme	5 mL
salt and freshly ground pepper	
8 cloves garlic, peeled	8
¾ cup dry white wine	175 mL

Rub lamb with 2 tablespoons (30 mL) of olive oil, rosemary, thyme, salt and pepper. Let stand 2 hours.

Preheat oven to 325°F (160°C). Place on rack in roasting pan. Insert meat thermometer into fleshy part of the meat — cooking time approximately 2½ hours or as desired.

Garlic Sauce

Heat remaining oil in a skillet, cook garlic cloves slowly until soft — do not brown garlic.

Remove lamb from roasting pan. Pour wine into pan, scrape bottom and sides of pan — reduce to about a ½ cup (125 mL). Add pan juices to garlic. Mash garlic, add salt and pepper.

LAMB ROASTED AND STUFFED WITH APPLES AND CIDER

Serves 8

5 pound boned leg of lamb	2.5 Kg
1 lemon (juice and peel)	1
1 pound cooking apples, peeled, cored, and sliced	500 g
2 tablespoons sugar	25 mL
3 cloves	3
2 teaspoons ginger	10 mL
salt and pepper, to taste	
2 tablespoons dripping or oil	25 mL
2 cups cider, or apple juice	500 mL

Rub the lamb inside and out with the lemon juice and peel, then lay the slices of apple inside the meat, sprinkle with sugar, dot with cloves and roll up, skewering or sewing up firmly. Rub the outside with the mixture of ginger, salt and pepper and brush over with oil. Put in a baking pan and roast in a moderate oven 350°F (180°C) for 20 minutes to the pound. Warm up the cider and baste with the warm juice every 20 minutes. Drain off any excess fat when it is cooked, reduce the gravy on a hot flame until it is about half, and serve separately in a gravy boat.

ROAST LEG OF LAMB WITH ORANGE-PEPPER SAUCE

Serves 8 to 10

5 to 6 pound leg of lamb	2.5 to 3 Kg
½ cup butter, melted	125 mL
½ cup olive oil	125 mL
¼ cup lemon juice	50 mL
2 teaspoons prepared mustard	10 mL
½ teaspoon pepper	2 mL
1 teaspoon dried sage leaves	5 mL
1 teaspoon salt	5 mL
2 cups dry white wine	500 mL

Sauce — Orange-Pepper:

¼ cup butter	50 mL
3 shallots, chopped	3
1 leek, sliced	1
¼ cup onion, chopped	50 mL
1 strip orange peel	1
2 cloves garlic, crushed	2
1 tablespoon lemon juice	15 mL
1 hot red pepper, cut into long thin strips	1
2 tablespoons flour	25 mL
1 cup dry red wine	250 mL
½ teaspoon salt	2 mL

Preheat oven to 550°F (290°C). Trim excess fat off lamb, place in a shallow roasting pan, no rack. Combine butter, olive oil, lemon juice, mustard, pepper, sage, salt, mix well. Brush lamb well with mixture. Pour remaining mixture over lamb.

Roast lamb uncovered 45 minutes. Pour off excess grease. Pour wine over lamb. Reduce oven to 400°F (200°C). Roast 45 minutes longer.

Baste with pan drippings several times.

Sauce:

In a saucepan sauté shallots, leek, onion, orange peel, garlic, lemon juice, red pepper in butter. Stir in flour, then stir in wine, 1 cup (250 mL) water, salt, simmer covered, stirring occasionally ½ hour. Add juices from lamb (approximately 1 cup (250 mL), simmer 3 minutes, stir well).

Pour sauce over lamb, return to oven, roast 20 to 30 minutes longer, or as desired.

SAVORY LAMB AND SPINACH ROLL

Serves 6

¼ cup pine nuts	50 mL
5 tablespoons butter	75 mL
1 pound lean ground lamb	500 g
2 large tomatoes, chopped, peeled, and seeded	2
1 teaspoon salt	5 mL
¾ teaspoon ground allspice	4 mL
¼ teaspoon freshly ground pepper	1 mL
1 tablespoon fresh lemon juice	15 mL
1 cup leeks, chopped, white part only	250 mL
½ cup minced onions	125 mL
2-10 ounce packages frozen spinach, thawed, well drained, and chopped	2-284 g
¾ cup grated zucchini	175 mL
5 tablespoons minced fresh mint	75 mL
¾ teaspoon salt	4 mL
¼ teaspoon pepper	1 mL
1 egg yolk, lightly beaten	1
12 sheets Phyllo pastry	12
melted butter, as needed	
1 egg, lightly beaten	1

In large skillet, sauté pine nuts in 2 tablespoons (30 mL) butter until golden. Crumble lamb and brown. Drain off grease. Add tomatoes, seasonings, lemon juice, and simmer 5 minutes. In separate skillet, sauté leeks and minced onions in remaining butter and combine with meat mixture. Blend in spinach, zucchini, mint, salt, and pepper. Simmer 7 to 10 minutes until spinach is tender, cool to room temperature. (Can be prepared up to here the day before.)

Stir in egg yolk. Preheat oven to 350°F (180°C). Keeping Phyllo sheets covered until ready, place 1 sheet at a time on tea towel and brush liberally with melted butter. Continue layering and buttering until 6 sheets are used. Spread half of the lamb mixture over sixth sheet, leaving 3 inch (7.5 cm) border around edges. Roll like jelly-roll, folding in sides as you roll. Seal seams with butter, place seam side down on baking sheet. Do other sheets and other half of mixture. Brush top with beaten egg and bake 350°F (180°C) for 45 minutes.

CROWN ROAST OF PORK WITH CRANBERRY-APPLE STUFFING

Serves 8 to 12

1 crown roast of pork (12 ribs)	1
¼ cup butter	50 mL
1 chopped onion	1
1½ cups chopped celery	375 mL
4 cups day old bread, cubed, no crusts	1 L
1 teaspoon salt	5 mL
poultry seasoning and pepper to taste	
1 cup fresh cranberries	250 mL
2 cups apples, sliced and pared	500 mL
¼ cup apricot preserve	50 mL

Brown onion in butter and combine remaining ingredients except apricot preserve. Reserve some apple slices for garnish. Brush inside of crown with sage. Mound stuffing inside crown with apple slices around edge. Cover ribs and stuffing loosely with foil. Roast in 325°F (160°C) oven for 3 hours. Remove foil. Brush apple slices with apricot preserve. Return to oven for 30 minutes. Brush roast with apricot preserve and return to oven for 10 minutes. Garnish ribs with cherry tomatoes and arrange watercress around the serving platter.

ED McMAHON'S "LOIN OF PORK"

loin of pork
seasoned salt
sliced onions
parsley
Grand Marnier

Wash and dry meat then cover with seasoned salt. Alternate on top (using skewers) slices of onion and parsley. Roast in normal fashion. During the last 45 minutes of cooking, baste frequently with Grand Marnier. This adds a delightful flavour to the pork and makes an incredibly good gravy.

Serve with scalloped apples and corn pudding.

HAM AND VODKA SPAGHETTI

Serves 2

¼ cup olive oil	50 mL
2 tablespoons butter	25 mL
1 medium onion, chopped	1
1 cup peeled tomatoes, chopped	250 mL
10 medium mushrooms, peeled and halved	10
4 ounces ham, cooked and chopped	125 g
6 ounces whipping cream	175 mL
½ cup red or white wine	125 mL
¼ cup vodka	50 mL
3 tablespoons Parmesan cheese, grated	45 mL
3 tablespoons Romano cheese	45 mL
salt and pepper to taste	
2 tablespoons fresh parsley, chopped	25 mL
8 ounces spaghetti, cooked	250 g

In frying pan, heat oil and butter. Sauté onions, garlic and mushrooms until golden brown. Add tomatoes and ham. Simmer for 10 minutes. Stir in cream, wine, vodka, cheese, salt and pepper. Bring to a boil. (If sauce is too thin, add a rounded teaspoon of cornstarch mixed with a little milk.) Turn to simmer and add parsley. Pour over cooked spaghetti.

Can be doubled or tripled.

A wonderful Sunday brunch!

APRICOT GLAZE

Yields 1 cup or 125 mL

1 cup apricot jam	250 mL
2 tablespoons dark rum	25 mL

Melt jam in saucepan over moderate heat. Add rum. Let mixture come to a boil, and strain through fine sieve. Glaze half an hour before ham or pork roast is cooked. Ham and apricot glaze — a perfect duo.

CHAFING DISH JAMBALAYA WITH CHAMPAGNE

Serves 4

1 cup cooked ham, shredded	250 mL
¼ cup green pepper	50 mL
¼ cup chopped onion	50 mL
3 tablespoons butter	45 mL
dash of Tobasco	dash
2 cups freshly cooked tomatoes	500 mL
18 oysters, shucked	18
18 shrimps, shelled and deveined and cooked	18
6 ounces dry sparkling wine or Champagne	175 mL
½ cup heavy cream	125 mL
3 cups cooked rice	750 mL
parsley for garnish	

Set pan over direct heat and sauté ham, green pepper and onion in 3 tablespoons (45 mL) butter. Add Tobasco, tomatoes, oysters and shrimps. Cook for 2 minutes or until oysters are plump.

Add the champagne and simmer until reduced by half. Add cream.

Immediately remove pan from heat and set over hot water. Add rice.

Heat mixture through. Sprinkle with parsley.

SWEET GINGER PORK CHOPS

Serves 6

6-1 inch thick pork chops	6-2.5 cm

Marinade

½ cup honey	125 mL
¼ cup cider vinegar	50 mL
2 tablespoons soya sauce	25 mL
2 tablespoons crystallized ginger, coarsely chopped	25 mL
½ clove garlic, minced	½
freshly ground pepper	

Mix all marinade ingredients together in a baking dish and add chops turning to cover with marinade. Refrigerate for about 8 hours, turning the pork chops occasionally.

Bake in same dish at 350°F (180°C) for 1¼ hours.

PORK WITH CREAMY MUSTARD SAUCE

Serves 6

2 pork tenderloins cut into twelve 1½ inch (4 cm) slices	
flour	
salt and pepper, to taste	
4 tablespoons butter	50 mL
½ cup chopped onion	125 mL
8 peppercorns	8
⅓ cup vinegar	75 mL
2 cups heavy cream	500 mL
⅓ cup Dijon mustard	75 mL
2 tablespoons butter	25 mL
½ teaspoon salt	2 mL
dash of garlic	dash
¼ teaspoon thyme	1 mL

Roll pork slices to ½ inch (1.2 cm) thickness. Dust pieces with flour, salt, and pepper. Brown on both sides in butter. When thoroughly cooked, remove from pan and keep warm. Add onion to drippings, and cook until transparent. Stir in peppercorns and vinegar, thyme and garlic and bring to a boil. Remove from heat and stir in heavy cream. Return to heat and cook until thickened. Remove from heat and discard peppercorns. Stir in mustard, butter and salt. Pour over pork and serve immediately.

CHARLEY PRIDE'S "SWEET AND SOUR BAKED BEANS"

Serves 12

8 bacon slices, pan fried until crisp, drained and crumbled	8
4 large onions, peeled and cut into rings	4
½ to 1 cup brown sugar	125-250 mL
1 teaspoon dry mustard	5 mL
½ teaspoon garlic powder (optional)	2 mL
1 teaspoon salt	5 mL
½ cup cider vinegar	125 mL
1-10 ounce can white lima beans, drained	284 mL
1-15 ounce can green lima beans, drained	1-425 mL
1-15 ounce can dark red kidney beans, drained	1-425 mL
1-28 ounce can New England style baked beans, undrained	1-796 mL

Place onions in skillet, add sugar, mustard, garlic powder, salt and vinegar. Cook 20 minutes, covered. Add onion mixture to beans. Add crumbled bacon. Pour into 3 quart (3 L) casserole. Bake in moderate oven 350°F (180°C) for 1 hour.

Use larger measure of sugar if you like beans on the sweet side.

PORK NORMADE
Serves 4

2 tablespoons butter or margarine	25 mL
2 large pork tenderloins	2
1 medium onion, thinly sliced	1
2 cooking apples, peeled, cored and chopped	2
1 tablespoon flour	15 mL
1 cup apple juice	250 mL
½ cup water	125 mL
1 chicken bouillon cube	1
½ teaspoon salt	2 mL
⅛ teaspoon pepper	pinch
¼ cup cream	50 mL

Heat butter in a large heavy skillet over medium heat. Add pork and brown slowly on all sides. Remove pork and set aside. Add onion to pan and stir 3 minutes. Add apple and stir 2 minutes. Sprinkle in flour and stir to blend.

Remove pan from heat and stir in next 5 ingredients. Return to heat and stir until boiling, slightly thickened and smooth. Return meat to pan, cover and simmer 30 minutes. Turn meat, cover and simmer until fork-tender, about 30 minutes more.

Cut meat in thick slices on the diagonal and overlap on a small platter.

Stir cream into sauce in skillet, pour over meat and serve immediately.

ROAST PORK TENDERLOIN, CHINESE STYLE
Serves 6

3 pork tenderloins, ¾ pound each	340 g each
1 cup chicken stock	250 mL
¼ cup soya sauce	50 mL
¼ cup honey	50 mL
2 tablespoons sherry	25 mL
1 tablespoon lemon juice	15 mL
½ clove garlic, crushed	½
1 teaspoon cinnamon	5 mL
1 teaspoon salt	5 mL
¼ teaspoon ginger	1 mL

Combine chicken stock, soya sauce, honey, sherry, lemon juice, garlic, cinnamon, salt and ginger. Marinate meat for 2 hours. Drain meat and reserve liquid. Preheat oven to 325°F (160°C). Place meat in shallow roasting pan. Bake for 1½ hours, basting frequently with marinade. To serve, slice on the diagonal and garnish with parsley.

ITALIAN STUFFED VEAL CHOPS
Serves 6

6 veal chops, 1½ inches (4 cm) thick	6
¾ teaspoon salt	4 mL
½ teaspoon black pepper	2 mL
6 slices Proscuitto (ham)	6
6 slices Fontina or Mozzarella cheese	6
¼ cup flour	50 mL
6 tablespoons butter	75 mL
½ cup dry vermouth	125 mL
¼ teaspoon thyme	1 mL
½ teaspoon crushed bay leaf	2 mL

Trim the fat from the chops and split each chop open by cutting through the middle horizontally, so that each chop opens like a book. Pound each side flat lightly. Season the outside of the chops with the salt and pepper. Place a slice of Proscuitto and cheese on the cut sides of the chops and close the chops, pressing the edges together. Dip the chops in the flour.

Heat the butter in a skillet and sauté the veal over medium heat until browned on both sides. Add the vermouth, thyme and bay leaf; cover and cook over low heat 30 to 40 minutes or until chops are tender. This is a fabulous recipe!

VEAL CONTINENTAL

Serves 4 to 6

1 pound veal cutlets, thinly sliced	500 g
2 teaspoons flour	10 mL
½ teaspoon salt	1 mL
1 clove garlic	1
3 tablespoons butter	50 mL
1 tablespoon vegetable oil	15 mL
½ pound mushrooms, thinly sliced	250 g
1 onion, finely chopped	1
½ cup water chestnuts, sliced	125 mL
2 tablespoons flour	25 mL
1½ cups milk	375 mL
½ cup sherry	125 mL

Pound cutlets until thin; cut into serving pieces. Dust with mixture of flour, salt and pepper. Brown garlic in 1 tablespoon (15 mL) each of butter and oil; remove garlic. Add veal and sauté quickly until browned. Place in baking dish. Melt remaining butter in saucepan. Add mushrooms, onion and water chestnuts and sauté. Blend in flour, then add milk. Simmer, stirring for 2 minutes; add wine. Pour sauce over cutlets. Bake in 350°F (180°C) oven for 30 minutes. Serve with noodles.

VEAL WITH CREAM AND BRANDY

Serves 4

3 tablespoons butter	45 mL
2 pounds veal, thinly sliced	1 Kg
1 teaspoon parsley	5 mL
1 teaspoon chives, or chopped onion	5 mL
salt and pepper, to taste	
½ cup whipping cream	125 mL
1 teaspoon brandy	5 mL

Melt butter in large skillet. Cook slices of veal slowly with parsley, chives or onion until slightly browned; add salt and pepper.

Place veal in baking dish, pour cream and brandy over meat. Bake covered at 300°F (150°C) for approximately 60 minutes. Serve with rice and a salad.

PAT BOONE'S "VEAL SUPREME"

Serves 4

2 pounds veal scallops	1 Kg
6 tablespoons sweet butter	75 mL
1 medium green pepper, cut in thin strips	1
1 small red onion, peeled and cut into thin strips	1
⅓ can (10 ounce size) condensed cream of chicken soup	⅓-284 mL
10 mushroom caps, cut in thin strips	10
seasoned flour (salt and ground pepper)	
¾ cup dry vermouth	175 mL
wild rice	

Melt 2 tablespoons (25 mL) sweet butter in a large skillet until sizzling; add mushrooms, green pepper and onion. Cook over medium heat, stirring until onions are transparent. Lift out mushrooms, green pepper and onions and set aside. Add remaining butter to skillet, heat until hot. Add veal scallops that have been dredged in seasoned flour. Brown quickly over high heat on both sides. Remove scallops to a heated platter. Deglaze skillet by adding vermouth and heating over low flame.

Add soup, stirring. Add veal scallops and mushroom mixture. Cover, simmer over low heat, stirring often. Cook about 10 minutes or until veal is tender. Correct seasoning to taste. Serve veal and sauce over cooked wild rice.

VEAL KIDNEYS WITH WINE SAUCE

Serves 4

4 veal kidneys	4
4 tablespoons butter	50 mL
3 tablespoons brandy, warmed	45 mL
¼ cup dry white wine or vermouth	50 mL
2 teaspoons Dijon mustard	10 mL
¼ cup port wine	50 mL
¾ cup light cream	175 mL
2 tablespoons flour	25 mL
1 tablespoon minced onion	15 mL
parsley	
salt and pepper	
dash of garlic	

For each serving, cut out fat and remove membrane from 1 kidney. Cut into bite-size slices. Melt butter in a small skillet, add onion and garlic. Sauté kidney slices over medium heat until browned. Add brandy. Ignite. Flambé until flame dies out. Add the white wine. Cover. Cook over low heat for 3 minutes. Do not overcook. Transfer kidneys, using a slotted spoon, to a small dish and keep warm.

Sauce
Cook liquid in skillet until reduced to almost nothing. Stir in mustard and port wine. Season with a little salt and pepper. Cook over low heat until port is slightly reduced. Combine cream with flour. Stir into sauce. Keeping heat low, cook and stir until sauce is slightly thickened. Continue to cook for 5 minutes. Pour sauce over warm kidney slices. Sprinkle with parsley. Best when served immediately, however, leftovers can be frozen and reheated slowly.

VEAL SCALLOPS WITH VERMOUTH

Serves 4

2 pounds of veal scallops, pounded very thin	1 Kg
2 tablespoons flour	25 mL
1 onion, chopped	1
4 tablespoons butter	50 mL
4 tablespoons oil	50 mL
⅔ cup sweet vermouth	150 mL
1 teaspoon tomato paste	5 mL
¼ teaspoon mace	1 mL
8 to 10 florets of cauliflower, lightly cooked	8 to 10
4 to 6 Brazil nuts, sliced	4 to 6
salt and pepper, to taste	

Season scallops with salt and pepper. Flour lightly and brown scallops and onions in oil and butter for 3 to 4 minutes on each side. Remove meat from pan. Add vermouth, simmer over high heat until reduced by one half. Stir in tomato paste and mace. Return veal to pan and heat thoroughly.

Garnish with nuts and cauliflower. Serve with rice or Duchess potatoes.

VEAL IN MUSHROOM SAUCE

Serves 4

4 veal cutlets	4
flour	
salt and pepper, to taste	
3 tablespoons vegetable oil	45 mL
1 medium onion, sliced	1
2 cloves garlic, minced	2
1-7½ ounce can tomato sauce	213 mL
1 cup mushrooms, fresh or canned	250 mL
½ cup water or dry white wine or mushroom liquid	125 mL
1 tablespoon Parmesan cheese	15 mL
¼ teaspoon dried basil	1 mL

Dip veal in flour. Brown in oil in skillet over medium to high heat. Sprinkle with salt and pepper. Remove meat, reduce heat and add onion and garlic. Cook 1 to 2 minutes, then stir in remaining ingredients. Return meat to pan. Cover and simmer about 30 minutes or until very tender.

Excellent served over rice or hot buttered noodles.

VEAL WITH CHERRIES

Serves 8

3 pounds veal shank, cut in ½ inch (1 cm) slices	1.5 Kg
3 tablespoons butter	45 mL
2 medium onions, chopped	2
2-14 ounce cans pitted cherries	2-398 mL
1¼ cup seedless raisins	300 mL
1 cup beef, or chicken stock	250 mL
⅓ cup dry red wine	75 mL
12 cardamon buds or 1 teaspoon powdered cardamon	12 or 5 mL
1 teaspoon salt	5 mL
pepper to taste	

Brown meat gently, in butter, in heavy 2 quart (2 L) casserole. Add chopped onions and sauté until tender, but not brown. Drain cherries, reserving liquid. Add pitted cherries, raisins, stock, wine, cardamon and ¼ of cherry juice. Season with salt and pepper.

Cover tightly and simmer 2 hours on top of stove. If sauce needs thickening make a roux by heating 1 tablespoon (15 mL) butter and 2 tablespoons (25 mL) flour in a small saucepan. Blend well, stir into sauce and bring to a boil. Serve with rice or buttered noodles.

VEAL MADELON

Serves 4

1 clove garlic, minced	1
2 tablespoons butter	25 mL
2 pounds boneless veal, cut in bite-size chunks	1 Kg
2 tablespoons flour	25 mL
1 teaspoon salt	5 mL
¼ teaspoon pepper	1 mL
2 lemon peels cut ¼ × 2 inch (.5 × 5 cm)	2
1 cup hot water	250 mL
1 cup whipping cream	250 mL

Sauté garlic in butter. Remove garlic and brown veal in same butter. Sprinkle veal with flour, salt and pepper; continue browning. Add lemon peels and water, mix, and cover. Simmer until tender, adding more water if needed. Remove lemon peels. Stir in cream; heat through. Serve with hot, buttered noodles.

BRENDA VACCARO'S "VEAL ROLL"

Serves 4

3 pounds veal, either the rump or the shoulder boned and rolled	1.5 Kg
2 cups chicken stock	500 mL
3 onions, chopped	3
4 stalks of celery, chopped	4
8 carrots, chopped	8
1 bay leaf, crushed	1
dash of thyme	dash
3 or 5 tablespoons sherry	45 to 50 mL
arrowroot, to thicken to taste, or cornstarch	
2 tablespoons butter	25 mL
2 slices bacon, cut up	2
salt and pepper, to taste	

Sauté all the above vegetables and spices in butter with bacon.

Salt and pepper veal, brown on all sides. Pour oil off browned veal.

Put vegetables in bottom of pot, veal on top of that and pour stock over everything.

Simmer until done. Take meat out. Pour stock through sieve, then vegetables to give richness. Add sherry and thicken to desired consistency with arrowroot or cornstarch.

VEAL MARENGO
Serves 6

3 pounds lean shoulder of veal, cut in cubes	1.5 Kg
1 onion, chopped	1
½ cup tomato purée	125 mL
1 cup of dry white wine	250 mL
2 cups chicken stock	500 mL
1 garlic clove	1
2 bay leaves	2
¼ teaspoon thyme	1 mL
salt and pepper, to taste	
12 small white onions	12
6 tablespoons butter	75 mL
12 button mushrooms	12
3 large tomatoes	3
3 tablespoons cooking oil	45 mL
1 tablespoon flour	15 mL
1 tablespoon sugar	15 mL
chopped parsley	

In heavy kettle brown meat in 3 tablespoons (45 mL) oil. Add onion and tomato purée, cook for 3 minutes. Stir in flour and add the stock and white wine gradually. Add garlic, bay leaves, thyme, salt and pepper to taste. Simmer slowly for 1 hour. Sauté onions in 4 tablespoons (50 mL) butter, sprinkle with 1 tablespoon (15 mL) sugar and cook until brown and glazed. Sauté mushrooms in 2 tablespoons (25 mL) butter for 3 minutes. Peel, seed and quarter tomatoes. Add onions, mushrooms and tomatoes to kettle, stew for 30 minutes. Sprinkle with parsley before serving with rice.

Poultry

CHICKEN NEW ORLEANS

Serves 4 to 6

2 pounds chicken breasts, boned and skinned	1 k
½ cup flour, seasoned with salt and pepper	125 mL
4 tablespoons cooking oil	50 mL
1 clove of garlic, crushed	1
2 medium onions, finely chopped	2
2 medium green peppers, finely chopped	2
½ pound mushrooms, sliced	250 g
½ pound dried currants	250 g
2 to 3 cups canned Italian tomatoes, pureéd	500-750 mL

Seasonings

½ teaspoon salt	2 mL
¼ teaspoon curry	1 mL
¼ teaspoon thyme	1 mL
½ teaspoon cayenne pepper	2 mL

Garnish

½ pound almonds, blanched and toasted	250 g
½ cup parsley, finely chopped	125 mL

Cut chicken into cubes (bite-size) and coat with seasoned flour. Melt oil in frying pan over medium heat 350°F (180°C), gently brown chicken, remove from pan. In the remaining oil (add more if necessary), add garlic, onions, green peppers, and mushrooms. Sauté until limp, add tomatoes, seasonings, and currants. Blend and cook for 5 minutes. Pour mixture over chicken and bake in oven at 325°F (170°C) for ¾ to 1 hour, until chicken is tender.

Serve on platter surrounded with fluffy cooked white rice. Garnish rice with almonds and garnish the chicken with parsley. Serve with crusty rolls and tossed salad.

ELIZABETH TAYLOR'S "CHICKEN WITH AVOCADO AND MUSHROOMS"

Serves 6 to 8

1 avocado (preferably the dark-skinned California variety)	1
1 tablespoon lemon juice	15 mL
2 (2½ pounds each) small chickens, cut into serving pieces	2 (1 Kg each)
salt and freshly ground pepper	
¼ cup butter	50 mL
3 finely chopped shallots	3
3 tablespoons cognac	45 mL
⅓ cup dry white wine	75 mL
1 cup whipping cream	250 mL
2 cups sliced fresh mushrooms	500 mL
1 cup chicken stock	250 mL
chopped parsley for garnish	

Peel and cube avocado, sprinkle with lemon juice. Cover and refrigerate.

Sprinkle chicken with salt and pepper.

In a large heavy skillet, over low heat, heat 3 to 4 tablespoons (45 to 50 mL) butter and sauté chicken until juices run yellow when it is pricked with a fork, about 35 to 40 minutes. (Use two skillets if necessary, adding more butter as needed.)

Transfer cooked chicken to a serving dish. Cover loosely with aluminum foil. Keep warm in a 300°F (150°C) oven for 15 minutes, while preparing sauce.

Add shallots to skillet. Cook over medium heat, stirring and scraping sides and bottom of pan with a wooden spoon. Add cognac and wine and bring to a boil. Boil until mixture has almost evaporated. Add cream and boil 5 minutes longer.

In a saucepan over high heat, sauté mushrooms in 3 tablespoons (45 mL) butter.

Add chicken stock to cream mixture. Cook over medium heat, stirring constantly, until thick. Add the mushrooms, remaining cognac and avocado cubes. Stir until well blended. Pour over chicken. Sprinkle with parsley. Enjoy!

CHINESE CHICKEN CASSEROLE
Serves 6

4 whole chicken breasts	4
¾ cup oil	175 mL
⅓ cup soya sauce	75 mL
1 tablespoon salt	15 mL
pepper, to taste	
2 tablespoons sherry	25 mL
2 cloves garlic, chopped	2
1 cup sliced water chestnuts	250 mL
1 cup bamboo shoots	250 mL
2 green peppers, diced	2
2 scallions, chopped	2
1 teaspoon monosodium gluatmate	5 mL
½ teaspoon sugar	2 mL
¼ cup cornstarch	50 mL
½ cup water	125 mL
2 cups toasted cashews	500 mL
1 cup sliced mushrooms	250 mL

Cut chicken into bite-size pieces. Marinate chicken in 6 tablespoons (75 mL) of the oil, 2 tablespoons (25 mL) of the soya sauce, 2 teaspoons (10 mL) of the salt, pepper, and sherry for half a day. Discard marinade.

Stir-fry chicken in 4 tablespoons (50 mL) of the oil and set aside.

Stir-fry garlic, water chestnuts, mushrooms, bamboo shoots, peppers, and scallions in remaining 2 tablespoons (25 mL) of oil. Add remaining 4 tablespoons (50 mL) soya sauce, monosodium glutamate, sugar, remaining teaspoon (5 mL) of salt, and cook 2 minutes. (Can be prepared ahead to this point.)

Just before serving, mix cornstarch and water. Add to vegetables. Heat through. Combine vegetable mixture with chicken and cashews. Heat and serve with rice.

4

Henry Winkler's Hawaiian Chicken
Recipe on page 99

CHICKEN WITH SPICY WINE SAUCE

Serves 4

4 half chicken breasts, skinned and boned	4
2 eggs	2
1½ tablespoons water	20 mL
1 tablespoon dry mustard	15 mL
1¼ cups fine dry bread crumbs	300 mL
1½ teaspoons Italian seasonings	7 mL
3 or 4 tablespoons vegetable oil	45 or 40 mL
3 or 4 tablespoons butter or margarine	45 or 50 mL
1-7½ ounce can tomato sauce	213 mL
⅓ cup white wine	75 mL
1 cup sliced fresh mushrooms	250 mL
3 green onions with tops, chopped	3

Place chicken pieces between sheets of waxed paper and flatten with a meat mallet.

Beat together eggs and water. Using whisk, add mustard. Combine crumbs and Italian seasonings.

Dip chicken in egg mixture, then in crumbs. Repeat dipping in egg and crumbs. In half the oil and butter, brown 2 chicken pieces on each side. Brown remaining chicken in remaining oil and butter. Place in single layer in a lightly greased casserole dish.

Combine tomato sauce, wine, mushrooms and onions and spoon evenly over the chicken. Cover and bake at 350°F (180°C) for 20 to 25 minutes, until chicken is done. Serve with buttered noodles and a green vegetable. Pass warm whole wheat rolls.

CHICKEN WITH HERBS AND WINE

Serves 6 to 8

⅔ cup butter, melted	150 mL
10 chicken pieces	10
½ cup bread crumbs	125 mL
2 tablespoons Parmesan cheese	25 mL
1 teaspoon oregano	5 mL
1 teaspoon basil	5 mL
1 teaspoon garlic salt	5 mL
¼ teaspoon salt	1 mL
¼ cup white wine	50 mL
¼ cup chopped green onions	50 mL
¼ cup chopped fresh parsley	50 mL

Dip chicken pieces in melted butter and roll in bread crumbs, Parmesan cheese, oregano, basil and garlic salt. Bake at 425°F (220°C) for 30 minutes. Using the remaining butter make a sauce adding: salt, white wine, onions and parsley. Baste the chicken — with half the sauce. Put in oven for 5 minutes. Serve remaining sauce in a gravy boat.

TROPICAL SLIM CHICKEN

Serves 8
(about 300 calories per serving)

2-3 pounds each frying chickens, cut up	2-1.5 Kg each
2 tablespoons soya sauce	15 mL
2 to 3 teaspoons seasoned salt	10-15 mL
¼ teaspoon thyme	1 mL
2-10 ounce cans sugar free carbonated drink, any citrus flavour	2-284 mL
2 tablespoons cornstarch	25 mL
½ cup chopped onion	125 mL
½ cup chopped celery	125 mL
2 cloves, garlic, minced	2

Brush chicken on all sides with soya sauce. Sprinkle liberally with seasoned salt. Arrange in single layer in large shallow baking pan. Place under broiler to brown lightly on all sides. Sprinkle with onion, celery, garlic and thyme. Pour soft drink over all. Cover with foil and bake at 350°F (180°C) for 45 minutes. Remove foil and stir in cornstarch mixed with cold water. Bake 1 hour and baste until chicken is tender. Garnish with a few pineapple bits, peach slices, lime and tomato wedges.

HENRY WINKLER'S "HAWAIIAN CHICKEN"

Serves 6

2 medium fryer chickens, cut up	2
¼ cup butter	50 mL
2 tablespoons flour	25 mL
1 cup orange juice	250 mL
1-10 ounce can condensed chicken broth	284 mL
1 teaspoon salt	5 mL
dash of cayenne, cinnamon, and garlic salt	
1-20 ounce can pineapple chunks	540 mL
½ cup raisins	125 mL
2 ounces slivered blanched almonds	50 mL
Parsley and orange slices for garnish	

Brown chicken pieces in melted butter in large Dutch oven or heavy skillet. Remove chicken as it browns. Pour off all but 4 tablespoons (50 mL) of fat. Stir in flour and cook and stir for 5 minutes. Gradually stir in orange juice and broth. Return chicken to Dutch oven, add salt, cayenne, cinnamon, pineapple, liquid and raisins. Cover and simmer over low heat 50 to 60 minutes, or until chicken is tender. Sprinkle with almonds. Garnish with parsley and orange slices.

Alternative suggestion: sprinkle raisins and pineapple chunks over chicken and sauce at serving time.

CHICKEN FONDUE
FOR FOUR PEOPLE

Serves 4

2 chicken bouillon cubes	2
4 cups boiling water	1 L
1 cup white wine	250 mL
1½ to 2 pounds chicken breasts, skinned, boned and cut into cubes	750 g to 1 Kg

Combine chicken bouillon cubes in boiling water in metal fondue pot. Add wine. Each person cooks their own chicken cubes.

Serve with 2 or 3 sauces — eg. curry powder and sour cream, crabapple jelly, sweet red pepper relish. Good with a tossed green salad and lots of French bread.

ELEGANT ROLLED CHICKEN
WASHINGTON

Serves 6

6 or 7 whole chicken breasts, skinned and boned	6 or 7
flour	
2 eggs, slightly beaten	2
¾ cup fine dry bread crumbs	175 mL

Cheese Filling

½ cup fresh mushrooms, finely chopped	125 mL
2 tablespoons butter	25 mL
2 tablespoons flour	25 mL
½ cup light cream	125 mL
½ teaspoon salt	2 mL
dash cayenne pepper	dash
1¼ cups sharp Cheddar cheese, shredded	300 mL

Sauté mushrooms in butter, blend in flour, and stir in cream. Add salt and cayenne, cook and stir until mixture becomes thick. Stir in cheese; cook over very low heat, stirring constantly, until cheese is melted. Turn mixture into pie plate. Cover and chill thoroughly, about 1 hour. Cut the firm cheese mixture into 6 or 7 equal portions; shape into short sticks.

Place a cheese stick on each chicken breast, tucking in the sides, roll up chicken as for jelly-roll. Press to seal well. Dust the chicken rolls with flour. Dip in slightly beaten egg, then roll in fine dry bread crumbs. Cover and chill chicken rolls thoroughly (at least one hour). About 1 hour before serving fry rolls in deep, hot fat 375°F (190°C) for 5 minutes or until crisp and golden brown. Drain on paper towels. Place rolls in shallow baking dish and bake in a slow oven 325°F (160°C) about 30 to 45 minutes.

Well worth the effort!

CHICKEN AND SPARERIBS
Serves 6 to 8

¼ cup chopped onion	50 mL
1 tablespoon oil	15 mL
½ cup water	125 mL
1 tablespoon vinegar	15 mL
1 tablespoon Worcestershire sauce	15 mL
¼ cup lemon juice	50 mL
¼ teaspoon salt	1 mL
¼ teaspoon paprika	1 mL
6 tablespoons brown sugar	90 mL
½ cup chili sauce	125 mL
½ cup ketchup	125 mL
½ cup molasses	125 mL
1 chicken, cut up	1
5 to 6 sliced pork ribs per person	5 to 6

Sauté onion in oil until transparent. Add all other ingredients except chicken and ribs. Cook over medium heat until blended. Simmer on low heat for 30 minutes, stirring occasionally. Arrange chicken and ribs in large casserole. Pour on sauce and bake in 350°F (180°C) oven for 1 hour.

ITALIAN CHICKEN

Serves 8

¼ cup olive oil	50 mL
2 cloves, garlic, quartered	2
8 medium chicken breast halves, boned	8
1½ pounds Italian sausage	750 g
2 cups dry white wine	500 mL
1½ pounds sliced fresh mushrooms	750 g
1 teaspoon salt	5 mL
½ cup water	125 mL
2 tablespoons cornstarch	25 mL
2 chopped onions	2

In a large skillet, cook garlic and onions in hot olive oil until golden. Discard garlic. Brown chicken and sausage in same skillet over medium high heat. Pour off and discard all but 2 tablespoons (25 mL) of the pan drippings. Add wine, mushrooms, and salt. Heat to boiling. Cover and reduce heat. Simmer 30 minutes or until chicken is tender. Arrange chicken and sausage on a warm platter. Blend water and cornstarch. Stir gradually into hot pan drippings. Cook over medium heat until thickened. Spoon sauce over chicken and sausage. Serve. (Can be refrigerated and reheated at 350°F (180°C) for 30 minutes.)

ORANGE CHICKEN

Serves 4 to 6

Prepared in a matter of minutes —

4 pounds chicken pieces	2 Kg
1 envelope dry onion soup mix	1
1-6 ounce can orange juice, thawed	1-170 mL
1 tablespoon cornstarch	15 mL
1 teaspoon poultry seasoning	5 mL
orange slices	

In a bowl, combine soup mix, orange juice concentrate, cornstarch, and poultry seasoning. Place chicken pieces skin side up in a 13 × 9 inch (33 × 23 cm) baking dish. Pour juice mixture over chicken, cover and bake at 375°F (190°C) for one hour. Uncover and bake an additional 15 minutes before serving. Garnish with orange slices.

DOM DE LUISE'S "GINGER CHICKEN"

Serves 4

¼ pound melted butter	125 mL
1 tablespoon (heaping) fresh ginger or 1 teaspoon (5 mL) prepared ginger	15 mL
1 small bunch green scallions, cut into 1 inch (2 cm) pieces	1
1 small can water chestnuts, drained and sliced	1-284 mL
2½ cups cooked chicken, cut into two inch pieces (4 cm)	625 mL
½ cup chicken stock	125 mL
12 fresh button mushrooms	12
3 tablespoons sour cream (to mellow the taste of the ginger)	45 mL
salt and pepper to taste	

Combine all ingredients (in order listed) in a chafing dish and heat.
Serve with rice cooked in chicken broth. Top with a tablespoon (15 mL)
of sour cream and sprinkle with parsley.

CHICKEN PAPRIKA
Serves 6

3 tablespoons clarified butter	45 mL
10 to 12 pieces of breast and thigh meat	10 to 12
2 large onions, chopped	2
1 clove of pressed garlic	1
1 tablespoon paprika	15 mL
½ cup dry white wine	125 mL
1½ cups chicken stock	375 mL
2 bay leaves	2
¼ cup white roux	50 mL
½ cup tap hot water	125 mL
1 cup sour cream	250 mL

Put butter into a skillet. Heat it and add the chicken pieces.

Lightly brown on both sides and remove from pan. Put onions and garlic into pan and sauté for a few minutes and then stir in the paprika; cook for a minute. Return the pieces of chicken and add about half the stock and the wine. Cover and simmer for 25 to 35 minutes, or until tender.

Put the bay leaves in and allow them to cook with the chicken for the last ten minutes of cooking time. Check the meat and if the liquid has cooked away and the meat is again frying, add the rest of the stock or more water to loosen any meat particles or juice from the pan for gravy.

Put the roux into a 1 quart (1 L) bowl and slowly add the ½ cup (125 mL) hot tap water while stirring to a smooth paste. Blend in the sour cream and any remaining stock. Pour over meat and stir to blend. Allow to come to the boil and cook for about 2 minutes. Serve with dumplings.

White Roux (Basic thick white sauce)

¼ cup all-purpose flour	50 mL
3 tablespoons clarified butter	45 mL

In a small saucepan over very low heat melt the butter. Very slowly add the flour, stirring constantly for 5 to 10 minutes, until creamy but not brown.

Dumplings

2 eggs	2
½ cup cold water	125 mL
1½ cups all-purpose flour	375 mL
2 to 3 tablespoons butter	25 to 45 mL
salt and pepper, to taste	

Stir eggs, water, salt and pepper, and flour to a smooth mixture and gradually add additional cold water to make a thick paste. Drop by spoon into plenty of simmering salted water and cook five minutes after last dumpling is in. Drain and put into a warm dish. Add butter to dumplings and mix. Arrange to form a ring. Place meat in centre. Pour some sauce over and sprinkle some chopped parsley over all. Serve the rest of the sauce in a sauce boat.

CHICKEN LIVERS
Serves 4 to 6

1 pound chicken livers, wash, trim and cut in half	500 g
3 strips bacon, fried, crispy and cooled	3
2 cooking onions, chopped	2
4 stalks of celery, chopped	4
1 green pepper, chopped	1
1 sweet red pepper, chopped or substitute with 1 tomato	1
½ cup flour	125 mL
1 teaspoon ginger	5 mL
pinch garlic salt	pinch
pinch salt and pepper	pinch
1 lemon, grated	1
¼ teaspoon curry (optional)	1 mL
1 cup water	250 mL
½ cup red or white wine	125 mL
2 tablespoons soya sauce	25 mL

In a plastic bag, mix flour and spices and gratings from lemon. Shake together and add the chicken livers until well coated with flour mixture.

Sauté bacon in pan on stove, remove bacon from pan and add a little extra cooking oil. Add livers and cook over medium heat, keep stirring and cook for 15 to 20 minutes. Remove chicken livers from pan, add a cup of water, wine, red or white, soya sauce and cook until sauce thickens. Add livers and vegetables. Serve with rice. (Vegetables should still be a bit crispy.)

SUPERB TURKEY CASSEROLE

Serves 12

4 to 5 cups turkey, cooked, sliced	1 to 1.5 L
2-3 ounce packages toasted almonds	2-85 g
1 large green pepper, coarsely chopped	1
1 small jar pimentos, drained	1
1 pound mushrooms, sautéd in butter	500 g
1-10 ounce can water chestnuts, sliced	1-284 mL
1-10 ounce can condensed mushroom soup	1-284 mL
2-10 ounce cans condensed cream of chicken soup	2-284 mL
1½ cups mayonnaise	375 mL
4 tablespoons lemon juice	50 mL
12 ounces extra old Cheddar cheese, grated	340 g
1-8 ounce package herbed stove top stuffing mix	250 g

Spread turkey and almonds in a buttered flat casserole. Mix together in a large bowl green pepper, pimento, mushrooms, water chestnuts, mushroom and chicken soup, mayonnaise, lemon juice. Pour over turkey. Sprinkle with the cheese. Prepare stuffing mix as package directs and sprinkle over cheese. Bake at 325°F (160°C) for 1 hour.

ALL-OCCASION CHICKEN

Serves 4 to 6

6 chicken breasts, or pieces	6
1 pound mushrooms	500 g
2 Spanish onions, sliced	2
1 green pepper, sliced	1
1-28 ounce can whole tomatoes	796 mL
1 package wide noodles, cooked	1
1 pint whipping cream	500 mL
1 teaspoon chili powder	5 mL
salt and pepper to taste	
1 cup chicken stock	250 mL

Cook chicken pieces and remove meat from bones. Sauté mushrooms in butter. Add sliced onions, green pepper and 1 tablespoon (15 mL) flour. Add cream, chicken stock, chili powder, salt, pepper and tomatoes. Place half noodles, chicken and sauce in a 9 × 13 inch (23 × 33 cm) baking dish. Repeat. Bake at 350°F (180°C) for 45 minutes.

CAROL BURNETT'S "TURKEY FILLETS WITH PISTACHIOS"

1 cup butter	250 mL
6-6 ounce turkey fillets, cut from breast	6-170 g
salt and pepper to taste	
4 finely chopped shallots	4
4 large mushrooms, sliced	4
2 tablespoons flour	25 mL
⅓ cup dry white wine	75 mL
⅔ cup chicken broth	150 mL
2 egg yolks	2
½ cup whipping cream	125 mL
⅓ cup chopped pistachios, shelled	75 mL
¼ teaspoon dried tarragon	1 mL
1 tablespoon lemon juice	25 mL

Melt ¼ cup (50 mL) of butter in a large skillet, sauté the turkey on both sides until golden. Season with salt and pepper. Remove from pan and set aside. Add shallots to pan and sauté for 5 minutes. Add the mushrooms and cook for another 5 minutes, adding more butter if needed. Sprinkle in the flour and cook for about 3 minutes. Add the wine and broth, stirring until slightly thickened. Return the fillets to the pan and cover and cook for 15 minutes on low heat. Beat the cream and the egg yolks together. Add some of the hot sauce to cream mixture, then stir into the hot sauce. Stir until thickened. Add pistachios, tarragon and lemon juice. Correct seasoning.

MOZZARELLA CHICKEN

Serves 4 to 6

6 chicken breasts, boned and skinned	6
½ cup butter, melted	125 mL
½ cup flour	125 mL
2 cups chicken stock	500 mL
1 cup table cream	250 mL
1 cup white wine	250 mL
1 teaspoon Worcestershire sauce	5 mL
salt to taste	
1½ cups fresh mushrooms, sliced	375 mL
1-8 ounce package Mozzarella cheese slices	250 g

Brown chicken breasts quickly in butter. Remove from heat and stir in chicken stock, cream and white wine. Return to heat stirring constantly, until blended.

Remove from heat and add remaining ingredients, except cheese. Pour sauce over chicken breasts in casserole and bake at 350°F (180°C) for 25 to 30 minutes.

Remove from oven and cover with Mozzarella cheese slices and continue baking for 5 to 10 minutes.

CHICKEN SALTIMBOCA

Serves 4 to 6

This recipe doubles (or triples) easily

3 whole chicken breasts, split, boned, and skinned	3
1 teaspoon salt	5 mL
6 thin slices of ham	6
1 medium tomato, peeled, seeded, and chopped	1
6 slices Swiss cheese	6
½ teaspoon dry sage	2 mL
⅓ cup dry bread crumbs	75 mL
2 tablespoons Parmesan cheese	25 mL
2 tablespoons minced parsley	25 mL
4 tablespoons melted butter	50 mL

Flatten chicken breasts between sheets of waxed paper. Sprinkle each piece with salt. Top each with a slice of ham, chopped tomato, Swiss cheese, and a dash of sage. Roll jelly-roll fashion, securing with toothpicks. Combine crumbs, Parmesan cheese, and parsley. Dip chicken in melted butter, roll in crumb mixture, and place in buttered baking dish. Bake uncovered at 350°F (180°C) for 40 to 45 minutes.

COQ AU VIN
Serves 8

½ cup butter	125 mL
1 cup flour	250 mL
10 to 12 chicken pieces (boned, if desired)	10 to 12
½ cup brandy	125 mL
12 ounces whole, fresh mushrooms	340 g
5 green onions, diced	5
1 bay leaf, crumbled	1
1 clove garlic, minced	1
2 cups white wine	500 mL
5 slices raw bacon, cut into ½ inch (1 cm) pieces	5
¼ cup chopped, fresh parsley	50 mL
1 teaspoon thyme	5 mL

Melt butter in a heavy skillet. Dredge chicken in flour. Brown in butter. Place browned chicken in a foil-lined baking dish. Reserve butter in skillet. Pour brandy over chicken and flambé. Mix together remaining ingredients. Distribute evenly around chicken. Pour on reserved butter. Bake at 350°F (180°C) for 2 hours.

CHICKEN BOURGEOIS
Serves 4

4 chicken legs	4
2 whole chicken breasts, halved, boned and split	2
3 slices of ham, ½ inch (1 cm) thick, cut in 1 inch (2.5 cm) pieces	3
6 tablespoons butter	75 mL
½ cup green onions, sliced	125 mL
12 mushroom caps, quartered	12
8 carrots, split lengthwise	8
potato balls (about 30)	
2 bay leaves	2
salt and pepper, to taste	
1 cup white wine	250 mL

In a frying pan, sauté onions and mushrooms in butter; remove and set aside. Brown chicken pieces in remaining butter. Place chicken, onions and mushrooms in a casserole dish. Add all vegetables, ham, bay leaves, salt and pepper. Pour wine over top; cover; bake at 350°F (180°C) for 1½ hours (or until carrots are tender).

CHICKEN MANDARIN

Serves 6

8 to 10 chicken pieces	8 to 10
1 teaspoon salt	5 mL
¼ teaspoon pepper	1 mL
1 cup chopped onion	250 mL
1 clove, garlic, crushed	1
1 tablespoon butter	15 mL
¼ cup ketchup	50 mL
¾ cup marmalade	175 mL
2 tablespoons soya sauce	25 mL
1 cup chicken broth	250 mL
2 teaspoons dry mustard	10 mL
1 green pepper, julienne strips	1
2 cans Mandarin oranges, drained	2-284 mL
rice, cooked	

Season chicken pieces with salt and pepper. Brown in butter. Place in casserole dish.

Sauté onion, garlic in butter until tender. Add ketchup, marmalade, soya sauce, broth, mustard, green pepper and Mandarin oranges. Simmer for 15 to 20 minutes. Spoon sauce over chicken. Can be made one day in advance. Bake, basting occasionally at 350°F (180°C) for 1½ hours. Serve with rice.

CRUSTY CHICKEN WINGS

Serves 6 to 8

2 pounds chicken wings, or drumsticks	1 Kg
½ cup butter or margarine	125 mL
2 teaspoons seasoned salt	10 mL
2 cups instant potato flakes	500 mL

Cut chicken at joints. Melt butter in a small saucepan, add 1 teaspoon (5 mL) of the seasoned salt. Spread potato flakes on a piece of wax paper. Dip chicken pieces in the seasoned butter and roll in potato flakes until coated. Place chicken in a 10 × 12 inch (25 × 30 cm) baking pan, sprinkle with remaining 1 teaspoon (5 mL) of seasoned salt. Bake in moderate oven 375°F (190°C) for 35 minutes, or until chicken is golden brown.

This may sound mundane but the potato flakes make the chicken very crisp and crunchy.

ART LINKLETTER'S FAVOURITE RECIPE "STEWED CHICKEN"

Serves 6

1-5 pound stewing chicken, cut up	2-5 Kg
1 carrot, sliced	1
1 small onion, sliced	1
3 cups water	750 mL
2 ribs celery, chopped (leaves included)	2
½ teaspoon salt	2 mL
⅛ teaspoon paprika	pinch

Clean and cut chicken into pieces. Bring water, carrot, onion, celery to a boil. Drop chicken, slowly and gently, piece-by-piece, into the boiling liquid. As mixture increases in volume, the chicken need only be covered to the depth of ½ inch (1 cm). Cover pan and let simmer for about two hours or until tender. After one hour, add salt and paprika. After two hours, lift the pieces from the pot and make a thick gravy of stock left in pan using a standard recipe. If gravy tends to separate, stir into it slowly two or more tablespoons (30 to 35 mL) of cream.

Serve with noodles, dumplings, boiled rice, spaghetti or baked macaroni. With a tossed green salad, milk for all and fruit for dessert, you've got a hearty and well-balanced meal.

CHICKEN A L'ORANGE

Serves 4

6 chicken breast halves, boned, skinned	6
½ teaspoon salt	2 mL
¼ cup butter or margarine	50 mL
2 tablespoons flour	25 mL
⅛ teaspoon cinnamon	pinch
dash of ginger	
1½ cups orange juice	375 mL
½ cup slivered almonds, toasted	125 mL
½ cup seedless raisins	125 mL
1 cup Mandarin oranges or fresh orange sections	250 mL
1 teaspoon Worcestershire sauce	5 mL

Sprinkle chicken with ¼ teaspoon (1 mL) of the salt. Brown chicken in melted butter. Remove from pan and set aside. Blend flour, remaining salt, cinnamon, and ginger into pan drippings to make a smooth paste. Gradually add orange juice and Worcestershire stirring constantly. Cook and stir until sauce thickens. Return chicken to pan. Add almonds and raisins. Cover and cook over low heat, about 45 minutes, or until chicken is tender. Add orange sections and heat through. Serve with rice, or noodles, and plenty of sauce!

DIJON CHICKEN

Serves 6

12 chicken breasts, boned	12
1½ tablespoons butter	20 mL
¾ cup whipping cream	175 mL
3 tablespoons Dijon mustard	45 mL

Sauté chicken in butter. Thoroughly mix Dijon mustard and whipping cream. Heat and reduce sauce to half. Ladle over chicken.

Seafood

SOLE PROVENÇALE
Serves 6

6 fresh or frozen sole fillets (1½ pounds)	6-750 g
¼ cup chopped onion	50 mL
1 clove garlic, minced	1
1 tablespoon butter	15 mL
2 teaspoons cornstarch	10 mL
1-7½ ounce can tomato sauce	213 mL
1-7½ ounce can tomatoes, chopped	213 mL
1-4 ounce can sliced mushrooms, drained	113 mL
½ cup dry white wine	125 mL
2 tablespoons chopped fresh parsley or	25 mL or
2 teaspoons dried parsley	10 mL
1 chicken bouillon cube, crushed	1
1 teaspoon sugar	5 mL
salt and paprika, to taste	

Sprinkle each fillet with salt and paprika. Roll up and place seam side down in a 10 × 6 × 2 inch (25 × 15 × 5 cm) casserole. Set aside.

Sauté onion and garlic in butter until onion is tender. Blend in cornstarch. Stir in remaining ingredients and simmer, about 5 minutes, stirring frequently.

Pour sauce over fish and cook covered for 7 or 8 minutes. Every 2 minutes turn dish a quarter turn, basting with sauce each time.

Serve hot over cooked rice, accompanied by a tossed green salad.

HERBED BUTTER

½ pound butter	250 mL
1 tablespoon chopped chives	15 mL
1 tablespoon chopped parsley	15 mL
1 teaspoon marjoram	5 mL
1 teaspoon basil	5 mL
1 teaspoon thyme	5 mL
1 teaspoon lemon juice	5 mL
⅛ teaspoon dry mustard	pinch

Combine and mix well. Cover and refrigerate. Serve on fish, steak, hamburgers, or hot biscuits.

CARROLL O'CONNOR'S "SHRIMP COCONUT"

Serves 4

24 medium size shrimp	24
⅔ cup flour	150 mL
¼ pound dry shredded coconut	125 g
some milk	
2 eggs	2
salt and pepper, to taste	
1 quart peanut oil	1 L

Clean and devein shrimp, leaving tails. Mix eggs, flour, and enough milk to have a heavy dough, add salt and pepper. Lay out coconut on tray, dip shrimp into dough leaving tails clean; roll shrimp in coconut and shake off excess. Up to this point, you can do ahead and refrigerate.

Orange Sauce

2-8 ounce jars orange marmalade	250 mL
2 tablespoons horseradish	25 mL
¼ cup dry sherry	50 mL
few drops of Tobasco	

Put marmalade through blender and mix with sherry, horseradish and Tobasco to make a spicy orange sauce.

Just before serving, heat oil to 375°F (190°C), sauté shrimp about 3 to 4 minutes until coconut is golden brown. Serve on a bed of rice, garnish with orange slices, and serve sauce on the side.

SHRIMP WITH FETA CHEESE
Serves 4

½ cup minced onion	125 mL
1½ tablespoons butter	25 mL
1½ tablespoons oil	25 mL
½ cup dry white wine	125 mL
4 ripe tomatoes, peeled, seeded and chopped	4
1 small clove of garlic, minced	1
1 teaspoon salt	5 mL
¼ teaspoon pepper	1 mL
¾ teaspoon oregano	4 mL
4 ounces Feta cheese, crumbled	125 g
1 pound raw large shrimp, shelled and deveined	500 g
¼ cup chopped fresh parsley	50 mL

Sauté onions in butter and oil until soft. Add wine, tomatoes, garlic, salt, pepper and oregano. Bring to boil, lower heat to medium, and simmer until sauce is slightly thickened. Stir in cheese and simmer for 10 to 15 minutes. Just before serving, add shrimp to hot sauce and cook for five minutes. Do not overcook. Garnish with parsley and serve in bowls with crusty French bread.

CRAB SHELLS AU GRATIN
Serves 6 to 8

4-7½ ounce cans crabmeat, drained	4-213 g
4 hard boiled eggs, chopped	4
3 tablespoons butter	45 mL
3 tablespoons flour	45 mL
1 cup whipping cream	250 mL
salt and pepper, to taste	
2 slices onion, minced	2
juice of small lemon	
2 dashes of Tobasco	
1½ cups grated Cheddar cheese	375 mL

Melt butter over medium heat and stir in flour. Remove from the heat and stir in cream. Return to low heat and stir constantly until thick and smooth. Add all other ingredients except the cheese. Place in greased casserole and cover with cheese. Bake in 350°F (180°C) oven for 30 minutes until the cheese melts and is slightly browned. Can be made the day ahead.

JOHNNY MATHIS' "CREOLE GUMBO"

Serves 6

3 tablespoons butter or margarine	45 mL
3 tablespoons all-purpose flour	45 mL
½ cup chopped onion	125 mL
1 clove garlic, minced	1
1-16 ounce can tomatoes, cut up	425 mL
1 cup water	250 mL
1½ cups chopped green pepper	375 mL
2 bay leaves	2
1 teaspoon dried oregano, crushed	5 mL
1 teaspoon dried thyme, crushed	5 mL
½ teaspoon salt	2 mL
½ teaspoon bottled hot pepper sauce	2 mL
1-10 ounce package frozen cut okra, thawed, or a heaping cup full of fresh zucchini	284 mL
2-4½ ounce cans shrimp, drained and cut up	2-128 g
1-7½ ounce can crabmeat, drained and cartilage removed	213 g

Hot cooked rice

In a large saucepan melt butter or margarine; blend in flour; cook, stirring constantly, until mixture is golden brown. Stir in onion and garlic; cook until onion is tender but not brown. Stir in undrained tomatoes, water, green pepper, bay leaves, oregano, thyme, salt, and hot pepper sauce.

Bring to boil; reduce heat and simmer, covered, about 20 minutes.

Remove the bay leaves, stir in okra or zucchini. Bring mixture to boil, then stir in shrimp and crab; heat mixture through. Serve the gumbo over hot cooked rice in soup plates. (Traditionally rice is mounded in a heated soup plate and the gumbo spooned around.)

SCRUMPTIOUS SCALLOPS

Serves 4

2 pounds scallops	1 Kg
juice of 1 lemon	1
4 tablespoons butter	50 mL
1 small onion, chopped	1
3 tablespoons flour	45 mL
¼ teaspoon celery salt	1 mL
¼ teaspoon thyme	1 mL
1 teaspoon salt	5 mL
½ teaspoon Worcestershire sauce	2 mL
1 cup mushrooms, sliced	250 mL
¼ cup vermouth	50 mL
½ cup bread crumbs	125 mL

Wash and drain scallops. Cover with water. Add lemon juice and simmer 3 minutes. Drain and save 1½ cups (375 mL) liquid. Melt butter, and sauté onions 10 minutes. Add flour and seasonings. Add liquid from scallops and cook until smooth. Add scallops, mushrooms and wine. Mix and pour into buttered baking dish. Cover with crumbs and bake at 350°F (180°C) for 15 minutes.

ELEGANT SCALLOPS AND MUSHROOMS

Serves 4

½ pound fresh mushrooms	250 g
3 tablespoons butter	45 mL
2 tablespoons flour	25 mL
1 cup whipping cream or half and half	250 mL
1 tablespoon dry vermouth	15 mL
salt and pepper, to taste	
1 pound fresh or frozen sea scallops, quartered or whole bay scallops	500 g
bread crumbs	
Butter	

Slice mushrooms and sauté in butter until limp, about 5 minutes. Blend in flour. Add cream slowly, stirring until a thin sauce is made.

Add vermouth, seasonings and scallops. Place in small, lightly buttered casserole. Top with bread crumbs and clot with butter. Cover and bake at 375°F (190°C) for 10 to 15 minutes.

LIONA BOYD'S
"QUICK COQUILLES ST. JACQUES"
Serves 6 to 8

1½ cups water (or half water, half white wine)	375 mL
1 pound scallops (halved if large, whole if bay)	500 g
1 pound cooked shrimps	500 g
1½ cups fish stock (from scallops)	375 mL
4 sprigs of parsley	4
4 small halved onions	4
5 tablespoons butter	75 mL
4 tablespoons flour	50 mL
salt and pepper to taste	
juice of ½ lemon	
1 cup cream or milk	250 mL
3 eggs	3
2½ cups sliced mushrooms	625 mL

Topping
½ cup butter	125 mL
3 cups bread cubes	750 mL
1 cup grated Parmesan cheese	250 mL
paprika	

Heat water, parsley and onions to boiling. Add scallops and simmer about 5 minutes. Drain scallops reserving liquid, and set aside. In a saucepan heat 5 tablespoons (75 mL) of butter. Sprinkle in flour, stirring all the time. Slowly add lemon juice and 1½ cups (375 mL) scallop stock. Lightly beat eggs with cream or milk and slowly beat in sauce.

Add mushrooms, scallops and shrimp and heat thoroughly. Do not overcook. Place in casserole and sprinkle with topping. Place under low broiler until golden brown.

PARTY SEAFOOD LASAGNE

Serves 12

12 lasagne noodles	12
1 cup chopped onions	250 mL
2 tablespoons butter or margarine	25 mL
1-8 ounce package cream cheese, softened	250 g
1½ cups cream style cottage cheese	375 mL
1 egg, beaten	1
2 teaspoons crushed basil	10 mL
½ teaspoon salt	2 mL
⅛ teaspoon pepper	pinch
¼ cup flour	50 mL
¼ cup melted butter	50 mL
2 cups milk	500 mL
⅔ cup dry white wine	150 mL
1 pound cooked shrimp, shelled and cut in half lengthwise	500 g
1-7½ ounce can crabmeat, drained and flaked	220 g
¼ cup grated Parmesan cheese	50 mL
½ cup shredded sharp processed American or Cheddar cheese	125 mL
fresh parsley	
extra shrimp for garnish	

Cook noodles according to package directions; drain. Put two layers of three noodles each on bottom of a greased 9 × 13 inch (23 × 33 cm) baking dish.

Sauté onion in melted butter until tender. Blend in cream cheese, then add cottage cheese, egg, basil, salt and pepper. Mix thoroughly. Spread half on top of noodles.

Make a white sauce by blending flour into melted butter and stirring in the milk gradually. Cook, stirring constantly until thickened. Combine white sauce and wine. Stir in shrimp and crabmeat; spread half over cottage cheese layer.

Repeat layers starting with remaining noodles, then cottage cheese mixture, then seafood mixture.

Sprinkle with Parmesan cheese.

Bake uncovered 350°F (180°C) for 45 minutes. Top with cheese, and bake 2 to 3 minutes until the cheese is melted. Let stand 15 minutes before serving.

Garnish with parsley and shrimp, as desired.

RICHARD ATTENBOROUGH'S "SCAMPI PROVINCALE"

Serves 4

1 pound scampi, in seasoned flour	500 g
2 tablespoons butter to sauté	25 mL
¼ cup button mushrooms, sliced	50 mL
3 tomatoes, skinned, seeds removed	3
3 cups boiled rice	750 mL
Sauce	
2 shallots, finely chopped	2
bouquet garni	
¾ cup white wine	175 mL
2 tablespoons butter	25 mL
1½ teaspoons flour	7 mL
1 clove garlic, crushed	1
1 teaspoon tomato purée	5 mL
1 cup stock	250 mL

Prepare the sauce:

Simmer the shallots with bouquet garni and wine until liquor is reduced by half, then remove bouquet garni and set sauce aside. Melt 1 tablespoon (15 mL) butter, add flour, brown lightly, then add garlic, tomato purée and stock. Simmer for 10 to 15 minutes then pour in reduced wine and cook a further 5 minutes. Draw aside and add small shavings of butter. Keep hot. Roll scampi in seasoned flour and sauté lightly in 1 tablespoon (15 mL) butter for 5 to 6 minutes. Lift into serving dish. Sauté mushrooms in the pan and add to sauce with tomatoes roughly chopped. Reboil for 1 minute, then spoon over scampi. Serve with rice.

SHRIMPS LOUISIANA

Serves 4

1 pound fresh, uncooked shrimp	500 g
1 cup ground pork	250 mL
2 eggs	2
2 cloves garlic	2
2 green onions	2
2 tablespoons corn oil	25 mL
1 tablespoon soya sauce	15 mL
1 tablespoon sherry	15 mL
½ teaspoon salt	2 mL
½ teaspoon sugar	2 mL
1 tablespoon cornstarch	15 mL

Shell and devein shrimps, wash and drain. Beat eggs. Mince garlic and cut green onions into 2 inch (5 cm) pieces. Dissolve cornstarch in 2 tablespoons (25 mL) cold water. Heat oil in skillet over high heat.

Add garlic stirring occasionally. Add pork and cook until it is completely white, about 3 minutes. Add shrimps and stir until they turn pink. Stir in sherry, soya sauce, sugar and salt. Add green onions.

Add ½ cup (125 mL) water, bring to a boil, cover and cook for 3 minutes. Add cornstarch and stir until it thickens. Stir in eggs and serve immediately.

LOBSTER IN PORT

Serves 2 to 4

2-1¼ pound cooked lobsters	2-625 g
5 tablespoons butter	75 mL
¾ cup chopped onion	175 mL
½ cup grated carrot	125 mL
1 teaspoon salt	5 mL
¼ teaspoon white pepper	1 mL
¾ cup port wine	175 mL
2 tablespoons flour	25 mL
¾ cup whipping cream	175 mL

Remove meat from shells. Melt 4 tablespoons (50 mL) butter and sauté onion and carrot for 5 minutes. Add lobster and cook for 3 minutes, turning it frequently. Add salt, pepper and port. Cook over low heat for 15 minutes. Transfer lobster to heated platter and keep warm.

Mix flour and cream until smooth. Add to the sauce with the remaining tablespoon of butter. Stir constantly to the boiling point, but do not boil. Cook over low heat for 5 minutes. Strain over lobster. Serve with rice and asparagus.

EASY SCALLOP CASSEROLE

Serves 4 to 6

1 pound bay scallops, if using larger scallops cut up	500 g
1 cup bread crumbs	250 mL
2 cups cracker crumbs	500 mL
garlic salt and pepper, to taste	
¾ cup melted butter	175 mL
1 cup whipping cream	250 mL

Combine all ingredients, except scallops and cream. Grease a casserole dish. Put a layer of scallops, a layer of dressing, a layer of scallops and a layer of dressing. Top with cream and bake at 350°F (180°C) for 25 minutes. Alternative: you can add a layer of sliced mushrooms on the scallops.

ZUCCHINI AND SHRIMP CASSEROLE

Serves 4

1 pound medium shrimp, cooked or frozen may be used	500 g
4 cups sliced zucchini	1 L
¼ pound fresh mushrooms	125 g
6 or 8 tomatoes, cut in wedges, about 4 cups or 1 L	6 or 8
2 thinly sliced onions	2
1 tablespoon Worcestershire sauce	15 mL
¼ cup white wine	50 mL
¼ cup grated Parmesan cheese	50 mL
salt, pepper, paprika and parsley, to taste	

Arrange zucchini in buttered flat baking dish. Spread cooked shrimp over.

Sauté sliced mushrooms in 2 tablespoons (25 mL) butter and layer on shrimp, then layer the tomatoes and finally the onion.

Mix together the Worcestershire sauce, white wine and salt and pepper. Pour over contents in baking dish.

Sprinkle top with grated Parmesan cheese, dust with paprika.

Bake 375°F (190°C) about 20 minutes. Sprinkle with chopped parsley before serving. Only a salad is needed. Can be made ahead.

ARTICHOKE AND SHRIMP CASSEROLE

Serves 4

1 pound medium shrimp, cooked	500 g
1-10 ounce can artichoke hearts, drained and cut in half	1-284 mL
¼ pound fresh mushrooms, sliced	125 g
4 tablespoons butter	50 mL
1½ cups milk	375 mL
¼ cup dry sherry	50 mL
2 tablespoons flour	25 mL
1 tablespoon Worcestershire sauce	15 mL
salt and pepper, to taste	
¼ cup grated Parmesan cheese	50 mL
paprika, to taste	
¼ cup chopped parsley	50 mL

Arrange artichokes in a buttered flat baking dish, cover with cooked shrimp. Sauté mushrooms in 2 tablespoons (25 mL) of butter, then spread in a layer over shrimp.

In a saucepan, melt remaining butter, stir in flour. Slowly pour in milk and stir carefully until sauce has thickened. Stir in Worcestershire, sherry, and season with salt and pepper. Pour over contents in baking dish. Sprinkle with cheese and dust with paprika.

Bake at 375°F (190°C) for 20 minutes. Sprinkle with chopped parsley before serving.

CRAB TERRAPIN

Serves 2

1 cup crabmeat	250 mL
2 tablespoons butter	25 mL
½ large onion, thinly sliced	½
2 tablespoons sherry	25 mL
⅓ cup whipping cream	75 mL
2 egg yolks, slightly beaten	2
salt, to taste	
dash cayenne pepper	

Sauté onion in butter until golden. Stir in crabmeat and sherry.

Cook for 3 minutes. Stir in cream and egg yolks. Heat gently, season, (do not boil). Serve with rice. A gourmet dish in five minutes!

HAGOOD HARDY'S "SHRIMP RICKERT"

Serves 10

5 pounds of raw shrimp	2.5 Kg
1½ cups of melted butter	375 mL
½ cup of lemon juice	125 mL
¾ cup of chopped chives, or green onion tops	175 mL
¼ teaspoon salt	1 mL
⅛ teaspoon pepper	pinch
½ cup of soft bread crumbs	125 mL
½ cup of sherry	125 mL
¼ cup of slivered almonds	50 mL

Shell and devein the shrimp. Arrange close together in a single layer in a shallow baking dish.

Combine the butter, lemon juice, chives, salt and pepper. Pour over shrimp. Top with bread crumbs and sprinkle with sherry. Bake 20 minutes in the oven at 400°F (200°C). Add the almonds during the last 5 minutes of baking time. Serve with rice, green salad and music!

PILAF OF SCALLOPS

Serves 10 as appetizer or
Serves 6 as entrée

16 medium scallops	16
4 tablespoons olive oil	50 mL
¼ pint dry white wine	125 mL
freshly ground pepper	
1 teaspoon lemon juice	5 mL
1 pound rice, uncooked	500 g
salt, to taste	
½ pound lean bacon	250 g
1 ounce butter (2 tablespoons)	25 mL
2 tablespoons tomato purée	25 mL
chopped parsley	

Wash and clean scallops, remove and set aside reddish coral. Leave small scallops whole. Cut medium scallops in half (making two round slices); large scallops can be cut into three slices. Marinate scallops in olive oil and white wine, generously seasoned with freshly ground pepper and lemon juice.

Cook rice with pinch of salt. It should be dry.

Dice bacon and cook gently in butter. When nearly cooked, add 4 tablespoons (50 mL) of marinade.

Chop corals and add to bacon; cook, turning gently, for additional 3 minutes. Put bacon and coral mixture into saucepan, add rice and tomato purée. Stir well; keep warm.

In second saucepan, poach scallops in remaining marinade. Cook slowly, turning frequently, for a total time of 6 minutes. Pour juice from scallops onto rice mixture and stir over flame, heating fast.

When hot, place rice mixture onto heated serving dish. Arrange scallops on top and sprinkle with parsley. Serve at once.

By adding a clove of garlic to the marinade, the dish becomes in the Provençal style. This is outstanding!

LEE REMICK'S
"SEAFOOD MARINARA"

Serves 4 to 6

2 pounds fresh fish or shellfish (halibut, swordfish, corbina, bass, snapper, or peeled and deveined raw shrimp, lobster or scallops.)	1 Kg
1 medium onion, chopped	1
2 tablespoons olive oil	25 mL
1 tablespoon soft bread crumbs	15 mL
¼ to ½ cup minced parsley	50 to 125 mL
1 small tomato, peeled and chopped	1
2 or 3 garlic cloves, crushed	2 or 3
¾ teaspoon salt	4 mL
½ cup water	125 mL
½ cup dry sherry	125 mL

Sauté the fish or shellfish in olive oil over moderate heat, just until delicately browned. As soon as the fish has started to brown, add onion, garlic, salt and crumbs. Cook about 1 minute. Add chopped tomato and parsley. Lower heat, simmer 3 minutes. Add sherry and water, simmer uncovered 3 minutes longer. They'll rave! Serves 4 to 6 as an entrée, 15 as an hors d'ouevre.

FILLETS OF SOLE WITH SHRIMP

Serves 4

16 ounces frozen sole fillets, thawed	500 g
1 tablespoon lemon juice	15 mL
¼ cup snipped parsley	50 mL
1-3 ounce can whole mushrooms, drained	1-85 mL
1 tablespoon Dijon style mustard	15 mL
1 teaspoon cornstarch	5 mL
1 cup light cream	250 mL
1 cup cooked tiny shrimp	250 mL
2 tablespoons fine dry bread crumbs	25 mL
1 teaspoon butter or margarine, melted	5 mL

Brush each fillet with lemon juice, season with salt and pepper.

Sprinkle one side with parsley. Cut fish in half lengthwise. Roll each up loosely, parsley side in, secure roll with wooden pick. Stand rolls up in 9 × 9 × 2 inch (23 × 23 × 5 cm) baking dish. Cover and bake 425°F (220°C) oven for 10 minutes.

Drain off juices, remove picks. Press a mushroom in each roll. Blend mustard into cornstarch, stir in cream. Cook and stir until bubbly.

Add the shrimp, heat through. Pour the sauce over fish. Mix the remaining ingredients, sprinkle over fish rolls. Bake uncovered 10 to 15 minutes. Serve with asparagus.

CRABMEAT PIES

Makes 6 pies

Pastry for double pie crust	
3-7½ ounce cans crabmeat	3-213 g
3 tablespoons butter	45 mL
2 eggs	2
½ cup whipping cream	125 mL
½ cup milk	125 mL
½ pound Swiss cheese, grated	250 g

Fit pastry into 6 individual pot pie dishes. Melt butter, mix in crabmeat, place in pie shells.

In a blender, mix eggs, whipping cream, milk and Swiss cheese. Pour over crabmeat. Preheat oven to 400°F (200°C); reduce to 375°F (190°C) and bake pies for 25 to 30 minutes.

5

Carroll O'Connor's Shrimp Coconut
Recipe on page 115

JOHNNY MATHIS' "LOBSTER WITH MUSTARD SAUCE"

Serves 2

1 live lobster (2 pounds)	1 Kg
3 tablespoons butter	45 mL
salt and pepper, to taste	

For the Sauce

1½ cups whipping cream	375 mL
3 tablespoons prepared mustard	45 mL
1 tablespoon capers, drained	15 mL
1 tablespoon cornstarch	15 mL

Place lobster into boiling salted water. Cook 5 minutes and drain.

Dot fleshy underside with salt and pepper. Butter a large sheet of foil. Place lobster in centre and wrap completely. Set in dish and bake for 45 minutes.

Prepare sauce: Mix cream with mustard, capers, and cornstarch, salt and pepper. Heat over moderate heat, stir constantly until boiling. Remove from heat. Cut lobster in half and serve with boiled rice. Pour sauce over lobster.

TUNA SOUFFLÉ CHEZ MOI

Serves 4 to 6

1 cup fresh mushrooms thinly sliced	250 mL
2 green onions, finely chopped	2
¼ cup butter	50 mL
fine dry bread crumbs	
1 teaspoon lemon juice	5 mL
1 teaspoon Worcestershire sauce	5 mL
dash of garlic powder	dash
⅓ cup flour	75 mL
¼ teaspoon salt	1 mL
¼ teaspoon dry mustard	1 mL
1¼ cups milk	300 mL
4 egg yolks, well beaten	4
1 cup soft bread cubes	250 mL
1-6½ ounce can flaked tuna	184 g
1 tablespoon chopped parsley	15 mL
4 egg whites	4

Heat oven to 350°F (180°C). Butter a 6 cup (1.5 L) soufflé dish and sprinkle in some bread crumbs, shaking to lightly coat bottom and sides.

Shake out excess.

Melt ¼ cup (50 mL) butter or margarine in a saucepan over medium heat. Add mushrooms and onions and stir 3 minutes. Add next 6 ingredients and stir to blend. Remove from heat and add milk. Stir continuously, returning to heat. Boil gently until very thick and smooth. Gradually stir in some of the hot mixture into egg yolks, then stir this mixture back into the pan. Remove from the heat and add bread cubes, tuna and parsley. Beat egg whites until stiff but not dry. Fold in tuna mixture, and pour into soufflé dish.

Bake until browned on top and set in the middle, about 1 hour.

VICKI LAWRENCE'S "CRAB ALLANDO"

Serves 6

1 pound fettuccine noodles	500 g

Tomato Sauce

1 tablespoon butter	15 mL
2 cups crushed tomatoes	500 mL
2 tablespoons fresh chopped garlic	25 mL
salt and pepper to taste	
1 ounce fresh chopped parsley	50 mL
1 ounce crab meat	30 g
⅛ teaspoon monosodium glutamate	pinch
12 crab legs	12

Sauté crushed tomatoes in a small amount of butter, and add crab meat, then seasonings, and let simmer for approximately 15 to 20 minutes. Set aside.

Fettuccine Sauce

¼ pound butter	125 g
1 egg yolk	1
¼ cup fresh whipping cream	50 mL
½ cup fresh grated Parmesan	125 mL
salt and pepper to taste	

Beat butter until fluffy. Still beating, add the egg yolk and then the cream. Finally beat in the cheese and season with salt and pepper.

To prepare the dish:

Boil 1 pound (500 g) of fettuccine noodles in a large kettle of salted boiling water for 7 to 8 minutes, or until done. Drain thoroughly.

Combine with the fettuccine sauce and cook very briefly, until the sauce becomes very creamy. Add the tomato sauce and toss thoroughly. Serve immediately, using 2 crab legs per person as garnish.

Super company dish. Serve with hot French bread and white wine.

TUNA ST. JACQUES
Serves 6

3 green onions, finely chopped	3
4 tablespoons butter	50 mL
4 ounces mushrooms, chopped	125 g
1-10 ounce can condensed cream of chicken soup	1-284 mL
½ cup dry vermouth	125 mL
white pepper, to taste	
finely chopped parsley	
2-7 ounce cans white tuna, drained and broken into chunks	2-184 g
2 tablespoons Parmesan cheese	25 mL
⅓ cup bread crumbs	75 mL

Sauté onions and mushrooms in 3 tablespoons (40 mL) butter until tender. Remove from heat.

Combine soup and vermouth. Bring to boil. Add half of the sauce to onion and mushroom mixture.

Into 6 buttered sea shells or ramekins add equal portions of sauce, then parsley and tuna chunks. Cover with remaining sauce. Combine cheese and bread crumbs and sprinkle over each serving. Drizzle remaining butter over crumbs. Heat in 450°F (230°C) preheated oven for 10 minutes or until browned. Serve with chilled white wine!

Vegetables

BARBECUED ONIONS

Serves 4

12 small white onions, 1½ inches (4 cm) in diameter, peeled	12
¼ cup ketchup	50 mL
2 tablespoons water	25 mL
1 teaspoon vinegar	5 mL
¼ teaspoon salt	1 mL
pinch of pepper	pinch
1 tablespoon brown sugar	15 mL
4 slices bacon, diced and cooked crisp	4

Parboil onions for 4 to 5 minutes. Drain and put in a buttered, shallow 1½ quart (1.5 L) casserole. Mix ketchup, water, vinegar, salt and pepper and spread over onions. Sprinkle mixture with brown sugar and bacon. Bake at 375°F (190°C) for 30 minutes uncovered or until tender.

Can be refrigerated and baked later. Good with grilled steak.

ALMOND POTATO BALLS

Serves 4

3 medium potatoes, boiled and mashed	3
2 egg yolks	2
¼ cup whipping cream	50 mL
pinch of salt	pinch
pinch of pepper	pinch
pinch of nutmeg	pinch
flour for dredging	
2 eggs, beaten	2
½ cup slivered almonds	125 mL

Mix the first six ingredients together and form the mixture into medium-sized balls. Dip in the flour, then in the beaten egg, and lastly in the almonds. Cook in medium-hot oil in a skillet for about 2 minutes (turning constantly) and then finish up in a 350°F (180°C) oven for 5 minutes.

ROGER MOORE'S
"CREAMED CHEESE POTATOES"

Serves 6

2 pounds potatoes	1 L
1 onion	1
1 ounce flour	50 mL
3 tablespoons chopped parsley	45 mL
¼ pint whipping cream	125 mL
¼ pint hot milk	125 mL
4 ounces grated Cheddar cheese	125 g
salt and pepper to taste	

Peel the potatoes and onion, and dice. Put into a mixing bowl and stir in the flour, parsley, salt and pepper, and half of the cheese. Spread the potato mixture in an ovenproof dish. Put the cream into a bowl and pour on the hot milk. Mix well, and pour over potato mixture. Sprinkle the remaining cheese on top. Bake for 1 hour at 400°F (200°C).

MUSHROOM STUFFED TOMATOES

Serves 6

6 even-sized, firm, ripe tomatoes	6
¾ pound fresh mushrooms	340 g
1 tablespoon lemon juice	15 mL
⅓ cup butter	75 mL
freshly ground pepper, to taste	
1 egg and 1 egg yolk slightly beaten	1 + 1
3 tablespoons tomato paste	45 mL
½ teaspoon dried basil, or thyme	2 mL
grated Parmesan cheese	

Cut a slice from top of each tomato and carefully scoop out centres, leaving shells unbroken. Sprinkle inside with salt and invert to drain.

Wash and chop mushrooms and sprinkle with lemon juice. Sauté in butter until most of liquid has evaporated. Sprinkle with salt and pepper to taste. Combine egg mixture and tomato paste, add basil or thyme and mix with mushrooms. Spoon into tomatoes and sprinkle with Parmesan cheese.

Bake at 350°F (180°C) until thoroughly heated and until cheese has browned slightly (about 15 minutes). The tomatoes should be cooked, but still firm.

GREEN PEPPERS ROMANO

Serves 4 to 6

3 green peppers, cut in half	3
1½ cups zucchini slices	375 mL
1 tablespoon butter	15 mL
1-10 ounce can whole kernel corn, drained	1-284 mL
1 cup chopped tomatoes	250 mL
¼ teaspoon salt	1 mL
⅛ teaspoon oregano leaves, crushed	pinch
Romano cheese	

Remove seeds from peppers; parboil 5 minutes. Drain. Sauté zucchini briefly in butter. Combine zucchini, corn, tomatoes and seasonings. Spoon mixture into peppers.

Place peppers in buttered baking dish; bake at 350°F (180°C) for 30 to 35 minutes. Sprinkle with cheese before serving.

A colourful addition to a meal.

SQUASH WITH BAKED WALNUTS

Serves 8 to 10

2 pounds (approximately) of fresh squash, cooked and mashed fine or 1 package frozen squash, cooked	1 Kg
½ teaspoon salt	2 mL
dash of pepper	
¼ cup whipping cream	50 mL
1 cup walnut halves	250 mL
2 to 3 tablespoons butter	25 to 45 mL
⅛ teaspoon cinnamon	pinch
¼ cup packed brown sugar	50 mL

Lightly butter a 9 × 10 inch (23 × 25 cm) casserole dish.

Spread walnuts on baking sheet and brown lightly in oven. Melt butter in small saucepan. Stir in sugar, cinnamon and nuts. Cook over low heat, stirring constantly.

Spoon squash into baking dish. Sprinkle cinnamon and nut mixture over top.

Bake at 300°F (150°C) for 25 minutes, or until very hot. This freezes well.

GOURMET POTATOES

Serves 6

6 medium potatoes	6
2 cups shredded Cheddar cheese	500 mL
¼ cup butter	50 mL
1½ cups sour cream (at room temperature)	375 mL
⅓ cup green onions, chopped	75 mL
1 teaspoon salt	5 mL
¼ teaspoon pepper	1 mL
2 tablespoons butter	25 mL
milk	

Cook potatoes in skin. Cool. Peel and shred.

In pot over low heat combine and stir in cheese and butter until almost melted. Remove from heat and blend in cream, onions, potatoes and seasonings.

Add enough milk for desired consistency. Turn into casserole. Dot with butter and bake 25 minutes at 325°F (160°C), or until heated through.

Turn on broiler long enough to brown the top.

FESTIVE SCALLOPED POTATOES
Serves 25

30 new potatoes	30
20 onions	20
7 to 8 cups medium white sauce	1.75 to 2 L
1 pound Havarti cheese, grated	500 g
1 pound medium Cheddar cheese, grated	500 g
½ teaspoon cayenne pepper	2 mL
½ cup lemon juice	125 mL
2 tablespoons parsley, chopped	25 mL
½ cup red pepper, chopped	125 mL
salt and pepper, to taste	

Preheat oven to 300°F (150°C). Thoroughly butter very large casserole dish. Peel, and slice, enough new potatoes to almost fill the casserole you wish to use. Fill a roasting pan with cold water, add lemon juice. Add potatoes and let soak 1 to 3 hours. Peel and thinly slice onions; enough to alternately layer with potatoes. Set aside.

In a large saucepan, prepare medium white sauce. Add salt, pepper, and cayenne. When cooked, stir in all the grated Havarti cheese, and ¾ cup (175 mL) of the grated Cheddar. Stir constantly over medium heat until cheese is completely melted.

Drain potatoes. Layer potatoes, onions, and white sauce; repeat layers ending with potatoes and a top layer of sauce. Cover tightly with aluminum foil. Bake for 4 hours (time may have to be adjusted depending on size and depth of casserole dish). Remove foil for last ½ hour, sprinkle with remaining Cheddar cheese, parsley, and red pepper.

TURNIP AND APPLE CASSEROLE
Serves 6

1 turnip peeled and chopped	1
2 apples peeled, cored and chopped	2
¼ cup butter	50 mL
salt and pepper, to taste	

Cook turnip. Add apples near end of cooking time and continue cooking turnip and apples until both are soft. Drain and mash, or put in food processor. Add butter and seasonings. Put in buttered casserole and refrigerate. Bring to room temperature about 30 minutes before baking and reheat uncovered in 325°F (160°C) oven until hot in centre, about 35 minutes.

FRANK SHUSTER'S "RICE CASSEROLE"

Serves 6

1-10 ounce tin water chestnuts, thinly sliced	284 mL
2 cups long grain rice (mix brown with wild rice if desired)	500 mL
2 cups fresh mushrooms, sliced	500 mL
1 cup spanish onion, diced	250 mL
½ pound butter	250 mL
salt and pepper to taste	
pinch oregano (optional)	pinch

Prepare rice as per package instructions. Cook until slighly firm.

Sauté onions in half the butter. When golden, add mushrooms and sauté until slightly cooked.

Add mushrooms and onions to rice. Mix well. Add remaining butter, salt and pepper to taste, (oregano, if desired) and mix.

Add water chestnuts and mix thoroughly.

Place mixture into buttered covered casserole and bake in 400°F (200°C) oven for approximately 1 to 1½ hours, until edges begin to brown. (If too dry, add small amount of water.)

CORN FRITTERS
Serves 6

1-10 ounce can kernel corn, drained	1-284 mL
2 eggs	2
¾ cup flour	175 mL
1 tablespoon baking powder	15 mL
salt and pepper, to taste	
butter	
maple syrup	

Make a batter of corn, eggs, flour, and baking powder; season. Drop batter by the tablespoon onto a medium hot skillet, greased with butter. Pat down, brown slowly (like pancakes). When brown on one side, flip; brown the other side. Serve hot with maple syrup. Marvelous with ham or chicken!

MIXED VEGETABLE CASSEROLE
Serves 6

1-10 ounce can condensed cream of chicken soup	1-284 mL
¼ cup milk	50 mL
½ pound package Velveeta cheese, crumbled	250 g
3 tablespoons chopped onion	45 mL
1½ teaspoons oregano	7 mL
1-10 ounce package frozen cauliflower	283 g
1-10½ ounce package frozen broccoli	300 g
1-14 ounce can baby carrots, drained	1-384 mL
1-10 ounce can button mushrooms, drained	1-284 mL
½ cup bread crumbs	125 mL

Sauce

Combine first five ingredients in a saucepan, using only 1 cup (250 mL) of cheese. Stir over low heat until smooth.

Cook cauliflower and broccoli until crisp. Place vegetables in a buttered casserole and cover with sauce.

Sprinkle casserole with ½ cup (125 mL) bread crumbs, dot with butter and sprinkle with remaining cheese. Bake at 350°F (180°C) for 30 to 40 minutes.

DEVILLED GREEN BEANS

Serves 4

1 medium sized onion, chopped	1
1 clove garlic, minced	1
½ green pepper, chopped	½
2 canned pimentos, sliced or chopped	2
3 tablespoons butter	45 mL
2 tablespoons prepared mustard	10 mL
1-7½ ounce can tomato sauce	213 g
1 cup (¼ pound) Cheddar cheese, shredded	250 mL
1-10 ounce package frozen cut green beans, cooked and drained	1-284 g

Sauté onion, garlic, green pepper, and pimentos in butter until onions are limp. Stir in mustard, tomato sauce and beans. Turn into a greased 1 quart (1 L) casserole. Bake, uncovered in a moderate oven, 350°F (180°C) for 25 minutes, or until cheese is melted.

This recipe can be doubled as many times as desired or frozen for a large party. (Thaw and then cook.) Good with roasted or barbecued meat. This dish looks as good as it tastes.

BROCCOLI CASSEROLE

Serves 8

2 packages frozen broccoli, cooked, or equivalent fresh	2-300 g
12 to 18 sliced onions, cooked briefly	12 to 18
White sauce	
¼ cup butter	50 mL
⅓ cup flour	75 mL
1 cup milk	250 mL
Add	
⅔ cup consommé	150 mL
½ cup white wine	125 mL
salt and pepper, to taste	
⅓ cup sliced, blanched almonds	75 mL
½ cup Cheddar cheese, grated	125 mL

Cook broccoli and place in casserole, cover with onions and sauce. Sprinkle with cheese. Bake at 350°F (180°C) for 25 to 30 minutes.

ORANGE CARROTS

Serves 4 to 6

2 pounds baby carrots	1 Kg
¼ cup butter, melted	50 mL
¼ cup brown sugar	50 mL
¼ cup orange juice concentrate, thawed	50 mL
½ cup Mandarin orange pieces	125 mL
½ teaspoon salt	2 mL

Boil whole carrots until tender; drain. Combine remaining ingredients until well-blended. Place carrots in buttered baking dish and cover with sauce.

Refrigerate overnight.

Turn carrots to coat with sauce. Bake at 350°F (180°C) for 20 to 25 minutes.

GREEN BEANS AU GRATIN

Serves 10

2-10 ounce packages frozen French-style green beans	2
½ pound mushrooms, sliced	250 g
¼ cup butter	50 mL
1 onion, chopped	1
¼ cup flour	50 mL
1 cup milk, warmed	250 mL
½ cup light cream	125 mL
½ pound medium Cheddar cheese	250 g
1 teaspoon soya sauce	5 mL
½ teaspoon salt	2 mL
¼ teaspoon pepper	1 mL
½ teaspoon monosodium glutamate	2 mL
few drops of Tobasco sauce	
1-10 ounce can water chestnuts, sliced	1-284 mL

Sauté mushrooms in butter, add onion and sauté until clear. Add flour and cook until smooth. Add milk and cream, stirring constantly until thick. Add cheese, soya sauce, salt, pepper, monosodium glutamate and Tobasco. Cook beans. Drain and add water chestnuts. Put all ingredients in casserole dish. Cook until bubbly, about 20 minutes, at 325°F (160°C).

CANDIED SWEET POTATOES

Serves 10

3½ cups mashed sweet potatoes	875 mL
½ cup sugar	125 mL
2 eggs	2
1 teaspoon vanilla	5 mL
½ cup milk	125 mL
¼ cup softened butter	50 mL
Topping	
½ cup brown sugar	125 mL
⅓ cup flour	75 mL
¼ cup melted butter	50 mL
1 cup pecans, chopped	250 mL

Bake sweet potatoes at 450°F (230°C) for 1 hour. Scoop potato from shells. Combine potatoes, sugar, eggs, vanilla, milk and butter. Place in a large buttered casserole.

Topping
Combine brown sugar, flour, butter and pecans. Place on top of potatoes in casserole. Cover casserole. (This can be made a day ahead up to this point.)

Bake in 275°F (140°C) oven for 50 minutes. Uncover for last 10 minutes of baking.

STIR-FRY GREEN BEANS

Serves 6 to 8

2 pounds beans, cut diagonally into 1 to 1½ inches (2.5 to 4 cm) long	1 Kg
3 tablespoons peanut oil	45 mL
½ cup chicken broth	125 mL
1 teaspoon cornstarch	5 mL
2 tablespoons soya sauce	25 mL
1 teaspoon sugar	5 mL
⅛ teaspoon monosodium glutamate	pinch
7 scallions, sliced	7

Blanche beans, 2 to 4 minutes. Heat heavy skillet on top of stove to 350°F (180°C). Add oil and sauté scallions until golden. Add beans and stir-fry 2 minutes. Mix soya sauce, sugar, broth, monosodium glutamate. Add cornstarch and let the sauce thicken. Add to beans and stir-fry for additional 2 minutes.

ORANGE-GLAZED BEETS

Serves 6

24 to 30 small beets or canned beets, drained	24 to 30
¼ cup butter	50 mL
2 teaspoons sugar	10 mL
1½ to 2 teaspoons orange juice	7 to 10 mL
1 tablespoon grated orange rind	15 mL

Trim all but 1 inch (2.5 cm) of the stems from 24 to 30 small beets and place in a large saucepan. Add water to cover, bring to a boil and simmer the beets for 15 to 20 minutes, or until tender. Plunge into cold water and trim off the roots and stems. Peel the beets and cut into thin slices.

In a large skillet melt butter over moderately high heat; add the beets, tossing to coat. Sprinkle beets with the sugar and cook for 2 to 3 minutes, or until glazed.

Transfer beets to a serving dish and toss gently with the orange juice and rind.

CRUNCHY CELERY CASSEROLE

Serves 8 to 12

8 cups celery, sliced on diagonal	2 L
2-10 ounce cans condensed cream of chicken soup	2-284 mL
½ cup pimento	125 mL
1 cup water chestnuts, drained and sliced	250 mL
⅓ cups slivered almonds	75 mL
1 cup buttered bread crumbs	250 mL

Parboil celery. Drain. Reserve almonds and bread crumbs. Combine celery with remaining ingredients. Place in casserole. Top with almonds and crumbs. Bake at 350°F (180°C) for 30 minutes.

GRATED ZUCCHINI

Serves 4 to 6

2 zucchinis	2
salt, to taste	
3 tablespoons butter	45 mL
black pepper, to taste	

Grate zucchinis. Salt and leave 15 minutes. Squeeze dry. Heat butter until sizzling. Toss in zucchinis and stir-fry about 1 minute. Serve with black pepper. Simple and quick!

TED KNIGHT'S
"CABBAGE AND MUSHROOMS"

Serves 4

1 small head cabbage	1
1 finely chopped small onion	1
2 cups fresh mushrooms	500 mL
2 tablespoons sour cream	25 mL
butter	
salt and pepper	

Quarter cabbage and steam over water for 5 minutes. Cool and chop fine. Sauté onion in butter, add chopped mushrooms and sauté 5 minutes. Add chopped cabbage and continue to sauté a few minutes until the flavours blend. Add sour cream and serve. Can also be served cool.

STUFFED MUSHROOMS PARMEGIANA

Serves 6 to 8

16 large mushrooms	16
2 tablespoons butter or margarine	25 mL
1 medium onion, chopped	1
½ cup diced pepperoni	125 mL
¼ cup chopped green pepper	50 mL
1 garlic clove, minced	1
12 Ritz crackers, crushed	12
1 tablespoon Parmesan cheese	45 mL
1 tablespoon parsley	15 mL
½ teaspoon seasoned salt	2 mL
¼ teaspoon oregano	1 mL
pepper to taste	
⅓ cup chicken broth	75 mL

Chop mushroom stems and save mushroom caps. Melt butter, add onion, pepperoni, green pepper, garlic and stems, cook until tender. Add remaining ingredients. Stuff mushroom caps. Place in pan with ¼ inch (.5 cm) water. Can be used as a vegetable as well. Bake at 325°F (160°C) for 25 minutes.

CURRIED CAULIFLOWER

Serves 8 to 10

2 cauliflowers	2
1-10 ounce can condensed cream of chicken soup	1-284
1 cup Cheddar cheese, shredded	250 mL
½ cup mayonnaise	125 mL
1 teaspoon curry powder	5 mL
¼ cup dry bread crumbs	50 mL
2 tablespoons melted butter	25 mL

Break cauliflower into florets and boil for 10 minutes. Drain. In a 2 quart (2 L) casserole, mix soup, cheese, mayonnaise, and curry. Stir in cauliflower. Sprinkle bread crumbs on top and drizzle with melted butter. Bake at 350°F (180°C) until hot and bubbly for 20 to 30 minutes.

May be frozen without bread crumbs.

RED CABBAGE
Serves 6

1 red cabbage	1
1 onion	1
3 to 4 tablespoons lard	45 to 50 mL
3 to 4 sour apples	3 to 4
½ cup water	125 mL
2 tablespoons vinegar	25 mL
1 bay leaf	1
several cloves	
sugar, to taste	
salt, to taste	

Remove outside leaves from cabbage, quarter and remove stem. Slice in very fine pieces. Slice onion finely. Place lard in a pot and brown onion. Add cabbage and heat for a few minutes. Dice apples.

Add apples, water, vinegar, bay leaf, cloves, salt and sugar to cabbage. Cook slowly for 1 to 1½ hours.

SAUCY SWEET POTATOES
Serves 6 to 8

4 medium sweet potatoes	4
½ cup brown sugar	125 mL
1 tablespoon corn starch	15 mL
¼ teaspoon salt	1 mL
1 cup orange juice	250 mL
¼ cup seedless raisins	50 mL
¼ cup butter	50 mL
3 tablespoons sherry	45 mL
2 tablespoons pecans	25 mL

Boil, peel, and split sweet potatoes. Place in a flat casserole dish.

In a saucepan mix sugar, cornstarch, and salt. Blend in orange juice, add raisins. Over medium heat bring to a boil. Stir in remaining ingredients. Pour over potatoes. Bake at 350°F (180°C) for 20 minutes.

Sweet success!

CAULIFLOWER CASSEROLE
Serves 6

1 medium-sized cauliflower	1
1½ cups cheese sauce (see below)	375 mL
1 can french fried onion rings	1
¼ cup slivered almonds, toasted	50 mL
½ teaspoon paprika	2 mL
2 tablespoons fresh parsley, finely chopped (optional)	25 mL

Trim cauliflower and separate into florets. Boil or steam until crisp and tender. Drain. Arrange cauliflower in buttered casserole.

Cheese sauce

2 tablespoons butter	25 mL
2 tablespoons flour	25 mL
½ teaspoon salt	2 mL
pinch of black pepper	pinch
¼ teaspoon dry mustard	1 mL
⅛ teaspoon garlic salt	pinch
1 cup milk	250 mL
½ to ¾ cup diced sharp Cheddar cheese	125 to 175 mL

In a saucepan, melt butter and blend in flour combined with seasonings. Stir in milk and cook, stirring, until mixture thickens and almost reaches boiling point. Add cheese and heat, stirring, until cheese melts and mixture is smooth.

To hot cheese sauce add almonds and half of the onion rings. Pour over cauliflower and sprinkle with paprika. Cover and bake at 400°F (200°C) for 15 minutes.

Sprinkle with parsley; add remaining onions and bake uncovered for 5 minutes.

EXOTIC IDAHOS

1 baking Idaho potato per person	

For each potato:

1 teaspoon unsalted butter	5 mL
2 teaspoons caviar	10 mL
1 teaspoon chopped green onion	5 mL
½ teaspoon chopped cooked egg white	2 mL
½ teaspoon chopped cooked egg yolk	2 mL
1 teaspoon sour cream	5 mL

Bake potatoes. Just before serving, cut lengthwise and pinch open. Layer above ingredients in centre. A very elegant vegetable!

LEO BUSCAGLIA'S "BARLEY CASSEROLE"

Serves 4

½ cup butter or margarine	125 mL
1 onion, chopped	1
1 cup chopped mushrooms	250 mL
1 cup barley	250 mL
4 cups bouillon (chicken or beef)	1 L
seasoning, to taste	

Sauté onion and mushrooms in melted butter until tender. Do not overcook.

Place barley in large casserole, add the above cooked ingredients and sauté about 2 minutes. Pour in bouillon and stir. Cover casserole and place in 350°F (180°C) oven for 1 hour and 15 minutes, or until liquid is absorbed and barley is al dente.

Then, prepare for exclamations of approval when served!

SQUASH PUDDING

Serves 6 to 8

2 cups squash, cooked, drained and mashed	500 mL
¾ cup sugar	175 mL
2 tablespoons cornstarch	25 mL
3 eggs, beaten	3
½ teaspoon nutmeg	2 mL
½ teaspoon salt	2 mL
3 cups light cream (half and half)	750 mL

Mix together, sugar and cornstarch. Add to squash and mix well. Stir in eggs, nutmeg and salt. Mix in cream. Pour into greased 1 quart (1 L) casserole.

Bake uncovered at 325°F (160°C) approximately 1 hour or until knife inserted in centre comes out clean.

Serve with ham or "barbecued" chicken. May be prepared in a food processor.

SQUASH APPLE BAKE

Serves 6

3 pepper squash, halved and seeded	3
2 tablespoons butter	25 mL
2 tablespoons brown sugar	25 mL
1 can apple pie filling	1-540 mL
¼ cup walnuts or pecans, chopped	50 mL
¼ cup raisins	50 mL
1 tablespoon brandy	15 mL
⅛ teaspoon cinnamon	pinch
⅛ teaspoon nutmeg	pinch

Plump raisins in brandy and set aside. Put 1 teaspoon (5 mL) of brown sugar and 1 teaspoon (5 mL) of butter in each half of squash. Mix apple pie mixture with raisins and nuts and fill each squash cavity. Sprinkle with spices and bake at 350°F (180°C) for 1¼ hours.

POTATO PANCAKES
Makes 24

1 large onion, peeled and finely grated	1
6 large potatoes, washed, peeled and finely grated	6
3 eggs, slightly beaten	3
¼ cup flour	50 mL
1 teaspoon salt	5 mL
1 teaspoon baking powder	5 mL
melted butter or oil for cooking	

Combine above ingredients, except butter. Ladle the batter (about ¼ cup (50 mL)) onto hot greased skillet. When the pancakes are nicely browned on one side, flip them over and brown the other side. Serve with sour cream or applesauce.

SPINACH TOMATO SOUFFLÉ
Serves 4

4 medium tomatoes	4
1 package spinach soufflé, thawed	1
4 teaspoons Dijon mustard	20 mL
4 slices bacon, crisply cooked and crumbled	4
grated Parmesan cheese	
paprika	

Hollow and drain tomatoes. Place teaspoon (5 mL) of mustard in bottom of each tomato. Place 1 strip of bacon in each tomato. Fill with spinach. Sprinkle with cheese and paprika. Bake at 350°F (180°C) for 25 to 30 minutes.

LAZY LIMAS
Serves 4 to 6

1-14 ounce package frozen lima beans, thawed	350 g
2-6 ounces package frozen onion rings	2-170 g
1-10 ounce can condensed cream of mushroom soup	1-284 mL
½ cup milk	125 mL
pinch of marjoram	pinch
½ cup Cheddar cheese, grated	125 mL

In a casserole, layer beans and onion rings. Mix milk, mushroom soup, and marjoram. Pour over vegetables. Top with grated cheese. Bake at 350°F (180°C) for 1 hour.

GERMAN SPINACH
Serves 4 to 6

1 pound fresh spinach	500 g
1 teaspoon salt	5 mL
2 medium onions, chopped	2
2 tablespoons butter	25 mL
1 tablespoon flour	15 mL
1 dash nutmeg	dash

Wash spinach thoroughly. Cook in small amount of water with salt. Drain, chop and set aside. Reserve liquid.

Chop 2 medium onions. Sauté in butter until soft but not brown. Add flour and mix well. Moisten with spinach water to make sauce consistency of a cream sauce. Cook 5 minutes, stirring constantly.

Pour sauce over spinach in top of double boiler. Mix well and add dash of nutmeg.

BROCCOLI SOUFFLÉ
Serves 6 generously

2-10 ounce packages, chopped frozen broccoli	2-284 g
1-10 ounce can condensed cream of mushroom soup	1-284 mL
1 cup mayonnaise	250 mL
2 eggs, beaten	2
1 cup grated, or shredded, sharp Cheddar cheese	250 mL
2 tablespoons onion, grated	25 mL

Cook broccoli and drain well. Mix everything together and put into a greased casserole dish 2½ to 3 quart (2.5 to 3 L) size. Cook in a 400°F (200°C) oven until the casserole sets as a custard mould, approximately 15 to 20 minutes.

Test with a knife, the knife should cut into soufflé and come out clean much like a custard.

Suppers and Luncheons

FETTUCCINE PRIMAVERA

Serves 4

1-16 ounce package fettuccine or egg noodles	500 g
1 cup freshly grated Parmesan cheese or ½ cup (125 mL) Parmesan and ½ cup (125 mL) Romano cheeses	250 mL
½ cup whipping cream	125 mL
2 egg yolks	2
2 tablespoons butter, softened	30 mL
½ cup snow peas	125 mL
½ cup broccoli florets	125 mL
½ cup sliced mushrooms	125 mL
1 large tomato, sliced into 8 wedges	1
1 teaspoon basil	5 mL
salt and pepper to taste	
Parmesan cheese for garnish	

Cream butter until it is light and fluffy. Beat in the cream a little at a time. Add the cheese and egg yolks, beating the mixture until all the liquid has been absorbed. Cover the bowl and set aside.

Set a large serving bowl in a warm oven to heat while you cook the fettuccine. Boil the pasta approximately 5 to 8 minutes or until tender. Immediately drain the fettuccine into a colander. Transfer it at once to the hot serving bowl.

In a covered skillet, sauté the vegetables in butter and 2 tablespoons (30 mL) water until barely tender, or if you prefer the vegetables may be steamed. Starting with the broccoli, then snow peas, mushrooms and finally the tomatoes.

Add the butter and cheese mixture to the pasta, then add the spices, tossing it with a fork to ensure every strand is well coated.

Arrange the vegetables on top of the fettuccine and serve. Serve the extra grated cheese in a separate bowl.

When in season, you can substitute vegetables with fresh zucchini, asparagus, or cauliflower.

JOHNNY WAYNE'S "PESTO PRESTO"

(The Famous Sauce From Genoa)
Serves 6

2 cups fresh basil leaves	500 mL
½ cup olive oil	125 mL
2 tablespoons pine nuts	25 mL
1 clove garlic crushed	1
1 teaspoon salt	5 mL
½ cup grated Parmesan cheese	125 mL
2 tablespoons grated Romano cheese	25 mL
3 tablespoons softened butter	45 mL

Blend basil leaves, pine nuts, olive oil and salt at high speed. Stop from time to time to push mixture down with rubber spatula.

Add cheese and blend. Add butter and blend.

Then take the delightful green mixture and spoon it over pasta.

EGGPLANT PIE

Serves 6 to 8

A crustless quiche, a delicious flavour — a cross between eggplant Parmesan and pizza — which can be frozen, baked or unbaked. You can substitute zucchini or even potatoes for eggplant.

1 medium to large eggplant, sliced crosswise in ½ inch (1 cm) slices	1
¼ cup oil, or as needed	50 mL
salt and pepper, to taste	
2 teaspoons dried thyme	10 mL
finely chopped parsley, to taste	
3 tomatoes, peeled, seeded, thinly sliced and drained on paper towels	3
½ medium onion, finely chopped	½
1 green pepper, finely chopped	1
¼ pound Mozzarella cheese, thinly sliced	125 g
3 eggs, lightly beaten	3
1½ cups light cream	375 mL

In a large skillet, sauté the eggplant slices in hot oil until soft and lightly browned. Place slices in a 9 × 12 inch (23 × 30 cm) ovenproof dish, overlapping them to make them fit. Season with salt and pepper and half of the thyme and parsley. Cover with a layer of sliced tomatoes. Sprinkle with salt, pepper, remaining thyme and parsley, the onion and green pepper. Cover with cheese slices. The pie can be frozen at this point.

When ready to bake, mix the eggs with the cream and pour over. Bake at 325°F (160°C) for 45 minutes or until firm in the centre, puffy and golden brown. Let stand a few minutes before cutting into squares.

ARTICHOKE FETTUCCINE

Serves 6

½ cup unsalted butter, softened	125 mL
1 cup whipping cream	250 mL
1 cup (4 ounces) freshly grated Parmesan cheese	250 mL
⅓ cup pimentos, chopped	75 mL
1-9 ounce package frozen artichoke hearts, thawed and halved	1
or	
1-14 ounce can artichoke hearts, water packed	398 mL
1¼ pounds fettuccine	625 g
salt and pepper to taste	

Combine butter, cream, cheese, pimentos and artichokes in a skillet. Heat thoroughly. Cook the fettuccine according to package directions. Drain. Pour sauce over hot pasta. Toss lightly until noodles are coated. Add salt and pepper to taste. Serve immediately.

CLAM SAUCE FOR SPAGHETTI

Serves 2

¼ cup olive oil	50 mL
1 clove minced garlic	1
¼ cup water	50 mL
½ teaspoon salt	2 mL
½ teaspoon oregano	2 mL
¼ cup chopped parsley	50 mL
¼ teaspoon ground pepper	1 mL
1-6½ ounce can minced clams with juice	177 g
Parmesan cheese, grated	
crushed red pepper	

Heat oil in a saucepan. Sauté garlic in oil until lightly browned. Remove from heat and cool slightly. Add water slowly, stirring. Add remaining ingredients; heat through.

Can be refrigerated and reheated slowly at serving time.

Serve over al dente (firmly cooked) spaghetti. Add grated Parmesan cheese and red pepper. If recipe is doubled, do not add juice from second can of clams.

EVERYONE'S FAVOURITE RICE CASSEROLE

Serves 8

¼ cup butter	50 mL
1 cup chopped onion	250 mL
4 cups rice, cooked and kept warm	1 L
2 cups sour cream	500 mL
1 cup cream style cottage cheese	250 mL
½ teaspoon salt	2 mL
⅛ teaspoon pepper	pinch
1 large bay leaf crumbled	1
1 medium green pepper, chopped	1
2 cups Cheddar cheese, grated	500 mL
parsley, for garnish	

In a large skillet melt butter. Sauté onion and green pepper for 5 minutes, until golden. Remove from stove. Stir in warm rice, sour cream, cottage cheese, seasonings and mix well. Layer half of mixture in a 12 × 8 inch (30 × 20 cm) baking dish. Sprinkle with half the cheese and repeat the previous layer. Bake at 375°F (190°C) for 25 minutes and garnish with parsley.

MUSHROOM CRUST QUICHE

Serves 6

5 tablespoons butter	75 mL
½ pound mushrooms, finely chopped	250 g
½ cup crushed soda crackers	125 mL
¼ cup green onions, finely chopped	50 mL
2 cups Swiss cheese, shredded	500 mL
1 cup creamed cottage cheese	250 mL
3 eggs	3
¼ teaspoon cayenne	1 mL
¼ teaspoon paprika	1 mL

Melt 3 tablespoons (50 mL) of butter in a frying pan, add mushrooms and sauté. Stir in crushed crackers. Mix well and press into a pie plate. Melt remaining butter and add onion; sauté. Spread onions over mushrooms. Sprinkle shredded cheese evenly over onions. In a blender whirl cottage cheese, eggs and seasonings. Pour into pie dish.

Bake at 350°F (180°C) for 20 minutes.

PRESIDENT REAGAN'S FAVORITE "MACARONI AND CHEESE"

½ pound macaroni	250 g
1 teaspoon butter	5 mL
1 egg, beaten	1
1 teaspoon salt	5 mL
1 teaspoon dry mustard	5 mL
3 cups grated cheese, sharp	750 mL
1 cup milk	250 mL

Boil macaroni in water until tender and drain thoroughly. Stir in butter and egg. Mix mustard and salt with 1 tablespoon hot water and add to milk. Add cheese leaving enough to sprinkle on top. Pour into buttered casserole, add milk, sprinkle with cheese. Bake at 350°F (180°C) for about 45 minutes or until custard is set and top is crusty.

STUFFED EGG CASSEROLE
Serves 18 to 20

24 eggs, hard boiled, shell and cut lengthwise	24
2¼ cups minced ham	550 mL
¾ cup sour cream	175 mL
1¼ teaspoons dry mustard	6 mL

Sauce

⅔ cup grated onion	150 mL
¾ cup butter	175 mL
¾ cup flour	175 mL
¾ cup vermouth	175 mL
4½ cups half and half cream	1.1 L
½ teaspoon salt	2 mL
¼ teaspoon pepper	1 mL
½ teaspoon seasoning salt	2 mL
1 teaspoon dry mustard	5 mL
2 teaspoons Worcestershire sauce	10 mL
2½ cups grated Gruyère cheese	625 mL
24 mushrooms, quartered, and sautéed in butter	24
¾ cup Parmesan cheese	175 mL
⅓ cup butter, melted	75 mL
paprika	

Mash egg yolks, combine with minced ham, sour cream and mustard. Stuff and reassemble eggs. Sauté onions in a large pot. Stir in the flour and gradually add vermouth and cream, stirring constantly. Add remaining ingredients, except the Parmesan cheese, butter and paprika. Cook until thickened. Cover eggs in a large casserole with the sauce and sprinkle with the remaining ingredients. Chill until ready to serve.

Heat at 350°F (180°C) until the centre is bubbly, about ½ hour.

6

Brunch Pie
Recipe on page 169

TOPLESS — BOTTOMLESS QUICHE
Serves 8

6 eggs, beaten	6
2 cups sour cream	500 mL
1 teaspoon Worcestershire sauce	5 mL
½ pound fresh mushrooms, sliced	250 g
½ pound bacon, cooked and crumbled	250 g
2 cups Swiss cheese, grated	500 mL
2 cans French fried onion rings	2
dash of Tobasco	dash

Mix all ingredients together. Pour into a buttered medium-sized casserole. Bake at 350°F (180°C) for 30 minutes.

May be prepared the day before.

DILLED RICOTTA TORTE
Serves 8 to 12

1½ cups stale whole wheat bread crumbs	375 mL
1 cup ground almonds	250 mL
½ cup unsalted butter, softened	125 mL
12 ounces cream cheese, softened	340 g
1 cup Ricotta cheese	250 mL
2 eggs	2
⅓ cup snipped fresh dill	75 mL
2 tablespoons half and half cream	25 mL
1 teaspoon salt	5 mL
1 teaspoon lemon rind	5 mL
½ teaspoon nutmeg	2 mL

In bowl combine the bread crumbs, almonds and butter. Press mixture into bottom and 1 inch (2 cm) up sides of a well-buttered 9 inch (23 cm) spring-form pan.

In food processor, with steel blade, blend butter, cream cheese, Ricotta cheese, eggs, dill, cream, salt, lemon rind and nutmeg, until mixture is smooth. Pour into shell, bake at 350°F (180°C) for 45 minutes or until knife inserted in centre comes out clean. Cool in pan on rack, remove sides of pan, transfer to board or tray and garnish with dill. Leave at room temperature or chilled.

AUTUMN PASTA

Serves 6

1 medium eggplant	1
1 medium carrot	1
1 large zucchini	1
1 large onion	1
1 medium green pepper	1
1 large clove garlic, finely chopped	1
3 tablespoons oil	45 mL
¼ cup fresh basil, chopped	50 mL
1 dried red pepper, crumbled	1
salt to taste	
1-14 ounce can tomato sauce	398 mL
1-14 ounce can stewed tomatoes	398 mL
1-16 ounce package of cut, tube-shaped pasta such as penne, ziti or mostaccioli	500 g
1 cup Parmesan cheese, freshly grated	250 mL

Cut eggplant into quarters and slice in processor or by hand. Repeat with carrot, zucchini, onion, green pepper. Chop garlic finely and sauté for 5 minutes with the cut vegetables in hot oil in a large skillet. Stir frequently. Add fresh basil, dried pepper, salt, tomatoes and tomato sauce and cook over high heat for 10 more minutes while cooking pasta.

Cook pasta "al dente", according to package directions. Drain well and serve with hot sauce. Sprinkle with grated cheese and pass around some additional grated cheese when serving.

CHICKEN SALAD PIE

Serves 6

1½ cups cooked chicken	375 mL
1-9 ounce can pineapple tidbits, drained	1-284 mL
1 cup walnuts	250 mL
½ cup sliced celery	125 mL
1 cup sour cream	250 mL
⅔ cup mayonnaise	150 mL
3 tablespoons sharp Cheddar cheese, grated	45 mL
1 cheese pastry pie shell, baked	1
black olives, pitted and sliced for garnish	

Combine chicken, pineapple, nuts and celery. In another bowl, combine sour cream and mayonnaise. Add mayonnaise to the chicken mixture. Combine. Fill pastry shell. Top with remaining cream mixture. Sprinkle with cheese. Garnish with sliced olives.

JOAN RIVERS' "TOAST"

Serves 2

This recipe has been in my family for generations.

Ingredients
Two slices white bread*

Butter or margarine

Take two slices of white bread. Place them in a toaster. Press down the handle. Wait two minutes or until toast pops up.

Spread butter over slices *after* removing them from the toaster.

* For holidays and special occasions raisin bread may be substituted but follow the same procedure as above. For these special occasions we call it "Joan Rivers Holiday Toast".

CHICKEN SALAD, WITH A DIFFERENCE!

Serves 4 to 6

1-3½ pound chicken; cut into serving pieces	1.5 Kg
1 cantaloupe	1
2 tomatoes, peeled, seeded, and chopped	2
3 tablespoons olive oil	45 mL
3 tablespoons vegetable oil	45 mL
3 tablespoons lemon juice	45 mL
¾ teaspoon tarragon	4 mL
½ teaspoon salt	2 mL
¼ teaspoon pepper	1 mL

Poach 3½ pounds (1.5 Kg) chicken 50 minutes. Remove large pieces of meat and set aside. Cook down the carcass and remaining broth until 1½ cups (375 mL) remains. Cool the chicken in the broth until ready to use. Mix oils, lemon, tarragon, salt and pepper. Chop up chicken and pour the dressing over the chicken. Cut up cantaloupe and tomatoes in cubes and add to the salad. Cover and refrigerate for 2 hours or overnight.

Dressing

1 large egg	1
1 tablespoon lemon juice	15 mL
1 teaspoon salt	5 mL
pinch pepper	pinch
1½ cups vegetable oil	375 mL
1½ teaspoons fresh ginger root, grated	7 mL
½ cup cream, stiffly whipped	125 mL

In a blender, slowly add oil to the egg and lemon juice mixture until you have the consistency of mayonnaise. Fold in whipped cream, seasoning and ginger. Serve with chicken salad. Fabulous.

CRAB SOUFFLÉ
Serves 12

Make the day before serving and enjoy the luncheon.

12 slices white bread, buttered and crusts removed	12
2-7½ ounce cans crabmeat, drained	213 g
½ cup mayonnaise	125 mL
1 small green pepper, chopped	1
1 large onion, chopped	1
1 cup celery, chopped	250 mL
4 eggs, beaten	4
3 cups milk	750 mL
1-10 ounce can mushroom soup, undiluted	284 mL
1-10 ounce can celery soup, undiluted	284 mL
¾ cup mild Cheddar cheese, grated	175 mL
paprika	

Dice 6 slices of prepared bread and place in 9 × 13 inch (23 × 33 cm) buttered baking dish. Mix crabmeat, mayonnaise, onion, green pepper and celery. Spread over bread. Dice remaining bread and put on top of crab mixture. Beat eggs and milk together and pour over entire mixture. Cover and refrigerate overnight.

Set dish in a pan of hot water and bake in 325°F (160°C) oven for 15 minutes. Remove from oven. Mix soups together and pour over entire dish. Top with grated cheese and paprika. Put back in oven for 1 hour to finish cooking.

SALMON MOULD
Serves 4 to 6

2-7 ounce cans salmon	2-270 g
2 cups white bread crumbs, moistened in milk	500 mL
½ cup milk	125 mL
2 tablespoons butter	25 mL
1 medium onion, chopped	1
3 eggs, separated	3
5 tomatoes, skinned, seeded and chopped	5

Shred, clean and bone salmon. Sauté onion in skillet, add tomato and salmon. Add moistened bread crumbs. Beat 3 egg whites until stiff, blend in egg yolks. Combine eggs and salmon. Pour into a greased ring mould. Cook in 2 inch pan of water at 350°F (180°C) for 1 hour. Cool and refrigerate. Unmould and serve with mayonnaise.

SHERRIED EGGS

Serves 12

4-10 ounce packages frozen, or 6 bags fresh, spinach	4-284 g
3 tablespoons melted butter	45 mL
15 hard boiled eggs	15
1-10 ounce can condensed cream of chicken soup	1-284 mL
mayonnaise	
salt and pepper, to taste	
dry mustard or curry powder, to taste	
¾ pound fresh or canned mushrooms, sliced	340 g
¼ cup chopped onion	50 mL
⅓ cup butter	75 mL
⅓ cup flour	75 mL
3 cups hot milk	750 mL
¼ cup medium sherry	50 mL
¼ cup buttered bread crumbs	50 mL

Cook and thoroughly drain spinach. Chop and toss with melted butter.

Sprinkle over two, 9 inch (23 cm) square, buttered oven dishes.

Shell eggs and cut in half. Remove yolks and mash. Add half the can of soup and enough mayonnaise so that yolk mixture sticks. Season to taste with salt, pepper and dry mustard.

Fill egg whites and place evenly on spinach.

Sauté mushrooms and onions in butter. Remove from heat and stir in flour. Gradually add hot milk and cook until thickened. Add sherry and remaining soup. Cool, pour over eggs. Sprinkle with bread crumbs.

Cover and refrigerate.

Bake, covered, 375°F (190°C) for 20 minutes, uncover and bake 15 minutes or until bubbly.

This can be made the day before. Serve with ham, crabapple jelly and muffins — marvellous. For a change, substitute cooked, chopped broccoli, or stuff egg yolks with pâté, smoked salmon or shrimp.

BEVERLY SILLS' "DUTCH BABIES" MIDNIGHT SNACK OR SUNDAY BRUNCH

Serves 2 to 4

Put an 8 inch (20 cm) iron skillet in freezer.

Pre-heat oven to 450°F (230°C).

Blend at low speed in blender:

3 eggs	3
½ cup flour	125 mL
½ cup milk	125 mL
½ teaspoon salt	2 mL

Pour 3 tablespoons melted butter into the cold iron skillet. Pour in batter. Bake in oven 350°F (180°C) until crust is brown.

This will puff up like a soufflé. Serve with jam, stewed fruit, maple syrup or butter.

SPINACH AND CHEESE PIE

Serves 16

4-10 ounce packages frozen spinach	4-284 g
3 to 4 tablespoons olive oil	45 - 50 mL
4 sweet onions, medium sized, chopped	4
4 teaspoons fresh dill weed	20 mL
1½ cups milk	375 mL
6 eggs, beaten	6
1¼ pounds Feta cheese	750 g
2 teaspoons salt	10 mL
¼ teaspoon pepper	1 mL
¾ package frozen Phyllo pastry sheets, thawed	¾

Cook spinach and drain well. Sauté onions in 3 to 4 tablespoons of oil. Add spinach and dill. Add milk, cooking over low heat for 10 minutes. Add cheese, salt and pepper and set aside. Grease a 13 × 9 inch (33 × 23 cm) baking dish with oil and line the pan with 8 sheets of Phyllo dough so that the sheets overlap edge of the casserole and can cover the top of the pie when completed. Brush leaves with oil and pour in the spinach mixture. Fold over the Phyllo sheets and brush the pie with oil. Add 6 more sheets of Phyllo dough on top of pie brushing with oil between each sheet. Cut into serving pieces before cooking. Cook at 300°F (150°C) for 45 minutes the day before serving. Reheat at 325°F (160°C) for 30 minutes on the day of serving.

THE CATERPILLAR

Serves 6 to 8

1 large Italian loaf, unsliced	1
5½ slices cooked ham	5½
5½ slices Swiss cheese	5½
1 tablespoon onion, finely chopped	15 mL
1 tablespoon Dijon mustard	15 mL
1 tablespoon poppy seeds	15 mL
½ pound butter, softened	250 mL

Cut crusts off bread. Slice into 12 slices, taking care not to completely sever bottom of loaf. Mix last 4 ingredients and slather all surfaces of bread, including between slices. Insert a half slice (triangle) of cheese and ham between each bread slice exposing tips of triangles. Sprinkle with additional poppy seeds. Wrap in foil until ready to bake. Place on cookie sheet. Open foil. Bake 15 to 20 minutes at 425°F (220°C). Freeze before baking if desired. Serve with tossed green salad. A family and crowd favourite.

MINUTE RICE LUNCH

Serves 6

Prepare minute rice, or regular rice for 6 people, salt if necessary.

½ pound lean bacon, sautéed, drained and chopped coarse	250 g
3 onions, chopped and sautéed	3
2 stalks celery, chopped and sautéed	2
½ cup home-made chili sauce	125 mL

Mix all together. Serve hot. May use more bacon if desired or economy allows.

BRUNCH PIE

Serves 4 to 6

10 slices bacon, cooked crisp and crumbled	10
1 tin crescent rolls	1
2 medium tomatoes, thickly sliced	2
3 eggs	3
salt and pepper	
½ cup flour	125 mL
¾ cup sour cream	175 mL
1 cup Cheddar cheese, grated	250 mL

Line crescent roll dough in an ungreased pie plate. Arrange bacon, tomato slices and cheese on crust. Beat egg whites until stiff. Combine egg whites with yolks, sour cream, flour, salt and pepper. Place on top of pie. Sprinkle with paprika.

Bake at 350°F (180°C) for 35 to 40 minutes.

CHICKEN CASSEROLE
Serves 10

4 cups diced cooked chicken	1 L
1¼ cups diced celery	375 mL
½ cup chopped onion	125 mL
2 cups Cheddar cheese croutons	500 mL
12 ounces Swiss cheese, grated	340 g
½ cup milk	125 mL
1 cup real mayonnaise	250 mL
1 teaspoon salt	2 mL
1-10 ounce can condensed cream of mushroom soup	1-284 mL
¼ cup slivered almonds	50 mL

Mix together mayonnaise, milk, soup, and salt. Lightly sauté celery and onions and add to the soup mixture. Place half the croutons, half the chicken, and half the Swiss cheese in a casserole. Add remaining chicken and croutons. Pour the soup mixture over the casserole, sprinkle with the remaining cheese and slivered almonds. Bake at 350°F (180°C) for 40 minutes, or until the casserole is bubbling. Popular with everyone!

DELUXE CHICKEN SALAD
Serves 4

4 cups cubed cooked chicken	1 L
salt, to taste	
½ cup chopped celery	125 mL
1 cup seedless green grapes, cut in half	250 mL
1 cup cubed pineapple	250 mL
toasted almonds for garnish	

Mix with:

⅓ cup mayonnaise	75 mL
⅓ cup sour cream	75 mL

Garnish with toasted almonds. Serve in lettuce cups or halved avocados.

Desserts

FROZEN COGNAC PIE

Serves 8

Pie Crust

1½ cups graham cracker crumbs	375 mL
¼ cup brown sugar	50 mL
⅓ to ½ cup soft butter	75 to 125 mL

Mix and line a 9 inch (23 cm) pie plate. Bake 10 minutes at 350°F (180°C). Cool.

Filling

1 cup whipping cream	250 mL
½ cup sifted icing sugar	125 mL
4 egg yolks	4
2 tablespoons sherry	25 mL
2 tablespoons brandy	25 mL

Whip cream until stiff. Blend in sugar gradually.

In a separate bowl, beat the egg yolks until light and creamy. Add sherry and brandy. Fold into cream mixture.

Pour into prepared crust. Freeze (will keep up to two weeks).

Note: Remove from freezer ½ hour before serving. Serve with hot fudge sauce.

INSTANTLY-HARD HOT FUDGE SAUCE

Yields 1 cup or 250 mL

2 ounces (2-1 ounce squares) bitter chocolate	2-28 g
⅓ cup boiling water	75 mL
2 tablespoons corn syrup	25 mL
1 tablespoon butter	15 mL
1 cup white sugar	250 mL
1 teaspoon vanilla	5 mL

Over very low heat, melt chocolate and add butter. Mix well, add hot water. Add sugar and syrup, continue stirring until well blended. Turn heat to medium. Bring sauce to a boil and let boil for 5 minutes, NO LONGER, WITHOUT STIRRING. Add vanilla and serve hot over ice cream.

Very easy and I strongly suggest you double it, it doesn't last long!

FROZEN STRAWBERRY SOUFFLÉ

Serves 12

Ingredients

1-15 ounce package frozen sliced strawberries (thawed)	425 g
6 eggs, separated	6
1¾ cups sugar	425 mL
½ cup orange flavoured liqueur	125 mL
⅓ cup fresh orange juice	75 mL
3 cups heavy cream	750 mL
red food colouring (optional)	

Garnish

1 cup toasted almonds, chopped	250 mL
whipped cream	
whole fresh strawberries	

Strawberry Liqueur Sauce

1 quart sliced fresh strawberries	1 L
½ cup sugar	125 mL
4 teaspoons orange flavoured liqueur	20 mL

Soufflé Directions

Place 2 to 3 inch collar on 2 quart soufflé dish. Oil dish.

Purée strawberries and set aside. Beat egg yolks with ¾ cup (175 mL) sugar until thick and lemon coloured. Stir in half strawberry purée. Cook in double boiler stirring 15 minutes, or until mixture thickens and coats spoon. Remove from heat and cool. Stir in orange flavour liqueur, set aside.

In sauce pan combine remaining 1 cup of sugar and orange juice. Heat, stirring to dissolve sugar. Cook without stirring at 232°F-234°F (110-113°C) on candy thermometer.

Beat egg whites until very stiff. In a thin stream, slowly add hot orange syrup to egg whites beating at high speed until peaks form. Set aside to cool.

Whip the cream, fold into cooled strawberry mixture along with remaining purée. Fold into meringue and mix gently. Stir in few drops of red food colouring.

Turn into dish. Freeze 6 hours, or overnight. To serve, remove collar and press nuts into sides of soufflé. Decorate with extra cream and strawberries. Serve with strawberry liqueur sauce.

Liqueur Directions

Combine strawberries and sugar in sauce pan and heat through.

Remove from heat and stir in liqueur.

ICE CREAM PIE

Serves 8

1 cup whipping cream, whipped	250 mL
6 Crispy Crunch chocolate bars	6
1 pint chocolate ice cream	.5 L
1 pint coffee ice cream	.5 L
1 pint vanilla ice cream	.5 L

Roll and crush chocolate bars into small pieces. Reserve a few pieces and mix the remainder with stiffly beaten whipped cream. Line an 8 inch (20 cm) spring-form pan with mixture (sides and bottom) and freeze.

Soften ice cream, one flavour at a time. Remove pan from freezer and put in a layer of vanilla ice cream and freeze. Follow with a layer of coffee ice cream, and then chocolate ice cream. Sprinkle with reserved chocolate pieces on top. Freeze until serving time.

Drizzle chocolate sauce over each piece as you serve.

Chocolate sauce

½ cup corn syrup	125 mL
1 cup chocolate chips	250 mL
1 tablespoon butter	15 mL
¼ cup cream	50 mL
¼ teaspoon vanilla	1 mL

Melt chips, syrup and butter. Add cream and vanilla.

MAPLE DESSERT

Serves 6 to 8

12 lady fingers	12
¾ cup maple syrup	175 mL
½ cup pecans	125 mL
maple ice cream or buttered pecan ice cream	
1 cup whipping cream (whipped)	250 mL
¼ cup toasted coconut	50 mL

Soak lady fingers in maple syrup. Line a rounded bowl with wax paper and lady fingers. Cover bottom of bowl with pecans and extra syrup. Add maple ice cream or buttered pecan ice cream. Freeze. Whip cream, cover and garnish with toasted coconut.

MRS. GERALD R. FORD'S "CHOCOLATE ICE BOX DESSERT"

1-12 ounce package chocolate chips	350 g
4 tablespoons sugar	50 mL
6 tablespoons water	75 mL
6 eggs, separated	6
1 cup whipping cream	250 mL
2 teaspoons vanilla	10 mL
1 teaspoon salt	5 mL
1 angel food cake, prepared	1

Line a flat 9 × 9 inch (23 cm) cake pan with waxed paper. Slice angel food cake and place a layer of cake in cake pan. (I find that angel food cake slices better if frozen.)

Separate 6 eggs. Beat egg yolks. Melt chocolate chips in a double boiler over hot water. When melted add sugar and water. Mix well. (Be sure sugar is dissolved.)

Remove from heat and stir the above hot chocolate mixture gradually into the beaten yolks of eggs. Beat until smooth. Cool chocolate mixture. Add vanilla and salt, mix.

Beat egg whites until stiff. Whip whipping cream until stiff. Fold egg whites into the cooled chocolate mixture; then the whipping cream.

Place a layer of the chocolate mixture on the sliced angel food cake, then another layer of cake, then a layer of chocolate. Place in refrigerator and chill overnight.

This may be frozen and used later. Be sure to chill overnight before freezing.

RAISIN CHOCOLATE MOUSSE

Serves 6

¾ cup raisins	175 mL
¾ ounce light rum	15 mL
3 ounces semi-sweet chocolate	3-28 g
1½ tablespoons boiling water	22 mL
¾ cup whipping cream	175 mL
⅓ cup sugar	75 mL
1 teaspoon vanilla	5 mL
pinch salt	pinch
¾ cup sour cream	175 mL

Soak raisins in rum. Melt chocolate over hot water. Stir in boiling water, continuing to stir until smooth. Whip cream with sugar, vanilla and salt. Add hot chocolate mixture slowly, beating at low speed, just until smooth. Add sour cream; mix just until blended. Fold in raisins by hand. Spoon into serving dishes. Chill.

BANANAS EN CASSEROLE

Serves 6

6 bananas	6
lemon or lime juice, a sprinkle	
2 tablespoons butter	25 mL
salt to taste	
1 cup sweet red wine (not port)	250 mL
½ cup brown sugar	125 mL
½ teaspoon nutmeg	2 mL
½ teaspoon cinnamon	2 mL
¼ teaspoon cloves	1 mL
1½ teaspoons grated orange rind	7 mL
6 macaroons, crushed	6
almonds sliced	
2 tablespoons dark rum	25 mL

Peel bananas, sprinkle with lemon or lime juice. Brown lightly in hot butter. Salt to taste.

Make a syrup of wine, brown sugar, nutmeg, cinnamon, cloves and orange rind. Put the bananas in a buttered casserole, pour the spiced syrup over the bananas. Cover with crushed macaroons and almonds. Brown in a moderate oven and just before serving add dark rum. Serve aflame.

Spectacularly easy!

STRAWBERRY CHARLOTTE

Serves 10 to 12

2 tablespoons of unflavoured gelatine	30 mL
¾ cup sugar (divided)	175 mL
¼ teaspoon salt	1 mL
4 eggs, separated	4
½ cup water	125 mL
2-10 ounce packages frozen sliced strawberries	2-312 g
2 tablespoons lemon juice	25 mL
2 teaspoons lemon rind, grated	10 mL
10 ladyfingers	10
1 cup whipping cream, whipped	250 mL

Mix gelatine, ¼ cup (50 mL) sugar and salt in top of double boiler. Beat egg yolks and water together. Add to gelatine mixture. Add strawberries and cook over boiling water, stirring constantly until gelatine is dissolved. Remove from heat, add lemon juice, rind and chill in refrigerator until mixture mounds when dropped from a spoon. Line ladyfingers around an 8 inch (20 cm) spring-form pan. Beat egg whites until stiff with remaining ½ cup (125 mL) sugar. Whip cream and fold into gelatine mixture with egg whites.

Turn into pan and chill until firm.

MAPLE MOUSSE

Serves 6 to 8

1 unflavoured envelope gelatine	15 mL
¼ cup cold water	50 mL
1 cup pure maple syrup	250 mL
3 eggs, separated	3
2 tablespoons Amaretto	25 mL
1 cup whipping cream	250 mL
shaved chocolate	

Sprinkle gelatine over cold water and allow to soften. Beat egg yolks and maple syrup together in top of double boiler. Cook over boiling water for 10 minutes, stirring constantly. Stir in gelatine and cook until dissolved. Remove from heat and set pot over cold water until cool. Do not allow mixture to set. Stir in Amaretto.

Beat egg white until stiff. Fold into maple syrup mixture.

Whip cream until stiff. Fold into mixture. Pour into a serving bowl and chill until set, at least 3 hours. Garnish with shaved chocolate just before serving.

INDIVIDUAL ORANGE SOUFFLÉS

Makes 8

8 large oranges	8
1 teaspoon cornstarch	15 mL
⅔ cup orange juice	150 mL
1 teaspoon grated orange rind	15 mL
¼ cup sugar	50 mL
1 teaspoon marmalade	15 mL
1 teaspoon butter	15 mL
4 eggs, separated	4
icing sugar for dusting	

Remove tops from oranges, scoop out flesh from base without piercing skin. Mix cornstarch with ¼ cup (50 mL) orange juice. Add to remaining juice and bring to boil, stirring constantly. Add rind, sugar, marmalade and butter, continuing to stir until thickened and smooth. Remove from heat and gradually beat in egg yolks. Beat egg whites until stiff and fold into yolk mixture. Fill orange shells ⅔ full with mixture and place on baking sheet, or muffin tin. Bake in 400°F (200°C) oven for 10 to 15 minutes or until puffed and golden. Sprinkle with icing sugar after removing from oven and serve immediately.

Mixture can be halved to serve only 4.

RUM SOUFFLÉ

Serves 10 to 12

4 eggs separated	4
1 cup white sugar	250 mL
1 package unflavoured gelatine	15 mL
¼ cup water	50 mL
¼ cup rum, dark or light	50 mL
½ pint whipping cream	250 mL
1 angel cake or orange chiffon cake, cubed	1
chocolate curls for garnish	

Soak gelatine in ¼ cup (50 mL) water. Place egg yolks and sugar in top of double boiler. Beat until light. While beating, heat mixture slowly over simmering water. When sugar is all dissolved and egg/sugar mixture partly thickened, add gelatine mixture and rum. Combine well. Remove from heat. Chill egg mixture until stiff but not jelled. Beat egg whites until stiff; whip cream until stiff. Combine mixtures; pour over thin layer of cake cubes in spring-form pan. Alternate cake and custard mix. Chill for a minimum of 4 hours. Garnish with chocolate curls. Freezes well.

CAROL BURNETT'S "FRESH PEACH SOUFFLÉ"

1½ cups peeled, pitted, peaches	375 mL
¾ cup macaroon crumbs	175 mL
3 tablespoons Amaretto	45 mL
½ cup butter	125 mL
½ cup sugar	125 mL
4 egg yolks	4
5 egg whites, stiffly beaten	5

Crush peaches — combine with macaroon crumbs soaked in Amaretto. Cream together butter and sugar. Add egg yolks, one at a time, beating well after each addition. Combine egg and macaroon mixtures, fold in egg whites. Pour mixture into a buttered and sugared soufflé dish and bake in 350°F (180°C) oven for about 35 minutes, or until it is well puffed.

HONEYDEW MELON WITH PORT WINE JELLY

Serves 6

1 Honeydew melon	1
2-3 ounce packages strawberry Jello	2-85 g
port wine	
pinch of cinnamon	

Remove top of Honeydew melon and scoop out seeds.

Dissolve 2 packages of Jello in 1 cup (250 mL) of boiling water and add 1 cup (250 mL) of cold water. Pour Jello into melon leaving a 1½ inch (3 cm) space at top.

Top with port wine and a pinch of cinnamon powder to required taste.

Allow to set overnight.

Remove skin (optional), cut melon into wedges and serve with a twist of orange.

ORANGE CREAM DESSERT CAKE

Serves 10 to 12

1½ dozen ladyfingers	18
2 envelopes unflavoured gelatine	30 mL
1 cup sugar	250 mL
6 eggs separated	6
1¾ cups orange juice	425 mL
2 tablespoons lemon juice	25 mL
1 tablespoon freshly grated orange rind	15 mL
1 teaspoon freshly grated lemon rind	5 mL
2 cups whipping cream, whipped	500 mL
1 can Mandarin oranges, drained	1-284 mL

Butter a 9 inch (23 cm) spring-form pan. Line bottom and sides with ladyfingers. In a saucepan, combine gelatine and ¾ cup (175 mL) sugar. Beat egg yolks and orange juice together and stir into gelatine/sugar mixture. Cook over medium heat, stirring constantly until mixture comes to a boil and is slightly thickened. Remove from heat and stir in lemon juice and grated orange and lemon rind. Chill until the consistency of unbeaten egg white. Beat 6 egg whites to form stiff but moist peaks. Gradually add ¼ cup (50 mL) sugar. Beat until stiff and shiny. Fold into gelatine mixture. Beat whipping cream until stiff. Reserve ⅓ cup (75 mL) for garnish. Fold remainder into gelatine mixture. Pour into pan. Chill until set. Remove from pan and garnish with whipped cream and Mandarin orange sections.

FESTIVE PARTY BOMBE
Serves 10 to 12

2 cups whipping cream	500 mL
1½ cups icing sugar, sifted	375 mL
2 tablespoons rum, or sherry, or Kirsh	25 mL
½ cup almonds, finely chopped	125 mL
¼ cup chopped maraschino cherries	50 mL
1 quart raspberry sherbet	1L

Whip cream until it begins to hold its shape. Gradually beat in the icing sugar and the rum. Whip the mixture until it is stiff and then fold in the almonds and the cherries. Line a 6 cup (1.5 L) melon mould with about ¾ of the mixture. Leave a hollow in the centre. Fill the hollow with slightly softened raspberry sherbet and spread the remaining whipped cream mixture over the top. Cover with a lid or foil and freeze overnight. Unmould onto a chilled platter and let sit for ten minutes out of freezer before serving for easier handling.

A raspberry sauce drizzled over each slice makes it even more delicious. Gorgeous at Christmas time.

CHILLED ZABAGLIONE CREAM
Serves 6

6 tablespoons sugar	75 mL
1 teaspoon unflavoured gelatine	5 mL
½ cup Marsala or sherry	125 mL
6 egg yolks	6
1 tablespoon brandy	15 mL
1 teaspoon vanilla	5 mL
½ pint whipping cream (chill up to 2 days in advance)	250 mL
3 egg whites	3
⅛ teaspoon salt	pinch
⅛ teaspoon cream of tartar	pinch
½ square semi-sweet chocolate	½

In the top of a double boiler mix together 4 tablespoons (50 mL) of sugar and gelatine; stir in wine. In a bowl, beat egg yolks until light and lemon coloured; fold into gelatine mixture. Cook over hot water stirring constantly until thickened. Remove from heat; add brandy and vanilla. Cool.

Whip cream until stiff and fold into cooled gelatine mixture. Beat egg whites until foamy, add salt and cream of tartar; beat until stiff. Beat in remaining 2 tablespoons (25 mL) sugar. Fold meringue into custard and spoon into tall slender parfait glasses. Chill for at least 1 hour. Garnish with chocolate curls.

FROSTED CANTALOUPE

Serves 4 to 6

8 ounces cream cheese, softened	250 g
2 tablespoons milk	25 mL
1 large cantaloupe or honeydew melon	1
6 cups mixed fresh fruit	1.5 L
¾ cup toasted coconut	175 mL
mint leaves for garnish	

Beat cream cheese and milk until smooth and set aside. Remove the rind from the melon, cut a little off one end so that it will stand up. Slice a two inch piece from other end, scoop out seeds, fill melon with 1 cup (250 mL) of mixed fruit. Replace top, frost the outside of the melon with the cream cheese and press toasted coconut all over the melon. Refrigerate. Cut into wedges and serve remaining fruit from a sauce boat.

A conversation piece!

STRAWBERRY ANGEL GRAND MARNIER PIE

Serves 6 to 8

⅔ cup flaked coconut	150 mL
¼ cup icing sugar	50 mL
¼ teaspoon cream of tartar	1 mL
3 egg whites	3
⅔ cup sugar	150 mL
1 quart fresh strawberries	1 L
½ cup Grand Marnier	125 mL
1 cup whipping cream, whipped	250 mL

Combine coconut and icing sugar and set aside. Sprinkle cream of tartar over whites and beat until foamy. Add sugar, a small amount at a time. Beat well after each addition. Continue beating until mixture stands in stiff peaks. Fold in coconut mixture. Spread in buttered 9 inch (23 cm) pie plate. Bake in preheated 325°F (160°C) oven for 30 minutes, or until meringue feels dry and firm. Cool.

Strawberries should be washed and hulled. Slice large berries and leave a few whole for decoration. Place sliced berries in bowl with Grand Marnier for 3 hours. Shortly before serving, drain berries and reserve liqueur. Whip cream until stiff and sweeten to taste. Fold in strawberries. Fill meringue shell with mixture. Decorate with extra strawberries.

Serve in slices and pour small amount of liqueur over each.

THE MUCH REQUESTED RECIPE FOR JEAN STAPLETON'S "CHOCOLATE FONDUE"

Makes 4 to 6 servings

6-1 ounce squares unsweetened chocolate	6
1½ cups sugar	375 mL
1 cup light cream	250 mL
½ cup butter	125 mL
⅛ teaspoon salt	pinch
3 tablespoons Crème de Cacao (optional)	45 mL

In crockpot, melt chocolate on high for 30 minutes. Stir in sugar, cream, butter and salt, cook on high, stirring constantly for 10 minutes.

Add Crème de Cacao, turn to low.

In standard crockpot, recipe can be doubled or tripled.

For fondue pot, make first as above in double boiler. Then transfer to fondue pot. Otherwise it takes forever.

Good dippers:

Squares of pound cake or angel food cake

Marshmallow

Fruit chunks

Almonds

Bananas

RUM PEARS
Serves 6 to 8

2-28 ounce cans pear halves, drained	2-796 mL
4 tablespoons butter	50 mL
12 tablespoons dark brown sugar	175 mL
6 to 8 tablespoons rum	75 to 125 mL
1 cup whipping cream	250 mL

Melt butter in large frying pan and add brown sugar and rum. Cook over medium heat until mixture turns into a thick syrup. Takes about 4 or 5 minutes. Add drained pears and swirl until well coated. Pour in cream and boil 2 to 3 minutes, until sauce thickens, stirring constantly. Serve in crystal bowl. Chill before serving.

EASY HOLIDAY DESSERT

1 jar prepared mincemeat	1
1 tin of Bartlett pear halves, drain and reserve	1
brandy syrup (optional)	
whipping cream (optional)	

Place a heaping spoonful of mincemeat in the centre of Bartlett pear halves. Place pears in a baking dish and pour some syrup around them. Bake for 20 minutes in 350°F (180°C) oven. Serve warm. Delicious flambéed with brandy and a dollop of whipped cream.

STRAWBERRY MOUSSE
Serves 6

1 tablespoon gelatine	15 mL
2 tablespoons cold water	25 mL
1 cup crushed strawberries	250 mL
1 cup heavy cream, whipped	250 mL
¾ cup fruit sugar	175 mL
ladyfingers	

6 whole strawberries
  (add little or no sugar if using frozen
  sweetened strawberries)
	6

Soften gelatine in cold water, dissolve the gelatine over hot water and in a medium size bowl add the gelatine to the strawberries. Chill until mixture thickens slightly. Fold in whipped cream, sugar (if required), chill until thick enough to hold its shape.

Line serving dish with ladyfingers, add strawberry mixture and decorate with whole strawberries. Chill several hours before serving.

MAGIC FROZEN MOCHA TREAT
Serves 8 to 12

2¼ cups chocolate wafer crumbs	200 g
¼ cup butter, melted	50 mL
2 teaspoons instant coffee	10 mL
1 cup milk	250 mL
1-1 litre carton vanilla ice cream	1 L
1-4 ounce package instant chocolate pudding	1-113 g
1 teaspoon vanilla extract	5 mL

Combine chocolate wafer crumbs with melted butter. Set aside ½ cup (125 mL) of mixture. Press the rest firmly into bottom of a 12 × 7 × 2 inch (20 × 30 × 2 cm) well buttered glass baking dish.

Stir instant coffee into milk until dissolved.

Put ice cream in a chilled bowl and mix with electric mixer at low speed until soft. Working quickly add milk mixture, pudding and vanilla. Beat just to blend. Pour into crust. Sprinkle with reserved crumbs. Cover and freeze. Cut into squares to serve.

PINEAPPLE BAVARIAN
Serves 8

1-14 ounce tin pineapple tidbits	1-398 mL
½ cup sugar	125 mL
2 tablespoons lemon juice	25 mL
pinch of salt	pinch
1 tablespoon unflavoured gelatine	15 mL
¼ cup cold water	50 mL
½ pint whipping cream	250 mL
1 package ladyfingers	1

Soften gelatine in cold water. Drain pineapple and set aside. In a saucepan, boil and then simmer for 2 to 3 minutes the sugar, salt, pineapple and lemon juice. Add gelatine to the sauce and refrigerate until it is as thick as the white of an egg. Fold in the whipped cream and pineapple tidbits.

Line a dish with split ladyfingers, break remainder in 1 inch (2 cm) pieces. Pour some of the pineapple mixture into the lined dish, top with broken ladyfingers; cover with the remaining pineapple mixture. Refrigerate 3 to 4 hours or overnight.

ORANGES CÔTE D'AZUR

Serves 8

8 medium oranges	8
½ cup butter	125 mL
grated rind of 1 lemon	1
⅓ cup lemon juice	75 mL
1½ cups sugar	375 mL
¼ teaspoon salt	1 mL
3 eggs, separated	3
1 cup whipping cream	250 mL
1 teaspoon cream of tartar	5 mL
5 tablespoons sugar	75 mL

Scoop out oranges. Freeze cases.

Melt butter in double boiler over hot water. Add rind, lemon juice, salt and 1½ cups (375 mL) sugar. Beat egg yolks. Add to lemon mixture and cook, stirring until shiny and thick. Cool.

Whip cream and fold into mixture. Pour into bowl and freeze for 3 to 4 hours. Fill orange cases.

Meringue

Whip egg whites with cream of tartar and gradually add 5 tablespoons (75 mL) of sugar and beat until stiff and moist peaks form. Put on top of oranges. Brown under broiler for about 2 minutes. Note: Dessert can be made weeks in advance and kept in freezer. Just before serving, top with the meringue and brown under the broiler.

GINGER CREAM

Serves 8

1 tablespoon unflavoured gelatine	15 mL
¼ cup cold water	50 mL
1 cup homogenized milk	250 mL
2 egg yolks, slightly beaten	2
¼ cup sugar	50 mL
¼ cup candied ginger, cut in pieces	50 mL
2 tablespoons ginger syrup	25 mL
2 cups whipping cream, whipped	500 mL

Soak gelatine in cold water. In a double boiler slowly cook milk, beaten egg yolks, sugar and gelatine, stirring constantly until it thickens to coat a spoon. Add ginger syrup and chill. When it begins to thicken, fold in whipped cream and ginger. Place in serving bowl and refrigerate.

GLENDA JACKSON'S "CASSATA DI MASCAPONI"

Serves 6 to 8

½ pound cream cheese	250 g
2 eggs separated	2
2 ounces sugar	50 mL
2 tablespoons of rum	25 mL
¼ pint of cream	125 mL

Beat cheese and cream until very smooth. Beat egg yolks and sugar. Add the rum and beat again. Add to cheese and mix until smooth, then beat the egg whites stiff. Fold into cheese mixture.

Refrigerate 3 to 4 hours in a clear glass bowl.

BLUEBERRY PUDDING

Serves 4 to 6

2 cups fresh blueberries	500 mL
1½ cups sugar	375 mL
1 tablespoon lemon juice	15 mL
⅓ cup shortening	75 mL
2 well beaten eggs	2
1 teaspoon grated lemon rind	5 mL
1¼ cups sifted pastry flour or 1⅛ cups (275 mL) sifted all-purpose flour	300 mL
1½ teaspoons baking powder	7 mL
½ teaspoon salt	2 mL
¼ teaspoon grated nutmeg	1 mL
½ cup milk	125 mL

Combine blueberries, ¼ cup sugar, lemon juice. Spread berry mix in 9 × 9 inch (23 cm) pan.

Cream shortening, blend in 1 cup sugar, well beaten eggs and rind. Sift flour, baking powder, salt and nutmeg. Add flour mixture to creamed mixture alternately with milk. Combine lightly.

Turn batter into pan over berries. Bake at 375°F (190°C) for 35 to 40 minutes or until golden brown.

GRAND MARNIER SAUCE

Serves 8

5 egg yolks, at room temperature	5
¾ cup sugar	175 mL
¼ cup Grand Marnier	50 mL
1 cup whipping cream	250 mL
1 tablespoon sugar	15 mL

Beat egg yolks until light in the top of a double boiler. Beat in ¾ cup (175 mL) sugar and place over simmering water, stirring constantly, until thickened, about 20 minutes. Remove from heat and beat until cool. Add Grand Marnier and refrigerate until chilled. Whip cream just until it begins to thicken, then add 1 tablespoon (15 mL) sugar. Continue beating until cream is medium thick but will still pour. Fold in egg sauce and pour into a serving dish. Chill until serving time, or freeze. Serve over fresh fruit. This sauce is wonderful over fresh berries or a colourful bowl of mixed fruits.

BLUEBERRY MOULD

Serves 6

1-10 ounce package frozen blueberries	1-312 g
½ cup sugar	125 mL
½ tablespoon lemon juice	7 mL
1 envelope unflavoured gelatine	15 mL
¼ cup water	50 mL
1 cup whipping cream, whipped	250 mL

In a blender, purée blueberries for 30 seconds. Pour into bowl. Add sugar and lemon juice to blueberries and stir until sugar dissolves. In top of a double boiler, sprinkle gelatine over water and let stand 5 minutes. Heat until gelatine dissolves, stirring gently. Stir gelatine into blueberry mixture. Chill until slightly thickened. Fold in whipped cream. Pour into wet mould and chill until firm. Decorate with whole berries and a dollop of whipped cream.

PEANUT BUTTER CREAM PIE

Makes 3-9 inch (23 cm) pies
1 pie serves 6

Make 3 of your favourite graham cracker crusts and refrigerate.

1-8 ounce package cream cheese	250 g
2 cups icing sugar	500 mL
1 cup milk	250 mL
⅔ cup chunky peanut butter	150 mL
2 quarts frozen dessert topping (found in freezer section in store)	2 L

Cream cheese and add icing sugar. Stir in milk and add chunky peanut butter. Fold in whipped topping. Fill pie shells. Freeze. Remove from freezer ½ hour before serving. Garnish with fresh strawberries, kiwi fruit slices or Mandarin orange sections.

MOCHA MERINGUE TORTE

Serves 10

10 egg whites (at room temperature)	10
½ teaspoon cream of tartar	2 mL
2¾ cups sugar	675 mL
⅓ cup water	75 mL
4 teaspoons instant coffee	20 mL
8 egg yolks	8
1 cup butter, softened	250 mL
4 squares semi-sweet chocolate, melted	4
2 cups whipping cream	500 mL
small amount of Tia Maria liqueur	

1) Grease and flour two large cookie sheets. Using a 9 inch (23 cm) cake pan as guide, outline a circle on each.

2) *Prepare Meringue* — Beat egg whites and tartar until soft peaks form. Gradually beat in 2 cups (500 mL) sugar, 2 tablespoons (25 mL) at a time, beating well after each addition until sugar is completely dissolved. Do not underbeat. Spoon or pipe meringue into circles. Cook at 200°F (100°C) for 2 hours. Turn off. Leave meringue in oven for at least one hour.

Steps 1 and 2 may be done the day ahead.

3) *Mocha Filling* — In heavy saucepan over medium heat, heat water, instant coffee and ¾ cup (175 mL) sugar to boiling, stirring until sugar dissolves. Using candy thermometer, continue cooking and stirring frequently until temperature reaches 250°F (120°C) or hard ball stage. Remove from heat. In small bowl with mixer at medium speed, beat egg yolks slightly. Beating at medium speed slowly pour syrup in thin stream into egg yolks. Beat in butter and chocolate until mixture is very thick, about 10 minutes. Refrigerate until mixture is of good spreading consistency, but not firm.

4) *Assemble Torte* — Place one meringue layer on cake plate. Spread with half of mocha filling. Repeat. Cover and refrigerate at least three hours or overnight.

A couple of hours before serving, whip cream, sweeten to taste and add some Tia Maria for flavour. Spread over top and sides of torte. Sprinkle chocolate shavings on top if desired.

Fantastic party dessert.

CHANTILLY MERINGUE

Serves 10 to 12

Meringue

10 egg whites	10
10 tablespoons white sugar	150 mL
1 teaspoon vanilla	5 mL

Cream Chantilly

2 cups milk	500 mL
1 cinnamon stick	1
½ teaspoon salt	2 mL
1 or 2 strips lemon or lime rind	1-2
10 egg yolks	10
½ cup white sugar	125 mL
¼ cup butter or margarine	50 mL
1 teaspoon vanilla	5 mL

Preheat oven to 400°F (200°C).

Beat egg whites until peaks form. Add one tablespoon (15 mL) of sugar at a time.

Carmelize an angel food cake mould (use about ¾ cup (175 mL) sugar for the caramel).

Pour the meringue on the caramel mould. Put it in the oven and immediately turn off the oven. Leave it for 4 to 6 hours in the oven that has been turned off, or you can do this overnight if you want.

For the cream, boil the milk with the cinnamon, salt and lemon rind. Let the milk cool down. Beat the egg yolks and the sugar. Add the milk. Pass the milk and egg mixture through a strainer into a double boiler and constantly move it until it thickens slightly. Add the butter and vanilla.

For serving, unmould the meringue by turning over on a round dessert dish. Serve it with the chilled cream.

TORTONI FRANGELICO

Serves 6

1 quart pistachio ice cream, slightly softened	1 L
½ cup heavy cream, whipped	125 mL
⅓ cup Frangelico (hazelnut liqueur)	75 mL
⅓ cup macaroon crumbs	75 mL

Turn ice cream into large chilled bowl. Fold in remaining ingredients. Spoon into chilled dessert dishes and freeze until firm. Garnish with more macaroon crumbs if desired.

FROSTY HOLIDAY PIE

Serves 8 to 10

¼ cup butter	50 mL
¼ cup corn syrup	50 mL
½ cup semi-sweet chocolate chips	125 mL
2 cups Special K cereal	500 mL
4-3 ounce packages cream cheese softened	4-125 g
¾ cup sugar	175 mL
2 tablespoons brandy	25 mL
½ cup maraschino cherries, quartered	125 mL
½ cup almonds, chopped	125 mL
2¼ cups whipping cream, whipped	550 mL

Melt butter, corn syrup, and chocolate chips in medium size saucepan over low heat stirring constantly until smooth. Remove from heat. Add cereal stirring until well coated. Gently press mixture in buttered 9 inch (23 cm) pie pan to form crust. Chill.

In small mixing bowl beat cream cheese until smooth. Gradually beat in sugar. Stir in brandy; fold in cherries, almonds, and whipped cream.

Spread filling in chilled crust. Garnish with maraschino cherry quarters and toasted almonds if desired.

Freeze at least 4 hours. For easier cutting, let stand at room temperature 15 to 30 minutes before serving.

CHILLED GRAPEFRUIT PIE

Makes 1 pie

1½ cups grapefruit sections, cut into pieces with juice reserved, approximately 2 large or 3 small grapefruits	375 mL
1 cup sugar	250 mL
1 envelope unflavoured gelatine	1
¼ cup cold water	50 mL
1 cup whipping cream	250 mL
2 tablespoons confectioners' sugar	25 mL
½ teaspoon vanilla	2 mL
1-9 inch (23 cm) Graham cracker pie shell	1

Combine fruit, juice and sugar. Let stand 5 minutes. Drain fruit and measure 1 cup (250 mL) of juice. Bring juice to a boil. Sprinkle gelatine over cold water to soften, add to hot juice and stir until dissolved. Chill until mixture is slightly thicker than consistency of unbeaten egg white. Beat cream with confectioners' sugar and vanilla until soft. Fold whipped cream and fruit into gelatine mixture. Turn into pie shell and chill.

Strawberry Meringue Cake
Recipe on page 234

BARBARA ANN SCOTT'S "LEMON DREAM"

Serves 4

3 egg whites	3
½ teaspoon cream of tartar	2 mL
1½ cups sugar	375 mL
4 egg yolks	4
5 teaspoons lemon juice	25 mL
4 tablespoons lemon rind, grated	50 mL
1 cup whipping cream, whipped	250 mL

Beat egg whites until frothy and starting to stand up. Add 1 cup of the sugar gradually. Beat until very stiff. Put meringue mixture on wax paper on a cookie sheet in pie shape, heart shape or individual shell shapes.

Bake in 275°F (140°C) oven for 60 minutes. Turn off oven and leave until oven has cooled.

Beat egg yolks until thick and lemon coloured. Gradually beat in ½ cup (125 mL) of the sugar. Blend in 5 teaspoons (25 mL) lemon juice and 4 tablespoons (50 mL) grated lemon rind. Cook over hot water stirring constantly until thick (6 to 8 minutes). Cool.

Spread half of whipped cream on meringue shell. Fill with lemon mixture and top with remaining whipped cream.

Chill 12 hours before serving.

Tint meringues with a few drops of food colouring to match table flowers or napkins.

CHILLED CHEESE SOUFFLÉ

Serves 12

1 cup blanched almonds	250 mL
2 tablespoons soft butter	25 mL
2½ pounds cream cheese	3-250 g
4 teaspoons vanilla	20 mL
½ cup plain yogurt	125 mL
juice of 2 lemons	2
2 cups sugar	500 mL
2 cups heavy cream	500 mL

Toast nuts on a cookie sheet in a 350°F (180°C) oven for 10 minutes. Grind in a blender. Butter a 10 inch (25 cm) spring-form pan and press ¼ cup (50 mL) ground nuts into butter to make a light crust. To the remaining nuts in blender, add cheese, vanilla, yogurt, lemon juice, and sugar. Blend well and remove to a large bowl. Whip cream until stiff and fold into cheese mixture. Pour into nut-lined pan and refrigerate for 4 to 6 hours. Serve with vanilla sauce.

Vanilla Sauce

2 pints whole milk	1 L
6 egg yolks	6
1 cup sugar	250 mL
4 teaspoons vanilla	20 mL
1 tablespoon cornstarch	15 mL

Scald milk. Place over hot, not boiling water. In a bowl beat egg yolks until light and add sugar and cornstarch. Pour slowly into hot milk, stirring constantly until thickened. Remove from heat and add vanilla. Chill and serve.

BANANAS IN RUM CARAMEL

⅓ cup butter	75 mL
¼ cup sugar	50 mL
4 firm bananas	4
⅓ cup orange juice	75 mL
1 tablespoon grated orange rind	15 mL
¼ cup dark rum	50 mL
heavy cream or ice cream	

In skillet or chafing dish cook butter and sugar over low heat for about five minutes or until the sugar just begins to carmalize. Add peeled bananas, halved lengthwise, cut side down and cook them, turning them once or twice, until they are almost tender. Add orange juice and rind and shake the pan to deglaze the caramel. Add rum, warmed, ignite it and spoon the flaming sauce over the bananas. Serve the dessert flaming with a pitcher of heavy cream, or over ice cream.

EASY FRUIT COMPOTE
Serves 6 to 8

1-14 ounce can pitted black cherries	1-398 mL
1-28 ounce can peach halves	1-796 mL
1-14 ounce can apricot halves	1-398 mL
½ pound pitted prunes	227 g
1 lemon, unpeeled	1
1 orange, unpeeled	1
1-6 ounce can concentrated frozen orange juice	117 mL
½ cup brandy	125 mL

Thinly slice orange and lemon, mix together all fruit (with syrup) and orange juice in a large baking dish. Bake in 350°F (180°C) oven for 2 hours. Cool and store in freezer (optional). Thaw (if necessary), add brandy before serving. For slightly sweeter dessert add ¼ to ½ cup brown sugar before baking. Serve with slightly whipped cream.

A 'make the day before' delight.

LEMONADE PIE
Makes 1 pie

1-9 inch (23 cm) Graham cracker pie shell	1
1 can condensed sweetened milk	300 mL
1-6 ounce can frozen lemonade (not defrosted)	170 mL
juice of 1 lemon	1
1-9 ounce carton Cool Whip, defrosted	500 mL

Fold frozen lemonade and condensed milk together. Add lemon juice.

Gently fold in Cool Whip and put in a Graham cracker crust, homemade or bought. Refrigerate several hours before serving.

BUTTERSCOTCH SAUCE

⅔ cup corn syrup	150 mL
1¼ cups light brown sugar	300 mL
¼ cup butter	50 mL
⅔ cup evaporated milk	150 mL
dash of salt	dash

Boil first three ingredients to syrup consistency. Cool to lukewarm. Add evaporated milk and salt. Serve hot or cold. Stir if it separates during storage. A delicious quick dessert sauce. Keeps at least 6 months without refrigeration.

RUM BUMBLE

Serves 4 to 6

1½ tablespoons unflavoured gelatine	22 mL
2 tablespoons cold water	25 mL
6 tablespoons boiling water	75 mL
1 cup sugar	250 mL
⅓ to ½ cup rum	75 to 125 mL
4 tablespoons rye whiskey	50 mL
2 egg whites	2
1 pint whipping cream, whipped	500 mL
½ cup slivered almonds, toasted	125 mL

Dissolve gelatine in the cold water in small saucepan. Place over simmering water and stir until dissolved. In mixing bowl, dissolve sugar in boiling water. Add rum, rye whiskey and gelatine mixture. As mixture thickens, beat until white and frothy. Beat egg whites until stiff and whip cream, fold into gelatine mixture.

Pour into lightly oiled mould and refrigerate 3 to 4 hours.

When ready to serve, turn out onto serving plate. Decorate with almonds. The almond crunch is good with creamy texture of dessert.

HOT RUM SAUCE

Yields 2 cups or 500 mL

1 cup granulated sugar	250 mL
1 cup water	250 mL
½ cup butter	125 mL
¼ cup rum	50 mL

Cook together, sugar and water. When syrup reaches the thread stage, remove from the stove and add butter. When that has melted, stir in rum. Serve immediately with hot mince pie or ice cream.

Baking

CHOCOLATE SQUARES

Makes 24 squares

1¼ cups crushed graham wafers	300 mL
¼ cup butter, melted	50 mL
1 cup powdered cocoa	250 mL
1-6 ounce package of chocolate chips	250 mL
4 ounces nuts, chopped	125 g
14 ounce can condensed milk	300 mL

Mix crumbs with melted butter and press into bottom of a 9 × 9 (23 × 23 cm) cake pan. Combine cocoa, chips and nuts and sprinkle over crumbs. Pour condensed milk over top.

Don't worry if some of the chocolate or nuts float.

Bake at 325°F (160°C) oven for 30 minutes, or until golden, cut into squares.

DATE SQUARES

Makes 32 squares

1 pound pitted dates, chopped	500 g
½ cup sugar	125 mL
½ cup water	125 mL
1 teaspoon lemon juice	5 mL
¾ cup butter	175 mL
1 cup brown sugar	250 mL
1½ cups rolled oats	375 mL
1½ cups flour	375 mL
¼ teaspoon salt	1 mL
½ teaspoon baking soda	2 mL

Combine dates, water and white sugar. Cook over medium heat until mixture is well blended and smooth. Remove from heat, add lemon juice and cool.

Cream butter and brown sugar. Add rolled oats, flour mixed with salt and soda; mix well. Place one half of mixture on bottom of well-greased 13 × 9 × 2 inch (23 × 33 cm) baking pan. Spread with cooled date filling and cover with remainder of oatmeal mixture.

Bake at 350°F (180°C) for 20 minutes. Cut into squares while still warm.

photo courtesy of Toronto Star

H.R.H. THE PRINCESS OF WALES' "FUDGE"

Makes approximately 36 squares

¼ cup butter	50 mL
2 cups sugar	500 mL
3 tablespoons of water	45 mL
1 tin condensed milk (10 ounces)	300 mL

Put the sugar, butter and water into a large saucepan, preferably a non-stick saucepan. Stir gently until the sugar is dissolved. Add the condensed milk and bring to the boil. Simmer on a very low heat until the mixture thickens and browns — this should take about 45 minutes. Stir occasionally during simmering.

Remove from heat, cool slightly and beat well.

Pour into a 9 × 9 × 2 inch (23 × 23 × 5 mL) greased tray. Wait until it is set and then cut into squares.

LEMON SQUARES

Makes 16 squares

¾ cup butter	175 mL
1¾ cups graham cracker crumbs	425 mL
¾ cup flour	175 mL
½ teaspoon baking powder	2 mL
½ cup white sugar	125 mL
pinch of salt	pinch
½ cup coconut	125 mL
Topping	
1 cup sugar	250 mL
1 egg, slightly beaten	1
1 tablespoon flour	15 mL
1 lemon, juice and rind	1
¾ cup water	175 mL
1 tablespoon butter	15 mL

Bottom Layer
Sift together baking powder, flour and salt. Add remaining ingredients and mix well. Pack crumbly mixture into 8 × 10 inch (20 × 25 cm) pan. Cover with topping.

Topping
Mix all ingredients together in a saucepan and cook until thickened. Cool and pour over cracker mixture. Bake at 350°F (180°C) until firm, about 20 minutes.

Everyone's favourite.

CARAMEL SQUARES

Makes 16 squares

½ cup white sugar	125 mL
½ cup corn syrup	125 mL
½ cup peanut butter	125 mL
3 cups Rice Krispies	750 mL

Bring sugar and corn syrup to a boil. Remove from heat. Add peanut butter and Rice Krispies. Pour into greased 8 × 8 inch (20 × 20 cm) pan and press down.

Frosting

½ cup chocolate chips	125 mL
½ cup butterscotch chips	125 mL

Melt together and spread on top. Serve at room temperature.

A favourite with the children.

FANTASTIC ALMOND SQUARES

Makes 30 squares

Cream
½ cup butter	125 mL

Add
1 cup sugar	250 mL
1 egg	1
1 teaspoon almond extract	5 mL
1 cup flour	250 mL

Put in ungreased 8 inch (20 cm) square pan. Sprinkle with slivered almonds. Bake at 375°F (190°C) for approximately 20 to 25 minutes or until lightly golden. Freezes well.

STAMPEDE FLAPJACKS

Makes 16

¾ cup melted butter	175 mL
2 cups oatmeal	500 mL
1 cup brown sugar	250 mL
1 teaspoon baking powder	5 mL
pinch of salt	pinch

Melt butter and add dry ingredients.

Put in ungreased 9 inch (23 cm) cake pan and bake at 350°F (180°C) for 10 to 15 minutes. Cool slightly and cut into squares.

Can be doubled easily and will freeze well.

CRISPIE CRUNCHIES

Makes 2 dozen crunchies

1 cup peanut butter	250 mL
1 cup icing sugar	250 mL
1 tablespoon butter	15 mL
1½ cups Rice Krispies	375 mL
dipping chocolate, 1-6 ounce package chocolate chips	175 g
¼ cup butter	50 mL

Mix well first four ingredients, roll into balls. Chill thoroughly. Melt chocolate and butter over hot water. Dip half of each cookie in chocolate, set on waxed paper. Refrigerate.

Always keep chocolate over hot water while dipping.

SESAME SEED CRACKERS

Makes about 9 dozen crackers

1 cup, plus 2 tablespoons, sesame seeds	275 mL
3½ cups sifted unbleached flour	875 mL
1½ teaspoons salt	7 mL
¼ teaspoon chili powder	1 mL
1 cup butter or margarine	250 mL
½ cup ice water	125 mL
Cheddar cheese, grated	

Toast sesame seeds in large skillet over low heat, stirring occasionally, until seeds are light brown. Turn into a large bowl, cool.

Stir in flour, salt and chili powder, cut in butter with pastry blender until mixture is crumbly.

Stir in water slowly, mixing lightly with fork just until pastry is thoroughly moistened. Gather dough into a ball. Cover. Chill 30 minutes.

Lightly dust 2 cookie sheets with flour. Divide dough in half. Roll each half out directly on cookie sheets, covering entire sheet evenly. Patch if necessary. Cut into 2 inch (5 cm) squares. Prick each square a few times with a fork. Top with sharp cheese.

Bake at 425°F (220°C) for 12 minutes or until lightly browned. Remove from cookie sheets to wire racks to cool completely. Store in tightly covered containers.

SHORTBREAD

Makes 75 cookies

1 pound unsalted butter (at room temperature)	454 g
1 cup powdered fruit sugar	250 mL
1 cup rice flour	250 mL
3 cups all-purpose flour, sifted	750 mL

Cream butter until soft and fluffy. Add fruit sugar by tablespoonful, mixing well after each addition. Add rice flour to sifted flour. Gradually blend into batter mixture with hands.

Shape dough into two round balls, wrap and place in refrigerator overnight.

Sprinkle small amount of icing sugar on board, roll out balls of dough ¼ inch (½ cm) thick. Cut into 1½ inch (3.5 cm) rounds. Prick with fork. Set on ungreased baking sheet and chill for 20 minutes in refrigerator (10 minutes in freezer).

Bake at 375°F (190°C) for 15 to 20 minutes, or until golden brown.

SWEDISH COCONUT COOKIES

Makes 4 dozen cookies

Cream well together:

1 cup of butter	250 mL
2 cups of sugar	500 mL

Add:

2 beaten eggs	2
2 cups shredded coconut	500 mL
dash of salt	dash
2½ cups flour, sifted several times	625 mL

Mould dough with hands, roll into little balls and flatten with a fork. (Dip fork in cold water between balls). Bake at 375°F (190°C) oven and watch carefully.

CARAMEL APPLE COOKIES

Makes 3 dozen cookies

½ cup butter	125 mL
1½ cups brown sugar	375 mL
1 egg	1
1 teaspoon baking soda	5 mL
2¼ cups flour	550 mL
½ teaspoon salt	2 mL
1 teaspoon cinnamon	5 mL
½ teaspoon cloves	2 mL
½ teaspoon nutmeg	2 mL
1 cup apple, grated	250 mL
1 cup raisins	250 mL
½ cup apple juice	125 mL

In a large bowl cream butter and sugar. Beat in egg. Sift together flour and spices and add to butter mixture. Stir in grated apple, raisins and apple juice. Drop on buttered cookie sheet by tablespoons. Bake at 350°F (180°C) for 12 minutes. Cool and ice.

Icing

¼ cup butter	50 mL
¼ cup brown sugar	50 mL
1½ cups icing sugar	375 mL
¼ teaspoon salt	1 mL
2½ tablespoons light cream	30 mL

Mix well and ice cookies.

CHOCOLATE COOKIES

Makes approximately 40 cookies

½ cup butter	125 mL
1 cup brown sugar	250 mL
2 eggs, separated	2
1¾ cups flour	425 mL
¼ teaspoon salt	1 mL
½ teaspoon baking soda	2 mL
½ cup milk	125 mL
2 squares unsweetened chocolate, melted	2
1 cup chopped walnuts	250 mL

Cream butter with sugar, add beaten egg yolks and beat well. Add flour mixed with salt and soda, alternately with milk. Blend well.

Add melted chocolate and fold in stiffly beaten egg whites and nuts. Drop by teaspoonful onto greased and floured cookie sheet.

Bake in 350°F (180°C) oven 6 to 8 minutes.

OATMEAL CHOCOLATE CHIP COOKIES

Makes 48 cookies

1 cup butter	250 mL
1 cup brown sugar	250 mL
1 teaspoon vanilla	5 mL
1 teaspoon baking soda	5 mL
¼ cup boiling water	50 mL
2 cups cake and pastry flour	500 mL
½ teaspoon salt	2 mL
2 cups oatmeal (not instant)	500 mL
½ cup coconut	125 mL
1 cup chocolate chips	250 mL

Cream butter and brown sugar. Stir in vanilla. Pour boiling water over soda and add to creamed mixture. Stir dry ingredients together and stir into creamed mixture, mixing until well blended. Add chocolate chips. Drop by teaspoon onto an ungreased cookie sheet, flatten with a fork dipped in cold water and bake at 350°F (180°C), 12 to 15 minutes or until golden brown.

GREETING COOKIES

Use 1 cup (250 mL) of dough for each cookie, flatten as above. Makes 4 extra large cookies — bake 2 cookies at once leaving at least 2 inches between to allow for spreading.

TOFFEE COOKIES
Makes 18 cookies

3 bars (2 ounces) toffee	3 (56 g)
3½ tablespoons butter	50 mL
1 tablespoon cream	15 mL
⅓ cup almonds, slivered	75 mL
⅓ cup coconut	75 mL
1 cup Corn Flakes	250 mL

Melt toffee in a heavy saucepan. Add butter and cream. When well mixed, remove from heat, stir in almonds and coconut, then Corn Flakes. Drop by heaping teaspoonful onto a lightly buttered cookie sheet and chill. Yum!

BRANDY SNAPS
Makes 2 dozen cookies

½ cup molasses	125 mL
½ cup butter	125 mL
1 cup flour	250 mL
⅔ cup white sugar	150 mL
1 tablespoon ginger	15 mL

Heat molasses to boil, add butter. Remove from heat and stir in flour, mixed and sifted with sugar and ginger. Drop small bits on a greased pan. Bake 300°F (150°C) 7 to 8 minutes (until they stop bubbling). Cool slightly before removing from pan.

GUM DROP COOKIES
Makes 2 dozen cookies

¾ cup butter	175 mL
½ cup brown sugar	125 mL
½ cup white sugar	125 mL
1 egg	1
1 cup oatmeal	250 mL
1 cup flour	250 mL
¼ teaspoon salt	1 mL
½ teaspoon baking soda	2 mL
½ teaspoon baking powder	2 mL
1 teaspoon vanilla	5 mL
3 cups gum drops, cut in thirds	750 mL

Cream butter and sugar together. Add rest of ingredients and mix well. Drop by heaping teaspoonful onto a lightly buttered cookie sheet. Bake at 350°F (180°C) for 10 to 12 minutes until light brown. Allow to cool slightly, then remove from pan and finish cooling on rack.

OATMEAL COOKIES

Makes approximately 50 cookies

1 cup butter (or half butter, half shortening)	250 mL
1 cup brown sugar	250 mL
3 cups quick oats	750 mL
1 cup flour	250 mL
½ teaspoon salt	2 mL
1 teaspoon baking soda	5 mL
¼ cup boiling water	50 mL
½ teaspoon vanilla	2 mL

Cream butter and sugar. Add oats and flour mixed well with salt and soda. Moisten with water, vanilla and mix well. (You may even have to use your hands.)

Roll into 1 inch (2.5 cm) balls and drop on greased cookie sheet.

Press very flat with fork dipped in boiling hot water. Bake at 325°F (160°C) until lightly browned, about 8 to 10 minutes.

SESAME CRISPS

Makes 5 dozen cookies

½ cup sesame seeds, toasted	125 mL
¾ cup butter	175 mL
1 cup brown sugar	250 mL
1 egg	1
1 teaspoon vanilla	5 mL
1 cup all-purpose flour	250 mL
½ teaspoon baking soda	2 mL
¼ teaspoon salt	1 mL

To toast sesame seeds:
Place in a small frying pan over medium heat. Stir constantly until seeds are golden (about 10 minutes).

Cream butter and sugar until smooth, beat in egg and vanilla. Sift together flour, soda and salt and blend into creamed mixture along with cooled seeds.

Drop rounded teaspoonfuls on ungreased cookie sheet. Flatten with a fork. Bake at 350°F (180°C) for 10 minutes or until edges are golden. Let set on cookie sheet for one to two minutes before serving.

SPICE COOKIES

Makes 30 to 35 cookies

1 cup butter, melted	250 mL
¾ cup brown sugar	175 mL
1 egg	1
1¾ cups flour	425 mL
½ teaspoon cream of tartar	2 mL
½ teaspoon baking soda	2 mL
¾ teaspoon cinnamon	4 mL
¼ teaspoon vanilla	1 mL
¼ teaspoon cloves, ground	1 mL

Combine brown sugar, butter and egg. Beat well. Mix dry ingredients and add to egg mixture. Blend well. Add vanilla. Chill. Drop in small spoonfuls on greased cookie sheet.

Bake at 350°F (180°C) for 5 to 6 minutes.

RUSSIAN ROCKS

Makes 4 dozen cookies

1½ cups brown sugar	375 mL
⅔ cup butter	150 mL
3 eggs, well beaten	3
1 teaspoon baking soda	5 mL
2 teaspoons vanilla	10 mL
3 cups flour	750 mL
1 teaspoon baking powder	5 mL
pinch salt	pinch
1 cup nuts, chopped	250 mL

Cream butter and sugar, then add well beaten eggs. Dissolve baking soda in 3 tablespoons (45 mL) of hot water. Sift flour with baking powder and salt and add to creamed mixture then add baking soda and vanilla, last the nuts. If dough is too stiff, a little milk may be added. Spices and glacé cherries may be added if desired. Drop on greased cookie sheets and bake 15 minutes at 325°F (160°C).

BROWN SUGAR COOKIES

Makes approximately 5 dozen cookies

1 cup butter	250 mL
2 cups light brown sugar	500 mL
2 eggs	2
1 tablespoon vanilla	15 mL
3 cups flour	750 mL
¾ teaspoon baking soda	4 mL
1½ teaspoons cream of tartar	7 mL
½ teaspoon salt	2 mL

Cream butter and sugar. Add eggs and vanilla and mix well. Combine flour, baking soda, cream of tartar, salt and add to other mixture. Roll into 1 inch (2.5 cm) balls and place on greased cookie sheet. Press flat with fork dipped in boiling hot water. Bake at 350°F (180°C) about 5 to 8 minutes, or until lightly browned.

If preferred this dough may be chilled for several hours and then rolled thin to cut with cookie cutters.

RICE COOKIES

Makes 3 dozen cookies

½ cup butter	125 mL
1 cup brown sugar, packed	250 mL
1 cup rolled oats	250 mL
1 cup Rice Krispies	250 mL

Melt butter in large pan and add brown sugar. Mix in oats and Rice Krispies. Spread onto cookie sheet with sides.

Cook at 350°F (180°C) for 10 minutes. Cut into squares and enjoy.

WALNUT SLICE

Serves 8

Base

1 cup flour	250 mL
6 tablespoons butter	75 mL
2 tablespoons brown sugar	25 mL

Combine above ingredients and spread into an 8 × 8 inch (20 × 20 cm) baking dish. Bake in preheated 325°F (160°C) oven until slightly brown.

Filling

1 egg	1
½ cup brown sugar	125 mL
¼ cup coconut, shredded	50 mL
½ cup chopped walnuts	125 mL
sprinkled with 1 tablespoon flour	15 mL
¼ cup corn syrup	125 mL

Combine above ingredients and spread over shell. Bake 30 minutes, until set. Cool. Spread orange butter icing.

Orange Butter Icing

2 tablespoons soft butter	25 mL
1 egg yolk	1
1 cup icing sugar	250 mL
2 teaspoons grated orange rind	10 mL
1 tablespoon orange juice	15 mL

Blend butter, yolk, sugar and orange rind. Add juice carefully until desired spreading consistency is achieved.

STRAWBERRY PIE

Serves 4 to 6

1 cup all-purpose flour, sifted	250 mL
½ cup sugar	125 mL
¼ teaspoon salt	1 mL
⅓ cup butter or margarine	75 mL
1 egg yolk	1
2-8 ounce packages cream cheese, softened	2-250 g
2 tablespoons grated lemon rind	25 mL
6 tablespoons lemon juice	75 mL
1 quart fresh strawberries	1 L
1 cup strawberry preserves	250 mL
2 tablespoons cornstarch	25 mL

Combine flour, ¼ cup (50 mL) sugar and salt. Cut in butter. Add egg yolk and 2 or 3 tablespoons (24 to 45 mL) of water; mix lightly. Press into ball. Roll out on lightly floured surface to ¼ inch (.5 cm) thickness. Press over bottom and sides of 9 inch (23 cm) layer cake pan. Prick well and bake in 450°F (230°C) oven for 15 minutes. Cool. Combine cheese, lemon rind, 3 tablespoons (45 mL) lemon juice and ¼ cup (50 mL) of sugar; mix well. Spread cream cheese mixture in bottom of pastry shell. Top with strawberries. Combine strawberry preserves, 3 tablespoons (45 mL) lemon juice, cornstarch and ½ cup (125 mL) water. Cook over low heat until thickened and clear, stirring constantly. Cool, pour over strawberries.

CHOCOLATE MINT SNAPS

Makes 5 dozen cookies

⅔ cup shortening	150 mL
½ cup granulated sugar	125 mL
1 egg	1
6 ounces chocolate chips, melted	175 g
¼ cup corn syrup	50 mL
¼ teaspoon peppermint extract	1 mL
1¾ cups flour	425 mL
2 teaspoons baking soda	10 mL
1 teaspoon cinnamon	5 mL
¼ teaspoon salt	1 mL

Beat shortening, sugar and egg until creamy. Blend in melted chocolate chips and corn syrup. Sift and stir in gradually the remaining ingredients. Shape dough into balls and roll in sugar.

Bake at 350°F (180°C) for 5 to 7 minutes on an ungreased cookie sheet, until cracks form on the surface. Watch closely.

LEMON BARS

Makes 5 dozen bars

1 cup butter, room temperature	250 mL
¼ teaspoon salt	1 mL
2¼ cups flour	550 mL
½ cup icing sugar	125 mL
2 cups sugar	500 mL
1 grated rind of lemon	1
6 tablespoons lemon juice	90 mL
4 eggs, beaten	4

Preheat oven to 350°F (180°C). Mix butter, salt and 2 cups (500 mL) flour with icing sugar. Press firmly into a 9 × 13 inch (23 × 33 cm) pan.

Bake 15 to 20 minutes until edges are golden brown.

Gradually add sugar, grated lemon rind and lemon juice to beaten eggs. Sift remaining ¼ cup (50 mL) flour and fold in gently. Pour onto slightly cooked crust.

Return to oven at 350°F (180°C) and bake 20 to 25 minutes longer.

Remove from oven. Sprinkle with icing sugar. Cool and cut into bars.

JEWEL BARS
Makes 30 bars

1¼ cups flour	300 mL
⅔ cup brown sugar, firmly packed	150 mL
¾ cup butter	175 mL
1 egg	1
½ teaspoon salt	2 mL
1½ cups salted mixed nuts	375 mL
1½ cups halved candied cherries	375 mL
1 cup chocolate chips	250 mL

Combine flour and ⅓ cup (75 mL) of brown sugar. Cut in butter until mixture is coarse and crumbly. Press mixture evenly in bottom of 15 × 10 × ¾ inch (38 × 25 × 2 cm) jelly-roll pan. Bake at 350°F (180°C) for 15 minutes. Beat egg in large bowl. Stir in remaining ⅓ cup (75 mL) brown sugar and salt. Add nuts, cherries and chocolate chips. Toss lightly to coat. Bake additional 20 minutes at 350°F (180°C). Cool.

Cut into bars.

PEANUT BUTTER BALLS
Makes approximately 5 dozen balls

2 cups Rice Krispies	500 mL
1 cup peanut butter	250 mL
1 cup icing sugar	250 mL
5 tablespoons butter, room temperature	75 mL
½ cup coconut	125 mL
1 package chocolate chips (350 g) or sweetened bar chocolate	1

Mix all the ingredients, except chocolate, together. Place in the refrigerator for one hour. Remove and with wet hands roll dough into small balls. Melt the chocolate in the top of a double boiler and dip balls in chocolate one at a time. Place each ball on wax paper to dry.

These can be frozen or will keep in the refrigerator.

TOFFEE BARS
Makes 50 cookies

28 to 30 graham crackers	28 to 30

Line a 10 × 15 inch (25 × 40 cm) jelly-roll pan with foil paper, shiny side down. Preheat oven to 375°F (190°C). Place graham crackers on foil.

In a pot boil together:

1 cup brown sugar	250 mL
1 cup unsalted butter	250 mL
2 tablespoons sesame seeds	25 mL
4 ounces sliced almonds (flat pieces)	113 g

Pour above mixture over crackers and bake for 8 minutes. Cut immediately into bars, refrigerate and or freeze.

CHOCOLATE RUM BALLS
Makes 2 dozen balls

1 cup vanilla wafers, crumbled	250 mL
1 cup chopped pecans	250 mL
2 tablespoons cocoa	25 mL
1 cup icing sugar	250 mL
3 ounces liquor (light rum or brandy)	75 mL

Mix all ingredients together. Refrigerate overnight. Roll mixture into small balls and roll in icing sugar.

CHOCOLATE PEANUT BUTTER BALLS
Makes 24 balls

¼ cup butter, melted	50 mL
2 cups walnuts, chopped	500 mL
⅔ cup crunchy peanut butter	150 mL
2 cups icing sugar	500 mL
12 maraschino cherries, chopped	12
pinch salt	pinch
dipping chocolate	

Mix together and roll into 1 inch (2.5 cm) balls. Melt semi-sweet chocolate in double boiler over hot, not boiling, water. Coat balls one at a time.

BARBARA ANN SCOTT'S
"NEVER FAIL MOIST BROWNIES"
Makes 8 brownies

½ cup soft butter	125 mL
1 cup sugar	250 mL
2 eggs	2
2 squares unsweetened bakers chocolate, melted	2 squares
½ cup flour (sifted once)	125 mL

Cream butter and sugar. Add eggs one at a time, stir. Add other ingredients. Put in 8 × 8 inch (20 × 20 cm) greased pan. Bake 20 to 30 minutes in 350°F (180°C) oven. When cool, sprinkle with powdered sugar.

MINT FROSTED BROWNIES

Makes 14 brownies

½ pound butter	250 mL
4 squares unsweetened chocolate	4
2 cups sugar	500 mL
4 eggs	4
2 teaspoons vanilla	10 mL
1 cup flour	250 mL

Melt butter and chocolate in double boiler. Cream sugar and eggs and add to chocolate mixture. Add vanilla and flour. Bake in ungreased 9 × 13 inch (23 × 33 cm) pan for 25 minutes at 350°F (180°C). Do not overbake.

Mint Frosting

½ cup butter	125 mL
2 cups icing sugar	500 mL
2 tablespoons milk	25 mL
1 teaspoon peppermint extract	5 mL
green food colouring	

Beat together until smooth. Spread over cooled brownies. Refrigerate until firm.

Chocolate Glaze

2 squares semi-sweet chocolate	2
2 tablespoons butter	25 mL

In a small saucepan over low heat melt chocolate. Add butter and stir until smooth. Spread over mint frosting and refrigerate. Tastes as delicious as it looks!

MEDIUM-RARE BROWNIES

Makes 2 dozen brownies

½ cup butter	125 mL
1 cup sugar	250 mL
2 eggs	2
2 squares unsweetened chocolate, melted	2
½ cup flour	125 mL
½ teaspoon vanilla	2 mL
dash of salt	

Mix all ingredients together. Pour into greased 8 inch (20 cm) square pan. Bake at 350°F (180°C) for 25 to 30 minutes.

PEANUT BUTTER BROWNIES

Makes 16 brownies

½ cup butter	125 mL
½ cup peanut butter	125 mL
1 cup firmly packed brown sugar	250 mL
1 teaspoon vanilla	5 mL
2 eggs	2
1 cup all-purpose flour	250 mL
1 teaspoon baking powder	5 mL
¼ teaspoon salt	1 mL
1 cup chocolate chips	250 mL
icing sugar	

Cream butter, gradually add sugar and peanut butter, beat until fluffy. Blend in vanilla and eggs, one at a time beating well after each addition.

Sift flour, baking powder, salt, add to creamed mixture, mix thoroughly. Fold in chocolate chips. Spread in 9 × 9 inch (23 × 23 cm) square greased pan. Bake at 350°F (180°C) for 30 to 35 minutes.

Cool. Top with sifted icing sugar.

MALLOW TOPPING FOR BROWNIES

Bake one 9 × 13 inch (23 × 33 cm) pan of brownies and top with . . .

Topping

40 marshmallows	40
½ cup water	125 mL
½ cup brown sugar	125 mL
2 squares grated unsweetened chocolate	2
3 tablespoons butter	45 mL
1 teaspoon vanilla	5 mL
2 cups icing sugar	500 mL

When brownies are baked, halve about 40 marshmallows and place cut side down on top of brownies in pan. Place pan back in oven and bake at 325°F (160°C) until marshmallows puff; watch carefully. Remove from oven and pour following mixture over marshmallows.

In a saucepan, mix water, brown sugar and grated chocolate. Boil for 3 minutes. Remove from heat. Stir in butter, vanilla and icing sugar. Add a little water if necessary.

Rich, delicious and worth every calorie.

TEXAS PANCAKE BROWNIES

Makes 4 dozen brownies

½ pound butter	250 mL
1 cup water	250 mL
4 tablespoons cocoa	50 mL
2 cups white sugar	500 mL
2 cups flour	500 mL
1 teaspoon baking soda	5 mL
½ cup buttermilk	125 mL
1 teaspoon vanilla	5 mL
2 eggs beaten	2

Bring butter, water and cocoa to a boil. Mix sugar, flour and baking soda and add to the cocoa mixture. Add buttermilk, vanilla and beaten eggs.

Pour into large pan 1 × 11½ × 17¾ inch (2.5 × 29 × 44 cm). May even use broiler pan. Bake at 350°F (180°C) for 25 to 30 minutes. Test for doneness.

Remove cake from oven and while hot top with icing.

Icing

6 tablespoons buttermilk	75 mL
¼ pound butter	125 mL
1 teaspoon vanilla	5 mL
4 tablespoons cocoa	50 mL
1 pound icing sugar	500 g

Bring first 4 ingredients to a boil and pour over icing sugar. Spread on brownies.

WHOLE WHEAT SODA BREAD

Makes 1 loaf

2½ cups whole wheat flour	625 mL
1½ cups white flour	375 mL
2 eggs, slightly beaten	2
2 cups buttermilk	500 mL
3 tablespoons sugar	45 mL
1½ teaspoons baking soda	7 mL
1 tablespoon salt	15 mL

Preheat oven to 350°F (180°C). Combine ingredients and put into loaf pan. Bake 15 minutes and then slit top and bake an additional 40 to 50 minutes and test.

GRAHAM BREAD

Makes 1 loaf

2 cups buttermilk	500 mL
2 teaspoons baking soda	10 mL
2 cups graham flour	500 mL
1 cup white flour	250 mL
½ cup white sugar	125 mL
½ teaspoon salt	2 mL

Preheat oven to 400°F (200°C).

Combine buttermilk and soda, mix until foamy. Combine dry ingredients, add to buttermilk mixture. Pour into loaf pan. Reduce oven to 350°F (180°C), put in bread, and bake 1 hour.

BROWN OATMEAL BREAD

Makes 5 loaves

2 tablespoons sugar	25 mL
2 cups lukewarm water	500 mL
3 tablespoons dry yeast	45 mL
2 cups rolled oats	500 mL
1 cup boiling water	250 mL
4 cups lukewarm water	1 L
½ cup shortening (room temperature)	125 mL
1 cup brown sugar	250 mL
1 cup molasses	250 mL
5½ teaspoons salt	25 mL
2 cups wholewheat flour	500 mL
white flour to mix (approximately 11 cups)	2.75 L

Mix the sugar in the 2 cups (500 mL) lukewarm water, sprinkle with yeast and let sit for 10 to 15 minutes. Pour boiling water on the oatmeal and add shortening and stir together to melt shortening and remove any oatmeal lumps. Add lukewarm water, brown sugar, molasses and salt and mix. When mixture has cooled to lukewarm add yeast mixture. Add wholewheat flour and mix thoroughly. Start adding white flour until the dough is thick enough to come away from the side of the mixing bowl. Turn out onto a floured board and continue adding more white flour, kneading as you go, until dough is rather elastic and not sticky. Then knead for about 5 minutes more. Set in greased mixing bowl, cover with a dish towel, and set in a warm place to rise until double in bulk, about 1½ hours. Punch down and knead again for a few minutes. Divide into loaves in well greased pans and set in a warm place to rise again. Bake in a 350°F (180°C) oven for about 20 to 30 minutes or until loaves sound hollow when rapped with a knuckle and shrink slightly from the sides of the pan.

FAVOURITE EGG BREAD

Makes 3 loaves

5½ to 6 cups all-purpose flour	1.4 to 1.5 L
2 packages active dry yeast	2
1½ cups milk	375 mL
⅓ cup butter or margarine	75 mL
½ cup white sugar	125 mL
1 teaspoon salt	5 mL
3 eggs	3
1 slightly beaten egg yolk	1
sesame seeds	

In a large bowl, combine 2 cups (500 mL) of the flour and the yeast.

In a large saucepan, heat milk, butter, sugar, and salt, until warm, stirring constantly. Add 3 eggs to the dry ingredients and beat at low speed for ½ minute. Then at high speed for 3 minutes. By hand stir in as much remaining flour as you can mix in with a spoon.

Turn out onto lightly floured surface. Knead in enough remaining flour to make a moderately soft dough that is smooth and elastic (8 to 10 minutes). Shape into 3 balls and place in a greased bowl. Cover and let rise until double (1 to 1½ hours). Punch down, cover and let rest for 10 minutes. Divide one of the portions into three parts, shape each into 16 inch (40 cm) ropes. Place ropes 1 inch (2.5 cm) apart on greased baking sheet. Braid loosely. Seal ends together and tuck under. Repeat with remaining dough.

Cover, let rise until nearly double (about 40 minutes). Combine egg yolk and 1 tablespoon (15 mL) water, brush on braids. Sprinkle with sesame seeds and bake 375°F (190°C) about 20 to 25 minutes. Remove to rack.

SPOON BREAD

Serves 4 to 6

1 cup yellow cornmeal (unsifted)	250 mL
4 eggs	4
4 cups milk	1 L
2 teaspoons salt	10 mL
1 teaspoon butter	5 mL

In a saucepan heat milk and butter to the boiling point. Place cornmeal in one bowl, crack eggs into another bowl. Pour boiling milk into cornmeal, add salt, and beat slowly. Beat cornmeal mixture into eggs and heat gently to keep from forming lumps over a low burner, stirring until thickened. Pour mixture into a greased and floured 2 quart (2 L) baking dish. Bake at 350°F (180°C) for one hour.

JIM NABORS'
"SOUTHERN STYLE CORNBREAD"

Makes 1 loaf

1 cup self rising cornmeal	250 mL
¼ cup self rising flour	50 mL
1 egg	1
½ cup buttermilk	125 mL
¼ to ½ cup water (to make batter consistency of cake batter)	50 to 125 mL

Preheat oven to 425°F (220°C). Mix all of the ingredients above. Pour into a cold cast iron skillet (small one) that has been greased and dusted with cornmeal. Bake for approximately 30 minutes.

SOUR CREAM SCONES
Makes 6 Scones

1¾ cups flour (all-purpose)	425 mL
1 tablespoon baking powder	15 mL
¾ teaspoon baking soda	4 mL
¼ cup sugar	50 mL
½ teaspoon salt	2 mL
1 teaspoon orange rind	5 mL
1 teaspoon lemon rind	5 mL
¼ cup currants or raisins	50 mL
2 tablespoons butter	25 mL
1 egg, beaten	1
⅔ to ¾ cup sour cream	150 mL to 175 mL
1 egg yolk with 2 tablespoons water	1 with 2 mL
sugar	

Sift dry ingredients into a bowl. Add orange and lemon rinds, currants or raisins. Cut in butter and add egg, together with enough sour cream to make a soft dough. Turn onto a lightly floured board and knead gently until smooth. Pat or roll into a circle about ¾ inch (2 cm) thick and mark in 6 sections with a knife.

Place on a greased cookie sheet and brush with egg yolk diluted with water. Sprinkle with sugar and bake at 400°F (200°C) for 15 minutes.

BARN BRACK (CAKE-BREAD)
Makes 1 loaf

1 cup prepared tea	250 mL
3 tablespoons butter	45 mL
½ cup brown sugar	125 mL
½ cup molasses	125 mL
¾ pound mixed fruit (1½ to 2 cups — raisins, candied peel, glacéd cherries, etc.)	375 to 500 mL
2 cups flour	500 mL
2 teaspoons baking powder	10 mL
pinch salt	pinch
1 egg	1
1 teaspoon cinnamon	15 mL

Overnight, soak butter, sugar, molasses and fruit in tea. Mix flour, baking powder, salt and cinnamon. Add egg and tea mixture. Mix well. Bake in well-greased loaf pan for 1½ hours at 325°F (160°C).

BATTER BROWN BREAD

Makes 4 loaves

2 packages dry yeast	2
1 cup warm water	250 mL
6 tablespoons sugar	75 mL
26 ounces milk	750 mL
2 teaspoons salt	10 mL
4 tablespoons salad oil	50 mL
6 cups white flour	1.5 L
4-1 pound coffee tins, well greased	4

Dissolve yeast in water with 2 tablespoons (25 mL) sugar (until it rises, about 10 minutes).

Stir together remaining sugar, milk, salt, and oil. Add raised yeast mixture. Mix in flour gradually. Mixture is very sticky. Divide into 4 tins. Allow to rise to top of tin.

Bake 350°F (180°C) for 45 minutes. Remove immediately from tins.

Can be frozen.

HERBED SODA BREAD

Makes 1 loaf

2 cups whole wheat flour	500 mL
2 cups all-purpose flour	500 mL
1 tablespoon salt	15 mL
2 teaspoons sugar	25 mL
1 teaspoon baking soda	5 mL
¾ teaspoon baking powder	4 mL
3 tablespoons chilled butter	45 mL
½ teaspoon each of a variety of dried herbs such as: sage, savory, basil, rosemary, thyme, marjoram and chives	2 mL each
2 cups buttermilk	500 mL

Sift dry ingredients together into a large bowl. Blend in butter until the mixture resembles meal and stir in herbs. Stir in buttermilk and form the dough into a ball. Knead the dough lightly on a floured surface for 2 minutes, or until it is smooth. Transfer to a greased baking sheet and form it into an 8 inch (20 cm) round. Cut a ½ inch (1 cm) deep "X" in the centre of the loaf with a sharp knife dipped in flour and bake the dough at 375°F (190°C) for 40 minutes or until the loaf sounds hollow when tapped. Cool on a rack and serve warm or at room temperature thinly sliced and with butter.

1-2-3 BEER BREAD

Makes 1 loaf

3 cups self-rising flour	750 mL
¼ cup white sugar	50 mL
1 can beer	1

1. Mix flour and sugar thoroughly

2. Add beer and stir

3. Turn batter into a greased loaf tin

Bake 350°F (180°C) for 1 hour. For variety, add to batter chopped dill, grated orange rind or chopped nuts.

Easy as 1, 2, 3.

SHREDDED WHEAT BREAD

Makes 2 loaves

3 shredded wheat	3
2 cups boiling water	500 mL
½ cup warm water	125 mL
1 package active dry yeast	1
1 cup milk	250 mL
¼ cup white sugar	50 mL
1 tablespoon salt	15 mL
½ cup molasses	125 mL
¼ teaspoon baking soda	1 mL
2 tablespoons melted margarine or shortening	25 mL
7 cups flour	1.7 L

Pour boiling water over shredded wheat and let cool, set aside.

Scald milk, add margarine, sugar, salt, and let cool, set aside.

In a warm bowl add warm water, 1 teaspoon (5 mL) sugar and the yeast, let rise 10 minutes. Stir down. Add milk mixture to shredded wheat, add soda and molasses. Stir in 6 cups (1.5 L) of flour and use the last cup to knead the dough on a floured surface.

Place dough into a greased bowl and cover with a greased piece of wax paper and a damp towel. Let rise to double, about 2½ hours, or leave in a cool spot overnight. Punch down and put in pans. Let rise again. Brush top with margarine and bake at 375°F (190°C) for ¾ hour. A lovely moist bread!

BANANA BRAN BREAD

Makes 1 loaf

1½ cups flour	375 mL
2 teaspoons baking powder	10 mL
½ teaspoon baking soda	2 mL
½ teaspoon salt	2 mL
¼ cup shortening	50 mL
1 cup sugar	250 mL
1 egg	1
1 cup bran flakes	250 mL
1½ cups mashed bananas (3)	375 mL
1 tablespoon orange rind (optional)	15 mL
2 tablespoons water	25 mL
½ tablespoon vanilla	7 mL

Cream shortening and blend in sugar and egg; beat until fluffy. Mix in bran flakes. Combine bananas, orange rind, water, and vanilla. Add dry ingredients to creamed mixture alternately with banana mixture. Combine only until mixed. Put into 8¼ × 4½ (20 × 10 cm) greased pan. Bake at 350°F (180°C) oven 1 to 1½ hours. Let stand 15 minutes.

PAN OF BRAN

Makes 1 loaf

¼ cup oil (vegetable)	50 mL
½ cup molasses	125 mL
¼ cup liquid honey	50 mL
2 eggs, beaten	2
1 cup milk	250 mL
1½ cups bakers bran	375 mL
1 cup unbleached flour	250 mL
½ teaspoon baking soda	2 mL
1½ teaspoons baking powder	7 mL
¼ teaspoon salt	1 mL
½ teaspoon cinnamon	2 mL
½ cup raisins or finely cut dates	125 mL

Combine vegetable oil and molasses. Mix well. Add remaining ingredients and combine lightly. Pour batter into a well buttered 16 × 11 × ¾ inch (40 × 28 × 2 cm) pan. Bake 400°F (200°C) for 20 minutes. Cut into squares when slightly cool. Spread with sweet butter and preserves or honey, or top a square with applesauce for a breakfast treat.

ZUCCHINI BREAD

Makes 2 loaves

3 eggs	3
2 cups white sugar	500 mL
1 cup vegetable oil	250 mL
1 tablespoon vanilla	15 mL
2 cups grated zucchini	500 mL
2 cups flour	500 mL
1 tablespoon cinnamon	15 mL
2 teaspoons baking soda	10 mL
1 teaspoon salt	5 mL
¼ teaspoon baking powder	1 mL
3 tablespoons sunflower seeds	45 mL

Beat eggs until frothy. Add sugar, oil, vanilla, and beat until thick and lemon coloured. Add zucchini and rest of ingredients. Mix well and pour into two greased and floured loaf pans. Bake at 350°F (180°C) for 1 hour or until cake tester comes out clean. Cool in pan for 10 minutes. Remove. Freezes well.

This recipe also makes wonderful muffins!

SOFT GINGERBREAD

Serves 12

1 cup molasses	250 mL
½ cup butter	125 mL
¾ cup brown sugar	175 mL
1 cup boiling water	250 mL
1 egg slightly beaten	1
2½ cups flour	625 mL
1 teaspoon baking soda	5 mL
2 teaspoons baking powder	10 mL
1 teaspoon cinnamon	5 mL
1 teaspoon ginger	5 mL
pinch of cloves, nutmeg and allspice	pinch

Pour boiling water over molasses, butter and brown sugar. Cool. Add egg. Sift dry ingredients together and add the liquid. Mix well. Pour into a greased and floured 9 × 13 inch (23 × 33 cm) pan. Bake 45 minutes at 350°F (180°C).

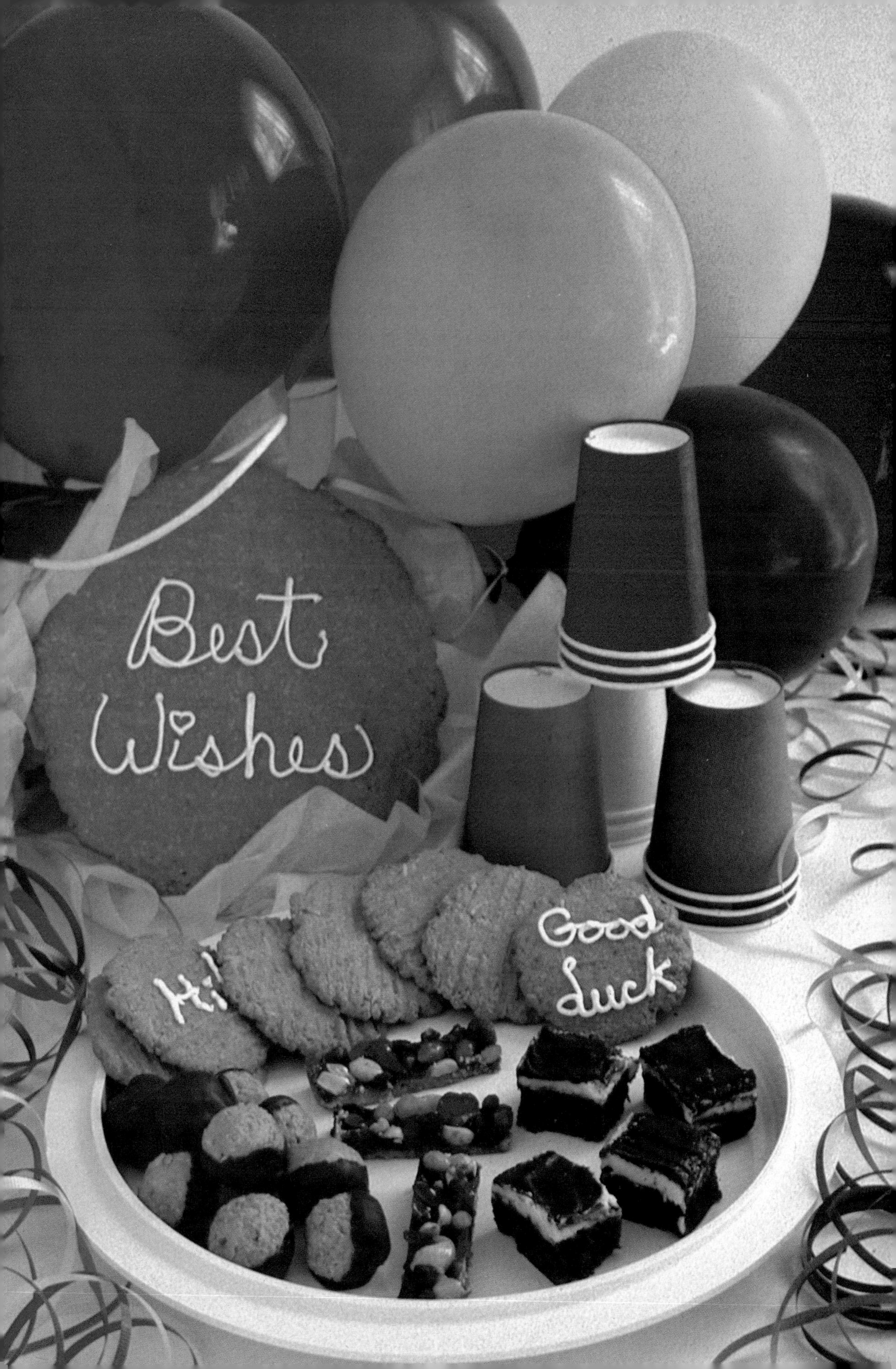
Best Wishes
Good Luck

8

Oatmeal Chocolate Chip Cookies
Greeting Cookies
Recipes on page 204

Chocolate Peanut Butter Balls
Recipe on page 212

Jewel Bars
Recipe on page 211

Mint Frosted Brownies
Recipe on page 214

CRANBERRY-PECAN LOAF
Makes 1 loaf

Cream together:

¼ cup butter or margarine	50 mL
¾ cup sugar	175 mL
1 teaspoon salt	5 mL

Beat in until all is foamy and smooth:

1 egg	1

Add:

1 teaspoon baking soda	5 mL
1 teaspoon baking powder	5 mL
¾ cup sour milk or buttermilk	175 mL
2 cups flour	500 mL

Mix until smooth, then fold in:

1½ cups cranberries, chopped	375 mL
½ cup broken pecans	125 mL

Bake in greased oblong loaf pan at 350°F (180°C) for 1 hour or until a toothpick inserted into the center comes out clean.

When cool, remove from tin, wrap in foil and store in closed container for a day or two before slicing. Serve buttered.

BANANA MUFFINS
Makes 18 muffins

¾ cup sugar	175 mL
¼ cup butter	50 mL
1 egg	1
1 teaspoon vanilla	5 mL
1 cup mashed bananas (Great for those "almost too ripe" bananas)	250 mL
1½ cups flour	375 mL
1 teaspoon baking soda	5 mL
1 teaspoon baking powder	5 mL
pinch of salt	pinch

Cream butter and sugar. Add egg and vanilla. Stir in bananas and soda dissolved in 2 teaspoons (10 mL) hot water. Add flour and remaining ingredients.

Fill greased muffin tins and bake at 350°F (180°C) for 15 to 18 minutes.

PINEAPPLE-CARROT MUFFINS
Makes 18 muffins

¾ cup sugar	175 mL
½ cup oil	125 mL
2 eggs	2
1½ cups all-purpose flour	375 mL
1 teaspoon baking powder	5 mL
1 teaspoon baking soda	5 mL
1 teaspoon cinnamon	5 mL
½ teaspoon salt	2 mL
1 teaspoon vanilla	5 mL
1 cup grated carrot	250 mL
½ cup crushed pineapple, drained	125 mL
⅔ cup raisins	150 mL

Combine and beat well, sugar, oil and eggs. Add combined dry ingredients, stirring just until dry ingredients are moist. Fold in the vanilla, carrot, pineapple and raisins.

Fill large, greased muffin cups ⅔ full and bake at 375°F (190°C) 20 to 25 minutes.

OATMEAL MUFFINS
Makes 12 muffins

1 cup rolled oats	250 mL
1 cup brown sugar	250 mL
1 cup buttermilk	250 mL
½ cup vegetable oil	125 mL
1 egg	1
1 cup all-purpose flour	250 mL
½ cup raisins or fresh or frozen blueberries	125 mL
½ teaspoon salt	2 mL
½ teaspoon baking soda	2 mL
1 teaspoon baking powder	5 mL
¼ teaspoon cinnamon	1 mL
¼ teaspoon nutmeg	1 mL

Preheat oven to 375°F (190°C). Pour buttermilk over quick cooking rolled oats. Add sugar, egg and oil. Beat well. Sift flour, salt, baking powder and baking soda together. Blend with rolled oats mixture. Fold in raisins or blueberries. Spoon into greased or paper-lined muffin cups.

Bake 30 minutes, or until golden brown. This recipe may be doubled.

NANTUCKET MUFFINS

Makes 20 large muffins

2 cups sugar	500 mL
4 cups flour	1 L
4 teaspoons cinnamon	20 mL
4 teaspoons baking soda	20 mL
1 teaspoon salt	5 mL
1 cup shredded coconut	250 mL
1 cup raisins	250 mL
4 cups shredded carrots	1 L
2 shredded apples	500 mL
1 cup pecans	250 mL
6 eggs	6
2 cups vegetable oil	500 mL
1 teaspoon vanilla	5 mL

Sift dry ingredients into a large bowl. Add fruit and nuts and stir well.
Add eggs, oil, and vanilla, stirring until just combined.

Spoon batter into muffin cups and bake at 375°F (190°C) for 20 minutes.
Muffins should ripen 24 hours before serving for blending of flavours.

BRAN MUFFINS

Makes 24 muffins

2 cups natural bran	500 mL
1 cup boiling water	250 mL
4 eggs	4
3 cups sugar	750 mL
5 cups flour	1.25 L
2 teaspoons salt	10 mL
3 teaspoons baking soda	15 mL
4 cups bran flakes	1 L
¾ cup melted butter	175 mL
1 quart buttermilk	1 L

In a large container soak bran and boiling water together. Beat eggs
with 3 cups (750 mL) sugar. Combine bran mixture with egg mixture.
Add flour, salt, baking soda, bran flakes, melted butter and buttermilk.
Bake 20 to 25 minutes at 400°F (200°C).

This mix will keep for 5 weeks in the refrigerator.

THE BEST REFRIGERATOR BRAN MUFFINS

Makes 7 dozen muffins

In a large container combine:

5 cups all-purpose flour	1.1 L
2½ cups sugar	625 mL
3 cups natural wheat bran (not cereal, buy in health food store)	750 mL
2 cups All-bran cereal	500 mL

In another large container:

1 quart buttermilk	1 L
3 tablespoons baking soda	45 mL

Add:

1½ cups cooking oil	375 mL
4 eggs	4
½ cup molasses	125 mL

Beat after each addition. Stir in 2 cups raisins. Make a well in dry ingredients; add wet ingredients. Mix. Store in large air-tight container. Keeps in refrigerator for 6 to 8 weeks.

Bake in teflon muffin tin at 375°F (190°C) for 20 minutes.

ORANGE CARROT MUFFINS

Makes 24 large or 30 medium muffins

1¼ cups oil	300 mL
2 cups white sugar	500 mL
4 eggs	4
2 cups plus a little more, all-purpose flour	500 mL
1 teaspoon salt	5 mL
2 teaspoons baking soda	10 mL
2 teaspoons baking powder	10 mL
2 cups grated carrots	500 mL
1 grated rind of orange	1

Combine and beat well, oil, sugar and eggs. Add combined dry ingredients, stirring just until dry ingredients are moist. Fold in the grated carrot and grated orange rind. Fill greased muffin tins ⅔ full and bake at 375°F (190°C) for 20 minutes or until golden brown.

BANANA RAISIN MUFFINS

Makes 12 muffins

3 medium ripe bananas, mashed	3
6 tablespoons melted shortening or oil	75 mL
½ cup white sugar	125 mL
1 egg, well beaten	1
1 teaspoon vanilla	5 mL
1½ cups whole wheat flour	375 mL
1 teaspoon baking powder	5 mL
1 teaspoon baking soda	5 mL
1 teaspoon salt	5 mL
½ cup raisins (optional)	125 mL

Combine mashed bananas, melted shortening and sugar until well mixed. Beat in egg and vanilla.

In a separate bowl sift together flour, baking powder, baking soda and salt; stir in raisins. Lightly stir flour mixture into banana mixture; stir as little as possible, only until moistened. Spoon batter into well-greased muffin pan. Bake at 350°F (180°C) for 20 minutes.

CRUNCHY APPLE MUFFINS

Makes 12 muffins

2 cups flour	500 mL
3 teaspoons baking powder	15 mL
½ cup white sugar	125 mL
½ teaspoon salt	2 mL
1 cup apples, chopped	250 mL
1 egg	1
¾ cup milk	175 mL
3 tablespoons butter, melted	45 mL
Topping	
⅓ cup dark brown sugar	75 mL
½ teaspoon cinnamon	2 mL
⅓ cup chopped nuts	75 mL

Mix together muffin ingredients. Fill muffin tins half full and top with topping.

Bake at 350°F (180°C) for 15 to 25 minutes.

CHOCOLATE MERINGUE PIE

Serves 6 to 8

Meringue

2 egg whites	2
¼ teaspoon salt	1 mL
½ teaspoon white vinegar	2 mL
½ cup sugar	125 mL
¼ teaspoon cinnamon	1 mL

Prepare 8 inch (20 cm) circle of cooking parchment and place on cookie sheet. Beat egg whites, salt and vinegar together until soft peaks form. Blend sugar and cinnamon together and gradually add to egg whites. Beat egg whites until stiff. Spread on parchment making base ½ inch (1.5 cm) thick and the sides of the circle high. Bake at 275°F (140°C) for one hour. Turn off heat and allow meringue to dry in oven for two hours or overnight. (If making ahead, keep in airtight container.)

Filling

1-6 ounce package semi-sweet chocolate chips	1-170 g
2 beaten egg yolks	2
¼ cup water	50 mL
½ pint whipping cream	250 mL
¼ cup sugar	50 mL
¼ teaspoon cinnamon	1 mL

Melt chocolate over hot water. Cool slightly and spread 2 tablespoons (25 mL) over bottom of meringue shell. To the remaining chocolate add egg yolks and water. Blend and then chill until mixture has thickened (not long — about the time it takes to do the next step). Combine cream, sugar and cinnamon and whip until stiff. Put a very small amount of mixture aside. Spread half of the remainder over the chocolate in the shell, fold the rest into the chocolate mixture and spread on top. With a fork, swirl the small amount of cream previously set aside on top of the chocolate mixture. Chill several hours.

BOB HOPE'S
"FAVOURITE LEMON PIE"

Serves 6 to 8

1 prepared 9 inch (23 cm) pie shell	
1 cup sugar, plus 2 tablespoons	265 mL
3 tablespoons cornstarch	45 mL
1 cup boiling water	250 mL
4 tablespoons lemon juice	50 mL
2 tablespoons butter	25 mL
4 egg yolks	4
pinch of salt	pinch
grated rind of 1 lemon	1

Combine cornstarch and sugar, add water slowly, stirring constantly until thick and smooth.

Add slightly beaten egg yolks, butter, lemon rind and juice, and salt. Cook 2 or 3 minutes. Pour into baked shell.

Cover with meringue made from 3 egg whites, beaten stiff, and 2 tablespoons (25 mL) sugar. Bake in 325°F (160°C) oven 15 minutes or until light brown.

YOGURT PIE

Serves 6 to 8

1¼ cup Graham crumbs	300 mL
6 tablespoons melted butter	75 mL
2 tablespoons sugar	25 mL

Combine and press into 9 inch (23 cm) pie plate.

Filling

2 eggs	2
1 cup yogurt	250 mL
1-8 ounce package cream cheese	1-250 g
⅔ cup honey	150 mL
½ teaspoon almond extract	2 mL
½ teaspoon vanilla	2 mL

Combine and put in pie shell. Bake at 350°F (180°C) for 40 to 50 minutes.

Topping

1 cup yogurt	250 mL
½ teaspoon vanilla	2 mL
½ teaspoon almond extract	2 mL

Serve with blueberry, raspberry, or strawberry preserves.

ARMENIAN ORANGE CAKE

Makes 1 loaf

2 cups brown sugar	500 mL
2 cups sifted all-purpose flour	500 mL
½ cup butter	125 mL
½ teaspoon salt	2 mL
2 teaspoons fresh orange peel, grated	10 mL
½ teaspoon allspice	2 mL
1 teaspoon baking soda	5 mL
1 cup sour cream	250 mL
1 egg, slightly beaten	1
½ cup almonds, chopped	125 mL

Combine first 6 ingredients in a bowl. Blend with a pastry blender until mixture is crumbly and completely blended. Grease a spring-form pan. Spoon in half the crumb mixture. Stir baking soda into sour cream and add egg. Add remaining crumb mixture. Pour batter over crumbs and sprinkle with almonds.

Bake 350°F (180°C) for 40 to 45 minutes. Serve warm with orange whipped cream.

Orange Whipped Cream

1 cup whipping cream, whipped	250 mL
2 tablespoons icing sugar	25 mL
1 teaspoon orange peel, grated	5 mL
2 tablespoons orange liqueur	25 mL

Whip cream until stiff. Stir in icing sugar, orange peel and liqueur. Let stand 1 hour to let flavours blend.

GREEK HONEY CAKE

Makes 1 cake

6 eggs, separated	6
1 cup, plus 2 tablespoons, sifted flour	275 mL
1 cup, plus 2 tablespoons, sugar	275 mL
grated rind of 1 lemon	1
1½ teaspoons baking powder	7 mL
¼ teaspoon baking soda	1 mL
½ cup melted butter	125 mL
chopped walnuts for garnish	
1 cup whipping cream	250 mL
1 cup fresh fruit	250 mL

Beat egg whites until stiff. In a large bowl beat egg yolks and add sugar. Mix together baking powder, baking soda, flour, and lemon rind. Add flour mixture to yolks and alternately fold in egg whites. Butter a 9 inch (23 cm) cake pan. Pour in cake mixture, then spoon melted butter over top. Bake at 350°F (180°C) for 35 minutes.

Syrup

2 cups sugar	500 mL
1½ cups water	375 mL
2 tablespoons lemon juice	25 mL
1 tablespoon rum or brandy	15 mL

Boil together in a saucepan for 10 minutes. Remove from heat and add 1 tablespoon (15 mL) rum or brandy. Cool.

Pour cooked syrup over hot cake. Sprinkle with walnuts, fresh fruit, and spread with whipped cream.

STRAWBERRY MERINGUE CAKE

Serves 10

2 cups sifted cake flour (sift before measuring)	500 mL
2 teaspoons baking powder	10 mL
⅛ teaspoon salt	pinch
½ cup softened butter	125 mL
1 cup sugar	250 mL
4 egg yolks, slightly beaten	4
¾ cup milk	175 mL
1 teaspoon vanilla	50 mL

Meringue

4 egg whites, room temperature	4
½ cup sugar	125 mL
1 quart strawberries, washed, hulled	1 L
1 cup whipping cream, whipped	250 mL
½ cup sugar	125 mL

Preheat oven to 375°F (190°C).

Sift flour, baking powder and salt, three times. Grease and flour, or line bottom with wax paper, two 9 × 1½ inch (23 × 3.5 cm) round pans.

In a large mixing bowl cream butter, gradually beat in sugar until light and fluffy. Beat in egg yolks until very light. At low speed, beat in flour mixture in fourths alternately with milk in thirds. Beginning and ending with flour. Add vanilla. Divide evenly into cake pans, smooth tops. Bake 20 to 25 minutes. DO NOT OVER-BAKE. Cool on rack for 10 minutes then turn cakes out of pan.

Preheat oven to 350°F (180°C).

At high speed beat egg whites until soft peaks form. Beat in ½ cup (125 mL) sugar, two tablespoons (25 mL) at a time, until stiff peaks form when beaters are removed. Spread meringue lightly on cake layers that have been placed on a cookie sheet. Bake until meringue is golden 10 to 15 minutes. Cool on racks.

Reserve half of the berries for the top of cake. Slice the rest into a bowl. Sprinkle with ½ cup (125 mL) of sugar and chill. Place one layer on cake plate. Spread with whipped cream. Top with sliced berries. Place second layer on top.

Halve the reserved berries and arrange on the cake. Serve within several hours. Do not refrigerate.

ORANGE MERINGUE CAKE

Makes 1 cake

1 large orange	1
5 egg whites	5
1½ cups fruit powdered sugar	375 mL
1 cup whipping cream	250 mL
½ ounce Grand Marnier	15 mL
bitter sweet chocolate	

Slice orange in even slices. Make a heavy syrup (1½ cup (375 mL) sugar to ¾ cup (175 mL) water). Add the orange and bring to a boil. Place in a sterile jar and keep refrigerated. Will keep for several months.

Preheat oven to 275°F (140°C).

Cover 3 cookie sheets with parchment paper. Beat egg whites until very stiff. Beat in 1 tablespoon (15 mL) of sugar. Fold in remaining sugar.

Fill pastry bag and pipe 3-7 inch (18 cm) disks onto the paper. Bake one hour and fifteen minutes, until they are slighly brown and completely dry.

Four hours before serving — Whip cream until stiff. Chop up a couple of the slices of orange in syrup and fold in whipped cream. Add Grand Marnier to cream.

Spread each meringue with the whipped cream mixture and stack on top of each other. Frost like a cake with the cream and cover with large chocolate curls. Refrigerate until serving time.

Chocolate Curls

Melt chocolate slowly in a heavy pot. Spread with a spatula on the back of a cookie sheet and work the chocolate until it is evenly spread. Chill until almost firm. Pull curls from the cookie sheet with the wide side of the spatula and keep refrigerated on parchment paper until ready to place on top of cake.

CHOCOLATE AMARETTO CHEESECAKE

Serves 10 to 12

Crust

1¼ cups chocolate wafer crumbs	300 mL
or	
1 cup graham wafer crumbs	250 mL
¼ cup cocoa	50 mL
2 tablespoons sugar	25 mL
¼ cup butter, melted	50 mL

Combine crumbs, sugar and melted butter. Press into bottom and halfway up sides of buttered 9 inch (23 cm) spring-form pan. Chill while preparing filling.

Filling

2-8 ounce packages cream cheese, softened	2-250 g
½ cup granulated sugar	125 mL
2 large eggs	2
6 squares semi-sweet chocolate, melted and cooled	6
½ teaspoon almond flavouring	2 mL
1 teaspoon vanilla	5 mL
⅓ cup Amaretto liqueur	75 mL
⅔ cup sour cream	150 mL

Beat cream cheese until smooth. Gradually beat in sugar, then eggs, one at a time. Add cooled chocolate, flavourings, Amaretto and sour cream. At low speed, beat until blended. Pour into pan. Bake at 300°F (150°C) for 1 hour. Turn off heat and leave in oven for 1 hour more. Cool to room temperature. Chill for 24 hours in refrigerator.

Add topping

2 squares semi-sweet chocolate, melted	2
1 teaspoon butter, melted	5 mL
whipped cream (optional)	
toasted sliced almonds	

Melt chocolate and butter. Spread over cake. Garnish with whipped cream (flavoured with additional Amaretto if desired). Sprinkle with almonds.

STEVE PODBORSKI'S "LEMONY CHEESECAKE"

Serves 10 to 12

1 cup graham cracker crumbs	250 mL
3 tablespoons sugar	45 mL
3 tablespoons margarine, melted	45 mL
3-8 ounce packages cream cheese	3-250 g
1 cup sugar	250 mL
3 tablespoons flour	45 mL
2 tablespoons lemon juice	25 mL
1 tablespoon grated lemon rind	15 mL
½ teaspoon vanilla	2 mL
4 eggs (one separated)	4
¾ cup sugar	175 mL
3 tablespoons cornstarch	45 mL
½ cup water	125 mL
¼ cup lemon juice	50 mL

Combine crumbs, sugar and margarine. Press onto bottom of 9 inch (23 cm) spring-form pan. Bake at 325°F (160°C), 10 minutes.

Combine softened cream cheese, sugar, flour, lemon juice, lemon rind and vanilla, mixing until well blended. Add 3 eggs, one at a time, mixing well after each addition. Beat in remaining egg whites, reserve egg yolk for glaze. Pour mixture over crumbs, bake at 450°F (230°C), 10 minutes. Reduce temperature to 250°F (120°C), continue baking 30 minutes. Loosen cake from rim of pan, cool before removing rim of pan.

Combine sugar and cornstarch, add water and lemon juice. Cook until clear and thickened, stirring occasionally. Add small amount to slightly beaten egg yolk, return mixture to pan and cook a few minutes longer. Cool slightly. Spoon over cheesecake, chill until firm. Garnish with lemon slices, if desired.

MISSISSIPPI MUD CAKE

Serves 14 to 16

3 squares unsweetened chocolate	3
1½ cups water	375 mL
¼ pound butter	125 mL
2 cups sugar	500 mL
2 cups flour, sifted	500 mL
2 eggs	2
1 teaspoon baking powder	5 mL
1 teaspoon baking soda	5 mL
1 teaspoon vanilla	5 mL
½ pint whipping cream	250 mL

In a large saucepan heat chocolate and water until chocolate is melted.

In a large bowl, cream butter and sugar. Beat in flour, eggs, baking powder, and soda; add vanilla. Beat in melted chocolate and water. Pour into 8 inch (20 cm) square pan and bake at 275°F (140°C) for at least 1½ hours. Cake tin will be very full but this cake does not rise.

Serve warm with lots of whipped cream.

BLUEBERRY CAKE

Serves 8 to 10

¼ cup shortening	125 mL
1 cup sugar	250 mL
1 egg	1
1¾ cups all-purpose flour	425 mL
¼ teaspoon salt	1 mL
2 teaspoons baking powder	10 mL
½ cup milk	125 mL
1 teaspoon vanilla	5 mL
1¼ cups fresh blueberries	300 mL

Beat shortening until light and fluffy. Add sugar, beat in egg.

Sift dry ingredients. Add vanilla to milk. Fold the dry ingredients alternately with milk into shortening mixture in thirds, beginning and ending with flour. Blend well.

Coat blueberries with a little flour so they will be dry; fold gently into cake batter. Pour into 9 inch (23 cm) square floured and greased cake pan. Bake at 350°F (180°C) for 50 minutes. Cool on a rack before removing from pan.

Don't forget this recipe during the blueberry season!

LEMON CUSTARD CAKE

1 large angel cake, baked and broken into pieces	1
6 eggs, separated	6
1½ cups sugar	375 mL
¾ cup fresh lemon juice	175 mL
1 tablespoon gelatine	15 mL
¼ cup cold water	50 mL
1 cup whipping cream	250 mL

Beat egg yolks. In top of double boiler cook 6 egg yolks with half of sugar. Add lemon juice and cook until thick — about 5 minutes.

Soak gelatine in ¼ cup of cold water.

Remove custard from heat and add gelatine. Beat the 6 egg whites until stiff and add remainder of sugar gradually. Pour custard over egg whites and mix well, add cake pieces and mix well again. Pour into a large angel cake pan and let stand in refrigerator overnight.

Just before serving remove from pan and frost with 1 cup (250 mL) whipping cream, whipped.

Garnish with lemon slices or desired fruit.

COLONIAL SEED CAKE

Makes 1 cake

½ cup poppy seeds	125 mL
¾ cup milk	175 mL
¾ cup soft butter	175 mL
3 eggs	3
1¼ cup sugar	300 mL
1 teaspoon vanilla	5 mL
2 teaspoons baking powder	10 mL
2 cups sifted all-purpose flour	500 mL

Combine poppy seeds and milk in mixing bowl and let stand at room temperature for 3 to 5 hours. Let butter and eggs stand at room temperature for easy mixing. Add butter, eggs, sugar, vanilla, baking powder and flour to poppy seeds and milk. Beat at medium speed with electric mixer for 1 minute, scraping side of bowl with spatula. Pour into greased and floured loaf pan 9 inches (23 cm) and bake in preheated 350°F (180°C) oven for 1 hour and 15 minutes. Let cool in pan for 5 minutes before removing. Sprinkle with icing sugar and serve plain or with whipped cream.

BLUEBERRY-LEMON LOAF CAKE

2 cups unsifted all-purpose flour	500 mL
1½ teaspoons baking powder	7 mL
¼ teaspoon salt	1 mL
½ cup butter or regular margarine	125 mL
1 cup sugar	250 mL
2 eggs	2
⅓ cup milk	75 mL
½ cup chopped walnuts (optional)	125 mL
2 teaspoons grated lemon peel	10 mL
1 cup washed fresh or frozen blueberries	250 mL
Syrup	
¼ cup lemon juice	50 mL
⅓ cup sugar	75 mL

Lightly grease a 9 × 5 × 2¾ inch (23 × 12 × 7 cm) loaf pan. Preheat oven to 350°F (180°C).

Sift flour with baking powder and salt; set aside.

In a large bowl of electric mixer, at medium speed, beat butter with sugar until light and fluffy. Add eggs, one at a time, beating well after each addition; beat until very light and fluffy.

At low speed, beat in flour mixture alternately with milk, beginning and ending with flour mixture; beat until just combined.

Stir in nuts, lemon peel and blueberries. Turn batter into prepared pan. Bake 60 to 65 minutes, or until cake tester inserted in centre comes out clean.

Make syrup: In small saucepan, combine lemon juice and sugar; cook, stirring, 1 minute, or until syrupy. Pour evenly over cake as soon as it is removed from oven.

Let cool in pan 10 minutes. Remove to wire rack; let cool completely.

HARVEY WALLBANGER CAKE

Makes 1 Cake

1 yellow cake mix	1
½ cup cooking oil	125 mL
1-4 ounce package instant vanilla pudding	113 g
4 eggs	4
¼ cup Galliano liqueur	50 mL
¼ cup vodka	50 mL
¾ cup orange juice	175 mL

Mix all ingredients together for about 4 minutes. Pour into a greased and floured Bundt pan and bake at 350°F (180°C) for approximately 40 to 50 minutes.

NEVILLE MARRINER'S
"EASY FRUIT CAKE"

12 ounces mixed, dried fruit (raisins, currants)	340 g
2 cups all-purpose flour	500 mL
½ cup sugar	125 mL
½ cup melted butter	125 mL
¾ cup milk	175 mL
2 eggs, beaten	2
½ teaspoon grated nutmeg	2 mL
½ teaspoon allspice	2 mL
pinch of salt	pinch

Mix all dry ingredients. Add beaten eggs, milk, and melted butter. Beat together for 4 minutes, by hand. Bake approximately 2 hours at 275°F (130°C). Allow to cool slightly, then turn out onto a wire rack until cold.

CARROT CAKE

Makes 1 large cake or 3 small cakes

1½ cup salad oil	375 mL
2 cups sugar	500 mL
4 eggs	4
2 cups sifted flour	500 mL
2 teaspoons baking powder	10 mL
2 teaspoons baking soda	10 mL
2 teaspoons cinnamon	10 mL
½ teaspoon salt	2 mL
¼ teaspoon nutmeg	1 mL
1 cup chopped pecans (optional)	250 mL
3 cups grated carrots	750 mL
1 cup golden raisins	250 mL
1 teaspoon vanilla	5 mL

Blend oil and sugar. Add eggs one at a time: sift together dry ingredients and add to mixture, blend well. Add remaining ingredients. Pour into 3-9 inch (3-23cm) greased and floured cake pans. Bake at 350°F (180°C) about 25 minutes or until done.

A larger pan 16 × 11 inch (40 × 28 cm) may be used. Bake for 45 minutes.

ICING FOR CARROT CAKE

¼ pound browned butter	125 g
1 pound confectioners' sugar	500 g
1 teaspoon vanilla	5 mL
3 or 4 tablespoons cream	45 to 50 mL
rum liquor to taste	

Combine ingredients, blend well and frost cake while warm.

CHOCOLATE PUDDING ICING

Makes 2 cups (500 mL)

1 cup white sugar	250 mL
1 cup hot water	250 mL
3 tablespoons cocoa	45 mL
3 tablespoons butter	45 mL
1 heaping tablespoon, plus ½ tablespoon cornstarch	25 mL

Mix sugar, water, cocoa, and butter in a saucepan. Bring to a boil, then thicken with cornstarch. Let cool, stirring often. Spread on favourite cake.

BANANA CAKE

Makes 1 cake

1½ cups white sugar	375 mL
½ cup butter	125 mL
1 cup mashed bananas	250 mL
½ teaspoon salt	2 mL
2 eggs	2
½ teaspoon mace, or nutmeg	2 mL
3 tablespoons sour cream	45 mL
1 teaspoon baking soda	5 mL
1 teaspoon vanilla	5 mL
1½ cups flour	375 mL

Mix all ingredients together.

Bake 45 minutes in greased pan in a 350°F (180°C) oven.

TOMATO SOUP CAKE

Makes 1 cake

1 cup sugar	250 mL
1-10 ounce can condensed tomato soup	1-284 mL
1¾ cups flour	425 mL
½ cup butter at room temperature	125 mL
3 teaspoons baking powder	15 mL
½ teaspoon ground cloves	2 mL
½ teaspoon cinnamon	2 mL
½ teaspoon nutmeg	2 mL
1 cup chopped nuts (optional)	250 mL
1 cup chopped dates or raisins (optional)	250 mL
2 eggs	2

In a large bowl, sift the dry ingredients together. Cut in butter and half the can of soup. Beat until smooth. Add remaining soup and eggs. Fold in nuts and dates or raisins. Pour into greased 9 × 9 inch (23 × 23 cm) pan. Bake at 350°F (180°C) for 35 to 40 minutes. Cool 10 minutes on rack and remove from pan.

Icing

1 small package cream cheese	1-125 g
2½ cups icing sugar	625 mL
1 teaspoon vanilla	5 mL
1 tablespoon milk	15 mL

Soften cheese with milk. Gradually add 2½ cups (625 mL) of icing sugar. Add vanilla and blend until creamy. Spread on top of cake.

RASPBERRY BAKED-ALASKA PIE

18 ladyfingers	18
⅓ cup orange-flavoured liqueur	75 mL
1-15 ounce package frozen raspberries (slightly thawed)	312 g
2 pints vanilla ice cream (slightly softened)	1 L
4 egg whites	4
¼ teaspoon salt	1 mL
⅛ teaspoon cream of tartar	pinch
⅔ cup sugar	150 mL

Up to two weeks before serving:

Line bottom and sides of 9 inch (23 cm) pie plate with about two-thirds of ladyfingers, allowing rounded ends to extend slightly over pie plate rim, then sprinkle with half of the liqueur.

In medium bowl, with potato masher, crush raspberries well to make a paste consistency.

In large bowl, stir softened ice cream slightly. Drop spoonfuls of raspberries onto ice cream then cut through mixture to get a rippled effect. Spoon half of ice cream mixture into pie plate. Layer remaining ladyfingers on top of ice cream, and sprinkle with remaining liqueur. Spoon rest of ice cream mixture onto ladyfingers.

FREEZE.

About 20 minutes before serving:

Preheat oven to 500°F (260°C).

Beat egg whites, salt, cream of tartar until soft peaks form.

Beating at high speed, gradually beat in sugar, 2 tablespoons (30 mL) at a time, until sugar is completely dissolved. Quickly spread meringue over top of pie, sealing to edge. Bake 3 to 4 minutes until meringue is lightly browned. Serve immediately.

LORNE GREENE'S "PECAN PIE"

Serves 8

Rub butter on the inside of a 9 inch (23 cm) or 10 inch (25 cm) pie plate.
Beat until stiff:

4 egg whites	4
pinch of baking powder	pinch

Let stand for half an hour.
Mix together:

1 teaspoon vanilla	5 mL
1 cup sugar	250 mL

Add to egg whites.
Break up into small not fine pieces:

30 Ritz crackers	30
1 pound unsalted pecan nuts	500 g

Mix everything together.

Pour into pie plate and press down. Don't pack too tightly but firmly.
Bake at 300°F (150°C) for 20 minutes.

Serve with whipped cream. Keep refrigerated.

A Bonanza!

YULE LOG

Sponge Roll

3 large eggs	3
1 cup sugar	250 mL
5 tablespoons water	75 mL
1 teaspoon vanilla	5 mL
1 cup all-purpose flour, sifted	250 mL
1 teaspoon baking powder	5 mL
¼ teaspoon salt	1 mL
icing sugar	

Heat oven to 375°F (190°C). Grease sides of 15 × 10 inch (37 × 25 cm) jelly-roll pan and line bottom with waxed paper. Beat eggs in small mixer bowl until very thick and fluffy. Add sugar gradually and beat well after each addition. Beat in water and vanilla.

Sift flour, baking powder and salt together into egg mixture and beat until smooth. Pour into prepared pan and spread evenly.

Bake 12 to 15 minutes or until top springs back when touched lightly in centre. Sift icing sugar over top of cake and turn out on tea towel. Roll cake and towel up together loosely from narrow end and let stand on cake rack until cool.

Unroll and spread with mocha cream (reserve ¼ cup (50 mL) and roll up again.

Mocha Cream

¼ cup sugar	50 mL
4 egg yolks	4
½ pound soft sweet butter	250 mL
4 tablespoons triple strength coffee	50 mL

Beat sugar and egg yolks until light and frothy. Add soft butter and beat on high speed for 5 minutes. While still beating, add coffee.

Chocolate Butter Cream

1-6 ounce package semi-sweet chocolate chips	1-175 g
¼ cup boiling water	50 mL
4 egg yolks	4
1 teaspoon vanilla	5 mL
1 stick soft butter (¼ pound)	125 mL

Empty package of chocolate chips into blender container. Add boiling water, cover, and blend on high for 20 seconds.

Turn off motor. Add egg yolks and vanilla. Cover and turn motor on high speed. With motor on, uncover and drop in butter. Blend for 15 seconds or until frosting is smooth.

To assemble: Cut a diagonal slice from each end of roll to give it shape of log. Stick cut pieces on top to make knots. Ice tops of knots and end of log with ¼ cup (50 mL) Mocha cream. Mark with fork to look like wood. Ice rest of roll thickly with Chocolate Butter Cream. Mark to look like bark with a fork.

IRISH WHISKY FLAN
Makes 1 pie

Graham wafer crust, 9 inch (23 cm) pie	1
½ cup sugar	125 mL
2 envelopes (½ ounce size) unflavoured gelatine	2
pinch of salt	pinch
pinch of nutmeg	pinch
5 ounces (⅔ cup) green glazed cherries	150 mL
2 cups milk	500 mL
6 egg yolks	6
2 cups whipped cream	500 mL
½ cup Irish whisky	125 mL
drop of green food colouring	drop
Graham wafer crust	
1½ cups crumbs	375 mL
¼ cup sugar	50 mL
⅓ cup melted butter or margarine	75 mL

Crust

Mix together and press mixture over bottom of 9 inch (23 cm) spring-form pan and bake at 350°F (180°C) about 5 minutes. Cool.

Filling

To prepare the filling, mix sugar, gelatine, salt and nutmeg in a bowl.Cut the glazed cherries into small pieces and set aside. In a saucepan,scald milk. Beat the egg yolks, and carefully whisk into the milk.Remove from heat and stir very quickly to prevent possibility of curdling. Pour over sugar mixture and stir until gelatine and sugar are completely dissolved.

Chill mixture until it starts to set, stirring occasionally. Then carefully fold in the whipped cream, whisky, colouring and cut-up cherries. Pour into wafer crust and chill about 4 hours, until firm. Remove spring-form ring with hot knife and decorate with whipped cream rosettes and glazed green cherries. Cut into 12 wedges.

COLONIAL MUFFINS

Yields 15 muffins

Cream together:

½ cup butter	125 mL
1 cup brown sugar	250 mL

Add:

1 egg, slightly beaten	1

Measure and sift together:

1 cup whole wheat flour	250 mL
1 cup white flour	250 mL
2 teaspoons baking powder	10 mL
½ teaspoon baking soda	2 mL
½ teaspoon salt	2 mL

Add alternately with:

1 cup buttermilk	250 mL

Bake at 425°F (220°C) for 15 to 20 minutes.

POPOVERS

Serves 4

1 egg, beaten well	1
⅓ cup half and half cream	75 mL
⅓ cup sifted flour	75 mL
pinch of salt	pinch
pinch of mace	pinch
butter	

Mix together egg and cream. Slowly add flour. Beat well, until consistency of heavy cream. Add salt and mace.

Preheat buttered pyrex custard dishes (6 small) until butter is sizzling.

Add approximately 2 tablespoons (25 mL) of batter to each dish. Bake at 450°F (230°C) for 10 minutes, reduce heat to 400°F (200°C) and bake for 10 minutes, then at 350°F (180°C) for 10 minutes.

Serve warm.

Note: This batter also makes a fine Yorkshire pudding when poured into baking pan containing juices from a roast.

Index